Chilling Confession of a Twelve-Year-Old Killer

"I called my grandparents yesterday to come to the school. The vice principal said he wanted to talk to them. Because the day before, that boy on the school bus said I choked him.

"We got home about two o'clock or two-thirty. They told me they was going to lock me in my room. They locked me in there until about eleven-thirty. My grandpa said if I came out, he was going to beat me with the paddle.

"When they went to bed, I waited about ten minutes. I got the shotgun out of the cabinet. I took it in my room and loaded it. I took a box of shells from the cabinet. I put three in it. Jacked one and put another one in. I went in their room. I just aimed at the bed. I shot four times. I turned the light on. My granddad's feet were hanging over the bed. My granddad's face was to the side. My grandmother was facing the closet. Her legs were in the bed. I picked up the shell casings. I threw them in the door of my room.

"Then I got some guns. I got a Ruger twenty-two from the gun safe. I got the four-ten out of the gun safe closet; I had laid it on the sofa. I got 2 twenty-two rifles and my forty-five. Then I loaded up my dog, Chrisdee, and I put him in the passenger's seat.

"I backed out. Then I turned the lights on. I drove. . . ."

DIE, GRANDPA, DIE

DALE HUDSON

PINNACLE BOOKS
Kensington Publishing Corp.
http://www.kensingtonbooks.com

For my aunt, Patsy Holden,
who has always loved me as her own.

Some names have been changed to protect the privacy of individuals connected to the story.

PINNACLE BOOKS are published by

Kensington Publishing Corp.
850 Third Avenue
New York, NY 10022

All Kensington Titles, Imprints, and Distributed Lines are available at special quantity discounts for bulk purchases for sales promotions, premiums, fund-raising, and educational or institutional use. Special book excerpts or customized printings can also be created to fit specific needs. For details, write or phone the office of the Kensington special sales manager: Kensington Publishing Corp., 850 Third Avenue, New York, NY 10022, attn: Special Sales Department, Phone: 1-800-221-2647.

Pinnacle and the P logo Reg. U.S. Pat. & TM Off.

First Printing: August 2006

10 9 8 7 6 5 4 3 2 1

Printed in the United States of America

PART I
THE CRIME

CHAPTER 1

Station 12, West Chester. You have a fire off Slick Rock Road.
It was 11:52 P.M., on November 28, 2001, when West Chester volunteer fireman Tommy Martin arrived at the firehouse. Because Tommy was the first person there, he quickly unlocked the door, walked inside, then punched the alarm button, alerting the community there was a fire somewhere that needed tending. The old rotary fire alarm wound up slowly, getting faster and faster, and louder and louder. Finally it cranked out a noise that sounded something like a twelve-year-old arthritic cat who had just gotten his tail pinned underneath a porch rocker. The siren shot out nine more squalls, just like the first one, into the darkened night, and the small cement-block firehouse, off Pinckney Road, was brought back to life again.

In 2001, at the time of the Slick Rock Road fire, the cost of operating the West Chester Volunteer Fire Department had nearly tripled. But it didn't matter. The dedicated men at Station 12 had an attitude about finances that sounded more like the Visa commercial: *the cost of a new water tanker, $12,000; the cost of one man's fire protective gear, $3,500; the cost of one life saved, priceless.*

Tommy Martin and his brother, Andy, lived off Pinckney Road, two-tenths of a mile in opposite directions of the Chester, South Carolina, fire station. Both were at home and asleep in bed when they got the call. Meeting at the firehouse, they stood outside for a brief moment and studied the fire, wondering if they were looking at the signs of a forest fire.

The Martin brothers had seen a lot of forest fires over the past forty years, and especially hated it when the flames were so out of control that they climbed like crazed monkeys up into the trees from the lower branches, then swung from tree to tree without ever touching the ground. They knew the only way to stop a forest fire was by getting a crew of men in there quick and cutting a lot of trees down.

But this was no forest fire Tommy and Andy were looking at. From the looks of the blaze in the sky, this was a structure fire. They fastened on their gear and prepared themselves for battle, knowing when they got there it would probably be an ugly situation.

Just down the road from the fire station, West Chester chief James "Red" Weir also heard the dispatcher's announcement. He and Lucy, his wife of fifty years, had just finished watching the evening news and turned in for the night when the emergency call came though their scanner at 11:50 P.M.

Red had retired as a mechanic and machinist more than a decade ago, but every day he still labored inside his shop on a steady flow of oily motors and greasy machines. In his spare time, he served as West Chester's Volunteer fire chief, a position he had held for almost forty years. At seventy-four years old, he was living proof that an active mind was a major source of wealth.

"Did you hear that?" Lucy asked, wide-eyed and looking over toward Red. Her husband had a rugged, open face she could always read. "Somebody's called in a forest fire near the Pittmans' house."

Red slid his tiny frame out of bed, hurried to the kitchen, then pulled back the curtains and peered out the window. Joe and Joy Pittman were his and Lucy's best friends and their house would be in grave danger if backed up against a forest fire. Red stared at the pillar of smoke that loomed high into the sky, then murmured to himself, "I don't believe that's a forest fire."

Red Weir had been on enough calls and eaten enough smoke in his lifetime to know the difference between a forest fire and a structure fire. "Yep, that's a structure fire, all right," he explained to Lucy as she dressed. Lifting his open hands above his head, he demonstrated how the smoke from a structure fire extended straight up, then said, "Think of it like steam from a boiling pot of water."

Since having a heart attack, Lucy had been accompanying Red on his fire calls so as not to be left at home alone. As soon as they stepped out the door, she could see the glare of the fire over the top of the hill toward the Pittmans' home.

Lucy sniffed the air. She had learned from her husband to recognize the distinct smell of a forest fire.

Red is right. Somebody's house is on fire.

And if Joe and Joy Pittman's house *was* on fire, then Lucy wanted to be there to comfort them. She could visualize them standing out on the lawn in front of their burning home: Joy would be holding her head in her hands and crying, while Joe and their twelve-year-old grandson, Christopher—who had come to live with them just five days ago—ran madly around the house trying to douse the flames with a half-inch garden hose.

Red saw his wife was as uneasy as a cat near water. "You saw Joe and Joy tonight at church, didn't you?" he asked, trying to reassure her.

She nodded. The Pittmans were all there, rehearsing for the upcoming Christmas play. Lucy played the organ and Joe sang in the choir. Christopher was sitting in the church auditorium, listening to the rehearsal.

"And they looked okay then, right?"

Lucy nodded a second time.

"And they'll be just fine when you see them again,"

Red continued, trying to gauge her reactions. "A little shook-up, maybe, but they are strong people. And they'll survive this."

Red helped his wife out of their home, down the back steps, and into his 1955 Chevrolet pickup truck. About forty years ago, he had salvaged the truck from a junkyard, paying only $35 for it, before completely restoring it into a classic beauty. When asked how long he planned to drive his pickup, Red would grin and say, "For a good while yet. I'm still trying to get my money out of it."

Somewhat of an icon in Chester County, the fire chief's '55 Chevy had gotten a lot of attention around town, mainly from admirers wanting to know if it was for sale. Red had upgraded it with power steering and power breaks, painted it pure white, rebuilt the Thunderbird engine 292, and equipped it with a '58 model Federal Fireman's siren he had salvaged from another wrecked fire truck. But more than anything else, he liked it because it had a souped-up engine that could turn 120 to 130 miles per hour in second gear. Not only was it a classic, but it was perfect for getting Red where he needed to be in a hurry.

In two minutes, the Weirs were at the fire station.

Tommy Martin drove the first pumper truck out of the fire station, peeling out in front of Red and Lucy, while Andy Martin and fellow firefighter Stuart Grant, who had arrived shortly after the Weirs, followed behind in the other tankers. Honking and wailing, the fire brigade quickly picked up speed and headed west, toward Highway 9 and Slick Rock Road. The highway was empty, as it should have been, for most people were at home, in bed, asleep at this hour.

Driving toward Slick Rock Road, Chief Weir thought about the time he had once asked Joe Pittman if he would consider becoming a volunteer fireman. Joe said he really wasn't interested, that it wasn't his thing. Finally, when Red put a little pressure on him, Joe answered, "I'm too old to fart around in a fireman's hat like that, Red.

I'm sixty-six years old and I'd probably just get in the way." Red smirked and reminded Joe that he had just celebrated his seventy-fourth birthday, and he didn't think he'd ever been in the way.

All this fire near his home might change Joe's mind about becoming a volunteer fireman, Red thought. *After he's experienced the dangers of a fire firsthand, he might realize the value of having a volunteer fire department.*

CHAPTER 2

Since Tommy Martin was the first to arrive at the fire station, he was given the honor of serving as "incident commander." Leading the fire brigade down the highway, Tommy gazed at the sky in front of him. It was lit up like a huge red rubber ball. By now, he was certain it was a structure fire, and from the looks of it, the thick plume of smoke was rising directly above the home of Joe and Joy Pittman. If the crimson cloud was any indication of the severity of the fire, he knew they would need additional help from other local fire departments. Just to be on the safe side, he alerted the North Chester Fire Department, then radioed the nearby Leeds Fire Department and asked for assistance.

Tommy Martin had fished with Joe Pittman more than a few times and visited with him in his home on 950 Slick Rock Road. It was painful to learn that the house of an old fishing buddy was on fire. Following the bend in the road, Tommy slowed down and searched in his head-lights for the address on the mailboxes. Up ahead, he spotted the number among a pair of mailboxes to his right, and someone standing at the driveway flagging him in. Tommy turned in the driveway on the opposite side of the road and headed up the drive toward the Pittmans' home.

Since there were no streetlights, Tommy believed the drivers behind him would not be able to see the driveway. Slowing his vehicle in the drive, he stepped out of his truck and attempted to flag them in. Andy Martin drove past the driveway and had to stop, then turn around. Red Weir also made the same mistake, having to stop and turn around behind Andy. Stuart Grant noticed Andy and Red making their U-turns and spotted Tommy Martin's vehicle in the driveway. He was able to adjust and turn in to the driveway, driving in ahead of the other two vehicles.

Tommy glanced at his watch. It was exactly one minute before midnight. He was pleased to know it had taken them only seven minutes to respond.

As the four West Chester firemen drove onto the Pittman property, they found themselves looking at the silhouette of what once had been a beautiful country home. An inky black cloud of smoke rose from the house, totally engulfed in flames, into the sky. The roof already had given way and caved in, and the long wooden porches across the front and back of the house were completely burned away. The fire was everywhere: the grass, the surrounding woods, the Pittmans' twenty-foot motor home parked next to their house.

Tommy Martin quickly assessed the situation. Considering the required water supply needed to douse the fire, he started assigning his men to tasks. Yelling out over the roar of a fire, which sounded like twin jet engines, he cautioned Andy and Stuart to be careful. Tommy understood the dangers associated with a house fire like this. Such fires had a reputation for melting wedding bands off fingers and burning the flesh off firemen until it hung from their bodies like limp dishrags. People, furniture, equipment—it didn't matter—nothing could survive in these billowing flames and intense heat.

Absolutely nothing.

Already tasting the smoke, Andy Martin pulled out one of the 2 ½-inch hoses connected to the truck and started knocking down the fire in the grass. Feeling the sting of the fire, Andy tucked his long black hair underneath his protective helmet and moved in closer. With his dark skin and chiseled frame, and a couple of months' worth of pumping iron in Gold's Gym, he could have passed easily as a stuntman for Sylvester Stallone.

Stuart Grant stood near the trucks, operating both the tanker and the pumper. Butch Craig, who had just arrived in his personally owned vehicle (POV) hurriedly joined Andy and Tommy on the fire hoses. Fire hoses swiveled across the lawn like big white boa constrictors atop a black river of water. The firemen moved in closer. Hungry flames hadn't reached them yet, but the trailing heat had.

Like all disasters, the fire off Slick Rock Road drew a growing number of spectators. Some were there out of curiosity, but, by and large, most were there out of love and concern for the Pittmans. Joe and Joy were good neighbors and had a lot of friends in the community. The Weirs were two of their closest.

Looking frantically for the Pittmans, Lucy Weir asked her husband, "Where is Joe and Joy?" By now, she was on the verge of tears. "Why aren't they here?"

Red didn't know the answer to that question. He did tell Lucy that Joy's car was missing in the driveway; on the positive side, that meant there was a good chance the Pittmans were out town. His face tensed suddenly. Shifting uneasily, he drew in a quick breath, then blew it out again. "There's nothing we can do but wait and see what happens," he said softly, trying to hide his frustrations.

Lucy stood anxiously by Red's Chevy and prayed. She always felt better when a Higher Power was involved.

A few minutes later, Shirley Carter, another friend and church member of the Pittmans', joined Lucy at the scene. The two women chatted briefly, discussing how the Pittmans had lost everything in the fire and would need help putting their lives back together. Shirley suggested they call their pastor, Chris Snelgrove, and tell him what was going on.

Snelgrove was in bed when his phone rang. "Are the Pittmans okay?" he asked, half-asleep.

"I don't know," Shirley responded. "Joy's car is missing and we're hoping they are out of town visiting relatives. But, at this point, we just don't know."

Snelgrove quickly dressed and drove the short distance across town to the Pittmans' home. When he arrived on the scene, he had to park his car at the end of the driveway and walk up the hill to the Pittmans' property. As he watched the flames shooting up in the sky, he remembered the Pittmans' country home was built so close to the woods that the squirrels would leap from the trees onto their house.

Snelgrove topped the hill; then he lost the breath he was holding. All he saw in place of the Pittmans' beautiful home was mayhem. Like some biblical disaster scene, everything was aflame. There were firemen, dressed in full gear—wearing their boots, protective gear, bunker pants, and yellow Nomex jackets—running and yelling. Someone, he couldn't tell who, was yelling to another fireman coming up the road behind him, asking if there were propane gas tanks around the home. If so, that had to be shut off or this place would soon look like Hiroshima.

From the pulpit, Snelgrove had preached about Hell many times in his sermons, but he never thought he'd actually experience it like this. Numb from it all, he made his way across the front of the property and to the familiar faces standing near Red Weir's truck. He was relieved to see he wasn't the only one having trouble finding words.

"Hey, folks, any more information on Joe and Joy?" he asked, eyes staring reflexively at the house fire.

Shirley Carter, her eyes red-rimmed and glistening, nodded nervously toward her minister. "We've called just about everybody who has a connection with them, but no luck so far. They're calling around at the local mechanic shops now, asking if maybe, by chance, Joy's car is in their shop being repaired. Hopefully, that will turn up something."

Snelgrove shook his head uncomprehendingly. He could feel a sharp pain suddenly growing inside his chest.

Tommy Martin and the West Chester firefighters remained focused on the burning home. Amazingly, it had taken them only about forty-five minutes to get this fire under control. After all the flames had been put out, Tommy gave the order to shut off the water.

Where there had been chaos, there was now a sense of order.

Since there was no life to protect, the firemen's last task was the salvage of personal property. It was so dark after the fire was extinguished that portable lights had to be set up so the firemen could see what they were doing. Because the five-eighth-inch decking boards on both front and back porches no longer existed, a ten-foot foldable ladder was placed at the bottom of the house, which enabled them to climb up on the foundation and walk around inside the smoldering shell. Surprisingly, the plywood floors to the main floor were still there, and in tact.

As the firemen searched the main floor of the home, they immediately noticed a five-foot-tall gun safe on the east end of the house. Smoke was seeping from inside this large, upright steel chest, and when Andy Martin cracked the door open, he saw a large collection of guns still inside. Thankful they had not blasted water inside the case and ruined the guns, Andy opened the door fully and inspected the contents. He counted out twenty-seven guns. Most of the guns were unharmed and still clothed in their protective stockings. Others were very hot to touch, but they were not in any way damaged or ruined.

Andy thought about what he would want if the situation

had been reversed, and this had been his home. "I'm sure Mr. Pittman would appreciate us saving his guns," he suggested without hesitation. He reached inside the cabinet and carefully handed out the guns one by one, to the other firefighters. Leaving no stones unturned, they documented the number of rifles, pistols, and other assorted items they removed from the steel safe. They then had their inventory witnessed and signed, before transferring it all into Tommy's vehicle. Tommy was still the incident commander and the person authorized to turn these weapons over to the authorities.

After all the weapons were locked away, Andy kept staring at a small wooden section jutting out over the gun case. It looked like a ten-by-ten piece of a loft or an attic, but, for some strange reason, it had not burned through and was still attached on top of the ceiling joists.

"I believe that's where Joe and Joy usually slept," Red Weir said, pointing to what remained of the second floor. "They added this on after their house was finished and used it as a bedroom. If I remember correctly, there was once a small staircase leading up to this loft."

In every house fire, one of the first things a fireman looks for, when all flames are knocked down and he boards the house, is the evidence of a bed. Almost always, it presents itself in the form of wire-type box springs. This was the first time Andy had heard about a second story inside the Pittmans' home. The wooden platform hanging above the gun case was about the size of a normal bed, and left just enough space for a double bed.

Andy set his attic ladder underneath the area and asked Stuart Grant to hand him the 110-volt portable light. "You weigh less than I do," Andy said, laughing. "Go up there and tell me what you see."

Stuart went up the ladder first and looked around, but didn't notice anything significant. "Look, I don't really see anything," he told Andy on the way down. "Just a bunch of rubbish, maybe parts of a bed, but nothing else."

Andy wanted to see for himself, so he grabbed a short light pole, climbed up the ladder, and pushed at the pile of rubbish. While moving the debris around, he spotted something unusual on top—something resembling an old piece of foam rubber that had aged and turned brown. He poked in and around the rubbish, pushing hard against the brown object. It didn't move. Stepping up higher on the ladder, he leaned forward and pulled a few charred pieces of wood toward him, then shone the light on the object protruding from the ashes.

"Oh, my God," Andy said, loud enough for only Stuart to hear. "I hope that is not what I think it is." With the blunt end of the pole, he raked away the remaining ashes from the pile, exposing what looked like the stomach area of a human being. The texture and color of the body reminded him of a turkey he had cooked in a deep fryer last Thanksgiving. The person's stomach had burst open like a ripe watermelon.

Andy closed his eyes. He opened his left eye. The blurry sight still loomed before him. Slowly he opened his right eye, hoping to corroborate what his left eye had seen. As he looked closer, he spotted, but couldn't swear to it, what he thought was a second body.

Stepping down from the ladder, Andy called a couple of other firefighters over to him. "How about you step up there and tell me if you see the same thing I am seeing," he said.

They climbed the ladder and confirmed that was indeed the remains of two adult bodies up there in the loft.

"Then go and tell Tommy," Andy whispered. "Tell him, I don't know if what we've found is one person, two persons, or three persons. I just know it's a body, and he'll want to notify the sheriff's department, the coroner's office, and probably the fire coordinator."

Tommy got the news and stepped in the area near the attic. He asked everyone to back out, giving further instructions to keep everybody out, unless a fire blazed up again. "We got dead bodies here, boys," he reminded his men. "We haven't seen one of these in about fifteen years, so let's treat it for what it is until the authorities get here."

Red Weir was stunned. He had never expected to find such stark horror inside of his friends' burned home. He turned and looked back toward his wife, who stood near his truck, still talking with Shirley Carter and Chris Snelgrove. He lumbered over toward where they stood, purposefully avoiding the firefighters in turnout gear who were still pulling hoses and adjusting their breathing apparatus.

"They've found some bodies up in the attic, where Joe and Joy slept," Red said under his breath. "Andy says they look like the bodies of an adult, so it's probably them."

A collective groan was heard.

Chris Snelgrove stood and talked with Lucy, Shirley, and Red at the top of the hill overlooking the Pittmans' property. He understood that something more ferocious was beginning to stir than the wind that had, hours ago, turned the Pittmans' house into a facsimile of King Nebuchadnezzar's oven. Even though he felt God's peace, he began bracing himself for an even deeper tragedy. There were a lot of questions among the firefighters as to where Christopher Pittman was when the home had caught fire. At this time of the night, it was normal to have expected him to be in bed, asleep, just like his grandparents.

Snelgrove bowed his head, then looked toward the sky. As he stood there with the members from his congregation, he noticed two shooting stars soar across the sky. Maybe the others hadn't noticed the stars, but he imagined that somehow God was sending him a message concerning the spirits of two people he had known and loved.

CHAPTER 3

It had been a bizarre morning for the men of the West Chester Volunteer Fire Department. After finding the Pittmans' charred bodies, the stunned crowd of firefighters and disbelieving spectators huddled together and discussed what they thought could have happened. There were more questions than answers. Where was Christopher Pittman? Had he escaped the fire? Or had his small body been consumed by the fire and lay buried somewhere deep in the ashes?

Tommy Martin radioed emergency 911 and asked that investigators from the Chester County Sheriff's Department (CCSD) respond to Slick Rock Road due to a fire fatality. Surely, they would be able to sort it all out.

Realizing there was nothing anyone could do but wait for the law enforcement to arrive, Andy Martin pulled out some money from his jacket pocket and sent a runner to the Hardees' restaurant. "Bring us a whole bunch of biscuits, as many as you can buy." He advised them he was going back to the fire station, mixing a pot of coffee, and bringing it back to the site. "We're going to be here for a while until everybody comes in, so let's keep ourselves comfortable."

Andy knew when most people get out of bed, the first

thing they want is a strong cup of coffee and a home-made biscuit.

Major James "Mac" McNeil, of the CCSD, was the first to receive the call from emergency 911. A twelve-year vet-eran with CCSD, McNeil had just been promoted to major of the crime investigative division and was offi-cially "the man" in charge of this investigation.

"What have we got here?" McNeil asked Sergeant Larry Thompson, who had arrived minutes before him.

"Well, the firemen told us they had found two bodies inside the burning residence," Thompson stated. "It's not a pretty sight, so we might want to call the sheriff and get him involved."

Before being transferred into the Chester Investiga-tive Division, McNeil had worked for 7½ years in a narcotics unit as a commander of a multijurisdictional task force involving covert-type investigations. Part of his responsibility during this tenure was to coordinate his in-vestigations with a federal metro narcotics unit comprised of six different agencies. McNeil not only had extensive training in narcotic investigation, but had also received extensive training in homicide and fire investi-gation at the South Carolina Fire Academy. It would serve him well in this meticulous investigation.

"Let's call the State Law Enforcement Division (SLED) arson division and ask them for assistance," McNeil instructed his right-hand man, Lieutenant Terry Love. "Also, go ahead and notify emergency nine-one-one. Ask them to issue a BOLO (be on the lookout) for the Pittman boy, as well as the missing vehicle."

At 1:50 A.M., Chester County sheriff Robby Benson was called. Early morning was not always the best time to learn that the bodies of two prominent citizens in the community had been discovered in a house fire. But after four years with the U.S. Air Force as a security and police (S&P) officer, fourteen years as an investi-gator with the Chester County Sheriff's Department, and now in his first term as sheriff, a phone call like this was routine.

Benson was asked by the dispatcher if he would meet Special Agent (SA) Scott Williams, an arson investigator with SLED, and lead him to the site. Benson climbed out of bed, dressed, and drove to meet Williams at their assigned meeting place.

Upon meeting Williams for the first time, Benson realized he was the prototypical rookie SLED agent: young, compact and athletic, his red hair cropped short in military style, he was uniformed and armed. Williams walked the walk and talked the talk. Benson was impressed.

Sheriff Benson and SA Williams arrived at the fire scene at approximately 2:45 A.M. The area around the burned house had been taped off and most of the CCSD investigators were already working out of this secured area. While Williams familiarized himself with the fire scene, Benson sought out Major McNeil, his chief of investigations, for an update. He and McNeil were accustomed to working together and immediately began a series of procedures they had perfected from years of investigation.

Standing beside each other, the two men were as physically different as any two men could be. Benson was five feet eight inches, a fast-talking Caucasian with dark hair and a blue-eyed, boyish squint. His face was decorated with a full, dark mustache and lines carved by years of too little sleep and too much coffee.

McNeil, on the other hand, was a slow-talking African American, not nearly as tall and big as Stephen King's character John Coffee in *The Green Mile,* but close enough. And he had the same kind and gentle heart as Coffee, the kind that loved animals of all kinds and children of all color.

Benson and McNeil began coordinating their normal tasks, which were considered standard common procedure for their initial investigation of a death scene. They initiated a search in and around the perimeter of the house for any evidence that would help shed light on the situation. Investigators sought the names and phone numbers of the Pittmans' family members and were busy trying to call them at their homes. Shirley Carter had already phoned Joe Pittman Jr., the Pittmans' son and Christopher's father, and informed him of the incident. Joe was only told about the house fire and that Christopher was missing. When Shirley inquired if he had any ideas as to where his son might be, the distraught father was clueless. But he assured Shirley he was on his way to Chester from Florida to find out.

While law enforcement waited for the heat to dissipate, they completed other tasks and phoned in additional officers to work the scene. SA Williams suggested to McNeil that they leave the two bodies undisturbed on the second floor, until SLED's senior arson agent Andy Weir arrived.

Williams walked around the house, then asked to speak with Assistant Fire Chief Andy Martin. During his walk-around, he had noticed there had been a number of items and guns taken from out of the top and the sides of the gun cabinet near the staircase. He saw the smoked outline of different collectibles, guns and other things that Joe Pittman had kept in his safe and had since been removed, and wanted an explanation as to where they were.

Andy admitted they had tried to salvage the items.

"Why on earth would you want to do that?" Williams asked Andy Martin and the group of firefighters who had begun huddling around them.

Red Weir looked at Andy, then turned and stared at Williams, as if to say, *Well, who just licked the red off your candy, boy?*

Williams was silent, waiting on an answer. He was not about to be intimidated by anyone. This was his job and he took it seriously.

Seeing that the agent didn't have a full understanding of what went on, Andy explained to Williams that which had motivated them to remove the guns and other items from the gun case.

"It wasn't like we found the bodies and then cleaned the guns out," Andy said as a matter of fact. "The gun safe was already open. We saw it was open and knew everything in it would get ruined. At that point in time, we didn't know about the Pittmans. There was no life to protect, so we attempted to save some of the man's property."

Williams explained the risk in disturbing potential evidence at a crime scene.

Andy accepted the criticism for removing all items from the gun case, and even though he thought Williams was a little badge heavy, he apologized. "You can blame all that on me, but we inventoried every gun and whatnot we took from the case. And we got it all stored in the back of my brother's truck, if you want to take a look at it."

Williams admonished Andy for removing the guns, then took his affidavit. He told him, "We at least would have liked to have gotten some prints before you took them out of the gun case. The person or persons who stole those guns just might be the same person who burned the Pittmans' house down. You know you will probably have to give an account of this in court."

Andy wanted Williams to know he wasn't afraid to tell the truth in court. He had directed the removal of the guns, as much for his men's protection as anything else. Who was to say that that entire arsenal of guns and ammo was only minutes away from exploding in the fire? Anyone worth his weight in salt would agree no one can predict what is going to happen in the midst of a burning fire. A lot of firefighters will never in their entire firefighting career come upon a scene that had the circumstances behind it like this one had. The Pittman fire was already an unusual case. What he did, he did with the best of intentions. So be it.

Williams finished taking Andy's statement, then asked, "Has anyone issued a search warrant and executed it to obtain entrance into the dwelling?" His question had a barb to it.

Andy shook his head no. "I didn't think a fireman had

to stop and get a search warrant before he entered a man's house to put out the fire."

Williams informed him it was required, especially when they had removed some of the property from the dwelling. Again there was a certain bite to his words.

"I don't know about all those technicalities. I'm *just* a volunteer fireman." Andy told Williams he would leave all that red tape up to him.

Tempers were beginning to flare. It had been a long night.

"Don't worry about it, Andy," Red said, pulling him away from Williams. "My nephew is also an arson agent with SLED. He's been dispatched to the scene and he'll take care of all that when he gets here."

CHAPTER 4

It was somewhere around 5:00 A.M. when the arson agent Andy Weir, Red's nephew, arrived at the fire scene. From the bottom of the driveway, he could see the flashing red lights of the fire truck. Once he climbed the driveway and reached the top of the hill, he quickly spotted the remains of the house fire and the yellow crime-scene tape strung around the trees and all along the perimeter of the fire. The firemen had set out generators and installed spotlights throughout the yard. With all the men still walking around in firefighting gear, all the firefighting and investigative equipment set out in the yard, and the steam rising from the burned ashes of the house, the scene reminded Weir of Steven Spielberg's *Close Encounters of the Third Kind*.

Like his uncle Red, Andy was one of the "old-timers" when it came to fighting fires. For seventeen years, he had been attached to the City of Chester Fire Department, until moving over to the division of the state fire marshal's office, and then on to SLED. His specialty for the past ten years had been handling the K-9s. He usually rode with his K-9, Trixie, who had been placed in service a year before to detect accelerants. She accompanied him this morning.

Shortly before daylight, and after the fire had cooled, arson agents Weir and Williams began their official investigation. While the firemen cleared the debris, Weir stood at what was once the front door of the Pittmans' home and tried to identify what type of furniture, if any, had survived the fire. In his walk-through, he came across what looked like a futon-type bed. It was lying at the back of the house and on top of some other furniture, which indicated that it probably had fallen from the upper level and down to the floor. The futon had taken a lot of intense heat. Weir deduced it had been in a fire for quite a long period of time, for some of the metal was already twisted and deformed.

After most of the debris from the fire was cleared, Weir decided it was time to let Trixie go in and do what she did best. If an accelerant had been used to start this fire, the odds would be overwhelmingly in her favor for detecting it. Like the pro he was, Weir worked Trixie on a leash, allowing her five minutes or so to become acclimated to the area. While the K-9 involved herself in the scene, Weir and Williams followed along behind, searching through the debris and observing any changes in her behavior.

"Trixie didn't detect anything," Weir reported to McNeil after his initial search. "I'm going to put her back in the vehicle; then we'd like to see the area where the bodies were found."

Several ladders had been placed along the path of the structure where the bodies had been found, and the two agents climbed up to take a look. At first, they, too, could see only one body clearly in the black rubbish. Weir suggested they put some additional ladders up, and asked Andy Martin to climb back up with them. Using flashlights as a guide, they moved a little more of the debris, and when they did, they saw the second body.

"You might want to call the county and get a backhoe in here to remove those bodies," Weir suggested to McNeil. "That structure is about as sturdy as a suspension bridge. It's going to be damn near impossible for any of us to stand up there and physically lift those bodies, then try and carry them down."

McNeil called the county maintenance supervisor and arranged for the backhoe to be brought to the fire scene. He had him drive the backhoe down toward the house and position it near the portion of the house where the Pittmans lay dead. The back bucket, which came to a height of about fifteen or sixteen feet, would be used like a giant hand to lower the bodies onto the ground. Knotting a rope to make a four-point harness, the rope was looped through the bedsprings, then tied together in the center with a center knot. A tag line, which was nothing more than a line extending down from where they had tied the bed and secured their ropes, was dropped down and the backhoe swung into place.

"Be careful, we don't want this bed to twist or turn." Weir shouted out his instructions to the backhoe operator.

Andy Martin tightened the tag line. The mattress springs and the bodies first shifted upward, then strained against the force of the rope harness and slowly eased to the ground.

The remains of Joe and Joy Pittman were spread out on a tarp before the investigators. Photographs were taken and the bodies were examined. Joe Pittman was lying on the bed, faceup, his legs hanging off the side of the bed. The smaller extremities of his body had been burned away. Because his body had received a lot more fire damage than his wife's, the arson agents believed he was probably closer to the main body of the fire than his wife.

Joy Pittman was found on the other side of the bed. She lay facedown with her head lowered in the prone position. The back of her head had a large, gaping hole in it. The agents pointed out that the heat of the fire often causes the brain to swell and eventually the skull cracks, but they weren't sure at this point if that was what had happened to Joy.

As the Pittmans' bodies were being examined, Andy Weir noticed one of the bodies had blood on it. In his thirty-plus years of investigation, he had seen many burned bodies with blood on them. Ultimately, it always indicated there had been some type of foul play before the fire.

Of course, *everybody knows that dead bodies don't bleed.*

Around daylight, CCSD deputies had discovered there were a lot of shotgun shells in the yard near the woodshed. Once an investigator himself, Sheriff Benson knew how important it was to find the facts and find them quickly. How critical it was that all physical evidence be gathered while the crime scene was fresh. Crime scenes never look the same on the second go-round.

In the smaller counties of South Carolina, law enforcement doesn't normally have a crime scene investigation team and depends on SLED for assistance in the meticulous cases. Andy Weir suggested to Sheriff Benson that he call for the assistance of SLED's senior crime scene investigator (CSI), sixteen-year-veteran David Black. With nearly five hundred crime scenes under his belt— and most of those death investigations—Black could be a valuable resource. Black's expertise was in the documentation and collection of any evidence, particularly those items that would have to go back to SLED's forensic laboratory for additional analysis.

CSI Black arrived around 9:15 A.M. and immediately started inquiring about the found evidence. After talking with CCSD investigators, he did a walk-through, just to see what they had and maybe identify any evidence that had been overlooked. Black located a number of spent .410 shotgun shells and a fired cartridge case found on the ground near the house and the motor home. A box of .410 shotgun shells was also found on a drum near the woodshed. All the items were labeled and photographed, as Black believed they were, more than likely, involved in the murders.

During Black's walk-through with the investigators

and firemen, he noticed Joe Pittman's utility shed was
unlocked. "Did Mr. Pittman normally leave this building
unlocked?" he asked no one in particular.

"Never!" Red Weir spoke up, insisting that Joe kept it
locked at all times. "Even when his wife called him to
come inside the house and eat lunch, he would lock it
before he left."

Black didn't know what had been taken from Joe
Pittman's utility shed, but he suspected if they could find
the character who had unlocked it, then they possibly
would have found their killer.

Under Black's supervision, law enforcement agencies
would spend the better part of the day collecting forensic evidence. They photographed and sketched the
scene, then started interviewing neighbors and friends
of the Pittmans to see if they knew anything about the
fire.

Arson agent Andy Weir told CCSD that after reviewing
all the evidence he believed the fire had been deliberately set. Based on all his training and experience as a
firefighter and an arson specialist, he deduced the fire
was a slow, built-up fire—definitely not an accelerated
one—and had originated somewhere near and on the
second-floor loft area. After the fire had been started, he
believed, it first burned upward and consumed the roof,
then started burning downward toward the first floor.

Weir then alluded to the .410 shotgun shells found
amongst the burned ruins and outside the home, hint-
ing that perhaps all was not well within the Pittman
house before it burned. The gathered evidence indicated foul play, but before anyone jumped to any
conclusions, he advised, they needed to make sure they
were absolutely right.

By now, Coroner Carter Wright had arrived on the
scene. Wright added he had also examined the bodies
after they were placed down on the ground and saw that
one of those bodies—Joy Pittman—had suffered great
trauma to the back skull. Joy's body was found with her

head facing down and there was blood on her body around the back and neck area. That could mean only one thing to him: she had been murdered.

Joe and Joy Pittman murdered? In their own home, and while they were asleep in their bed? Who could do such a thing? And why?

As Weir, Williams, and the investigators from CCSD stood there pondering these and other questions, they stared at what was left of the Pittmans' bedroom. The small charred area suddenly took on the appearance of an altar of death that had risen out of the ashes. This section of their bedroom was all that was left of the second-floor attic. Somehow, they couldn't help but think, it had refused to go down in the fire, as if, above everything else, it was there to reveal the truth of what had happened in the Pittmans' home the night of November 28, 2001.

CHAPTER 5

Life is strange and can change directions in a heartbeat.

There was nothing that Roland Pennington and Terry Robinson loved more than hunting. They had both started hunting as little boys and for twenty years or more had continued the sport. Every year, in the fall, the two hunters would suit up in their camouflaged outfits and head to the woods. For the last twelve years, they had been hunting at the Smokey Ridge Hunting Club in Gaffney, South Carolina, where they were two of ten members who paid for the exclusive rights to hunt deer, duck, and turkey on a secluded 469-acre reserve.

A little before 7:00 A.M., on November 29, Pennington and Robinson drove Terry's 1996 truck to the hunting club, parked it on a logging road, then proceeded on the four-wheeler a quarter of a mile down the logging road. Pennington took his usual spot at the intersection of two logging roads, where he had set up a camouflaged tripod deer stand in the swamp. After walking the short distance to the stand, he climbed the fifteen-foot ladder and prepared himself for a morning's wait on the deer.

Robinson's deer stand was on the opposite side of the woods. But this time, when he cut across the intersection and drove past a cemetery, he noticed a black SUV

Pathfinder parked on the left side of the road. Twenty feet away from the truck, he slowed and looked to see if anyone was in the truck. There was no one inside the truck that he could see. Apparently, Robinson figured, whatever persons were there had left, by now, and were out in the woods hunting.

The SUV would be a mental thorn for Terry to rub all day. He was president of their hunting club and usually received a printout of the vehicles and the people that hunted on the reserve. It was always a peeve of his that people were hunting where they weren't supposed to be. The members had bought that right and they didn't like it when someone tried to usurp that privilege. He made a mental note of the description of the car and the license plate number, then drove on down the road toward his deer stand near the creek.

Robinson parked the four-wheeler on the side of the logging road and walked another quarter of a mile through dense underbrush to his tree stand. He had been sitting in his deer stand for about an hour when he heard what sounded like a truck coming through the woods. He assumed it was the SUV he had spotted at the cemetery, but he wasn't sure. It was unusual for someone to drive down the old logging road, as it was grown over and tree limbs were hanging over the road. As the truck continued on the road, he could hear the limbs cracking and breaking underneath its weight.

A few minutes later, Robinson heard the truck stop. For the next three minutes, he listened as tires spun and some more limbs broke underneath the weight of the truck. He then heard the truck shut off—as if the person had gotten the truck stuck—followed by the sound of the truck door opening and closing. Someone was talking.

Robinson looked in the direction toward the vehicle and mumbled, "All this noise is messing up my hunting."

Pennington was about three hundred yards away from Robinson, on the other side of the swamp. He, too, had heard the spinning tires and noise from the vehicle out on the logging road, and he was relieved when it finally stopped. Then, about fifteen minutes later, he heard the crack of a small-caliber rifle about twenty-five yards behind him. It sounded as if the shot had been fired from a .22 rifle. Pennington was familiar with the different sounds of firearms and was certain the shot was not that of a high-powered deer rifle.

Somebody must be hunting rabbits or squirrels, Pennington thought as he scanned the woods. He was very nervous about someone shooting a rifle that close to him.

"Help, help!" The cry came from the area where Pennington had heard the spinning tires.

Pennington's head snapped forward. He looked from side to side, looking for the person who had called out. He couldn't swear to it, but it sounded like the voice of a little boy.

"Please, somebody help me—I'm lost." The weak voice cried out again.

Pennington cupped his hands to his ears and listened. When he heard the voice again and identified where the voice was coming from, he yelled out in that vicinity, "Over here. I'm over here in the tree stand. Just keep walking toward the sound of my voice."

Pennington could see the small figure of a little boy making his way through the woods toward him. Breaking branches and snapping twigs, the boy clawed his way through until he finally emerged in the clearing on the back side of Pennington's deer stand.

"How did you get out here?" Pennington asked the boy. The boy was dressed in hunting clothes and clutching a rifle to his chest. "And what's your name?"

"My name is Christopher Pittman." The words flew out of the boy's mouth, like he was overjoyed at just seeing another human being. "This—this black guy kidnapped me. He brung me here. He killed my grandparents and burned our house up, too."

Fearing the boy may have been followed, Pennington's eyes darted through the woods. "What about that shot I heard a while ago? Was that this guy?"

"It was that black guy. He shot at me."

Pennington was cautious. It wasn't every day that a little boy walks out of the woods, telling you he's been kidnapped by a man who has murdered his grandparents. He needed to be careful. If the black man had driven him here, that meant he was still out in the woods somewhere. Armed and dangerous. Who was to say the little boy wasn't in on some kind of setup?

Pennington grabbed his rifle and climbed down out of the deer stand. Once on the ground, he could see the boy was carrying a .45 lever-action rifle. It was cocked and the hammer was pulled back. The boy had his finger in the trigger hole and was waving the gun all around, as if the gun had a mind of its own. As he waved it out in front of Pennington like a flag, it continually fell backward and forward in the boy's hands, making Pennington very anxious.

It doesn't matter what that boy thinks he is aiming at, Pennington thought. *When he pulls that trigger, there is no telling where that bullet is going. One spastic jerk, a step in the wrong direction, and I'm in the hospital. Even worse, I'm in the morgue.*

Pennington stepped closer to the boy. "How about you handing me your gun?"

The boy gripped the gun tighter, as if to say he wasn't sure he trusted the stranger he had just met in the woods, but then unloosened his grip and handed it over to Pennington. As he stood there, looking a bit uneasy, he watched Pennington empty all the shells out of his gun.

Pennington took a deep breath. The boy's gun had been fully loaded—with a shell still in the chamber. Somebody could have been hurt, especially the way he was waving that gun. "Do you have any more guns on you?"

The boy shook his head. The .45 was the only weapon he had with him. Accepting that his gun had been confiscated by an adult, Christopher told Pennington, "I want you to show me how to get out of these woods."

Pennington stood talking with the boy near the deer stand. Still in a bit of a stupor, he attempted to direct Christopher out of the woods and toward the main highway. When Christopher raised his hand, Pennington noticed a cut, one he assumed he must have gotten while plodding through the woods.

The boy looked nervous and scared, like any little boy who had just spent a couple of hours lost and wandering in a strange place. Pennington knew it wouldn't be right to send this boy back into the woods and ask him to fend for himself. He'd never forgive himself if something happened to him.

"Why don't you follow me." Pennington coaxed Christopher through the woods and toward a path leading to Robinson's tree stand near the creek. "My partner is not too far from here. We'll walk over there to where he is hunting. He's got a four-wheeler over there and we'll all drive out of here and get you some help."

Pennington and Christopher crossed the woods and neared the creek. The hunter called out his partner's name, "Terry, Terry."

Robinson was crouched in his tree stand near the creek when he heard Pennington calling. He looked in the woods and saw Pennington walking toward him with some little boy.

"What the . . ." Robinson couldn't get the words out. He had never seen this boy before and had no idea where he came from. He quickly climbed down from his perch and met them in an open spot near the creek. When he was told what had happened to Christopher, he was as surprised as Pennington.

"So what did you say your name was?" Robinson asked.

"Christopher Pittman." The boy repeated the same information he had offered Pennington. "A black guy kidnapped me, killed my grandparents, and brought me down here."

Robinson and Pennington exchanged glances.

"He—he drove me down here," Pittman added, anxiety filling his voice. "We've been out there in the woods all night."

Pennington nodded at the four-wheeler, then said to Robinson, "I guess we're lucky he didn't see the four-wheeler or it would have been long gone by now."

"Yeah, that black guy stopped and looked at your four-wheeler when we first pulled in," Christopher chirped in. "He knows it's here."

"Well, if he knows it's here, then he knows we're here, and he'll be looking for us to drive it out." Robinson stepped over to the four-wheeler and removed the key from the ignition. "We've got no choice but to leave it sitting right here."

Pennington's eyes widened. "Wait a minute, we are going to drive out of here, aren't we? I don't think it is such a good idea just to leave the four-wheeler sitting here in the swamp."

Although Pennington was a larger man than Robinson, he was younger and less experienced. He usually went along with Robinson's ideas.

"Yes, we're going to leave it here, for now," Robinson said calmly, blankly staring back at him. "The last thing we need to do is let that guy know where we're at. If he's armed, he can pick us off, one at a time, as we drive out of the woods on the four-wheeler. We've got less of a chance of him spotting us if we walk out through the woods."

Robinson pointed toward a different trail, one they had not taken previously, but one that would lead them safely through the woods. He estimated it was about a twenty-five-minute walk before they reached the old logger road, where his truck was parked.

"We're also going to leave the four-wheeler because we don't want any noise," Robinson explained further as they walked away. He walked straight ahead on the footpath through the woods, turning his head only slightly to watch Christopher and Pennington pacing behind him. "I'm trying to get us out of here without anybody knowing it. I don't know if there is anybody else in these woods or not, but I don't want to find out there's a guy waiting for us behind some tree with a high-powered rifle as we come riding through on the four-wheeler."

Robinson kept watching Christopher. If some black guy was after him, he didn't show it. He wasn't fidgety or nervous, and he wasn't moving around, hiding behind trees or crying, begging for them not to move forward. He quietly fell in the middle and followed him and Pennington through the woods. When Christopher was asked a question, his response was always a polite "yes, sir/no, sir" every time.

The two hunters knew the property like the back of their hands. They led Christopher past the creek, around the swamp, and back toward the cemetery. During their twenty to twenty-five minutes walking in the woods, they looked but never saw any signs of a black man Christopher claimed was stalking him. Before they made it to the logging road, Christopher also told them he had a car somewhere on the other road over there. But he never asked the hunters to take him back to it. They just assumed, since it was his car, he wanted to go back there.

"Is your car on this road?" Robinson asked.

Christopher shrugged his shoulders. He didn't know if this was the road or not.

Robinson led them onto another road, where they spotted the vehicle fifteen to twenty yards up ahead. It was bogged down in the old logging road. He looked at the vehicle stuck in the mud, then asked Christopher how his car had gotten this far down the logging road.

"The black man . . . he took it and drove it here."

Suddenly a dog ran out from under the car and charged at Pennington. The dog was growling and barking. Pennington backed away from the dog. He had never seen the dog before and didn't know if it was going to attack him or not.

"We might have to shoot the dog," Pennington shouted.

Christopher never told Pennington that the dog belonged to him, and that his name was Chrisdee. "Go ahead and shoot it," he smirked. "If you'll give me the gun, I'll shoot it."

Pennington suspected the boy would have shot the dog, had he given him the gun. He didn't like the way the dog growled and barked at him, either, but he wasn't so eager to shoot and kill him as Christopher was. He waited until the dog calmed down, then told Christopher just to keep on walking and leave the dog be.

When they reached Robinson's Dodge Dakota at the end of the road, Christopher got in the truck, sitting in the backseat behind Pennington. Christopher was told he was being driven to the Corinth Fire Department, where Robinson served as a volunteer fireman. Robinson would have access to the building and would call 911 and get him some assistance.

"Just make certain you don't try anything up the road," Pennington warned, turning around in his seat to face Christopher. He was still suspicious of the boy and his intentions.

Christopher dropped his head and stared at the floorboard. He never said a word during the fifteen-minute trip. He never cried, whimpered, or showed any signs of being afraid.

Once they were inside the Corinth Fire Department, Pennington led Christopher into the office. He was told to stand near the desk and empty the contents of his pockets on the desk. Christopher jammed his hands in his pockets, pulled out a fistful of bullets, and dropped them on the desk.

"Is that all you got with you?" Pennington asked.

Christopher stared back at him with a blank expression.

"No, I got a bunch of guns and some money back there in my car."

When Robinson finished his 911 call, he walked back into the office and started asking Christopher for additional details. "So I can give the police the correct information when they get here, can you tell me again how you were kidnapped?"

Christopher looked up at Robinson, then began slowly telling his story again. "I was in the house cleaning the shotgun. I heard someone come inside the house. I just ran outside and this black guy started chasing me out of there. He told me if I didn't stop, he would shoot me. He killed my grandparents, took our car, and brought me out here." Christopher didn't mention anything about his grandparents' house on fire.

"Well, what did this black guy look like?"

Christopher paused. "He was tall. Probably somewhere around six feet two inches."

The boy looked like he was about five feet two inches and weighed a couple of Big Macs short of about ninety pounds. They could see him being overpowered by a larger man.

"Did you get any kind of name?"

"No, that black boy wouldn't tell me his name," he said. "He said he was scared if I got away from him, I would tell on him."

Robinson studied Christopher's face. He had been with him for about an hour now and didn't have any trouble understanding his story. Granted his story was bizarre, but it did sound somewhat believable.

CHAPTER 6

Darrell Duncan, a thirteen-year veteran with the Cherokee County Sheriff's Department in Gaffney, was in his office when the call came in from 911 about a juvenile being kidnapped and found in the woods. He was told the boy was being held at the Corinth Fire Department, approximately seven miles from the sheriff's office.

Duncan hooked up with Chief Deputy Joe Hill and they drove to the fire department, where they met with Pennington and Robinson outside the building. Christopher remained inside, in the office, waiting, while the hunters told law enforcement how they had found him roaming in the woods and what he had told them about being kidnapped.

After talking with the hunters, the officers walked into the office and saw a scrawny boy wearing hunting pants and a multicolored jacket. He didn't appear very upset to them, considering the information he had given the hunters. They considered him a young boy who was both a victim and a witness of a horrible crime.

"Son, we've got two guys outside this building who are very upset and concerned about you," Deputy Hill stated, pulling up a chair directly in front of Christopher.

"We're trying to figure out exactly what is going on here. We want to know if you can help us out?"

Christopher sat up on the couch. He looked a little nervous, but not frightened to the point where he couldn't carry on a normal conversation.

"I was at home during the nighttime," he began. "I heard someone come in the house. I slipped out the back door and was hiding. I heard two gunshots up in my grandparents' room and that's when a black male came out and found me. This black guy burned down my grandparents' house, then, forced me to get in the car with him. That is how we ended up in the woods. This black man took me against my will."

"Where do you live?"

"In Chester, South Carolina. I live with my grandparents." Christopher remained calm. He still was not crying, nor did he appear to be upset in any way. "Last night, I heard two gunshots in my grandparents' room. The black guy then came outside and poured gas around the house. He burned it that way."

"Did he pour gas on the house itself?" Hill wanted to know all the details.

"No, he just walked around the house and poured the gasoline on the ground. Then he set it afire and burned the house down."

"So, this black guy then takes you in the car and brings you up here?" Hill reiterated.

Chris nodded. "Yes, sir."

"And he had guns that he had stolen from your grandparents' house?"

"Yes, sir."

"And he drives up to the hunting lodge, where he holds you all night?"

"Yes, sir. That's right."

Hill lowered his voice. He moved in closer to Christopher, then asked, "Now, tell me how you got away."

Christopher's dark eyes narrowed. "This black guy got out to use the bathroom, and when he did, I took off running." He wiped his mouth with the back of his hand. "When he saw me running, he yelled out, 'You can't go anywhere,' then shot at me once."

Hill was having to pull this story out of him, and he didn't like what he was seeing. "So what did you do then?"

"I got his keys and I threw them keys into the woods. I just kept on running through the woods."

Hill thought about what he had been told: the story sounded a little screwy, but until he found out any different, he had to assume the boy was telling the truth. He excused himself and walked outside to speak with the hunters again and swap stories.

By now, Cherokee County sheriff Bill Blanton and local SLED agent Dewitt "Spike" McGraw had arrived and already begun to coordinate a search for the kidnapper. If the black guy Christopher spoke of was hiding out somewhere in the woods at the hunting club, then chances were very good they would spot him. Hill passed on what little information he had garnered to the sheriff.

"We're setting up our sheriff emergency response team (SERT)," Sheriff Blanton informed Hill. "Spike has requested SLED send a helicopter and it's on the way to search the area. We've also called out our tracking team of bloodhounds. We'll take them first to the car and go from there."

Cherokee County law enforcement considered the kidnapping of a twelve-year-old and double homicide a major event. The young boy was telling them a black male, armed and dangerous, had committed these crimes, and that he was still out there in the woods. Every available officer and all the resources they could muster were called out to help find this person. In situations like these, no expense was spared.

Wes Foster, a nine-year veteran with the Cherokee County Sheriff's Department, was also contacted that day and told that someone had been kidnapped near the Smokey Ridge Hunting Club. One of his many duties with the sheriff's department was assigning the sheriff's emergency response team and the bloodhound tracking team. The K-9 unit was especially needed to help track the suspect in the woods.

When Foster arrived at the Corinth Fire Department and went inside to wait on the other team members, he saw Christopher inside the office. The boy was sitting on the couch, with his head down, just staring at the floor.

In a brief five-minute conversation, Foster spoke with Christopher about the person who kidnapped him. "Christopher, I'm sorry you've had to go through all this," he said with great sympathy, "but I need you to help me find the guy that kidnapped you."

Christopher looked up from the floor and nodded.

"Can you give me a description of the guy who kidnapped you?" Foster asked. "Maybe what he looked like and what type of clothing he was wearing so we'll know who and what we're looking for?"

"All I can remember is that he was a tall black guy." Christopher looked confused. He swallowed hard before answering. "He was about six foot two inches. But I don't know anything about his clothing."

"Can you tell me the last place you saw him?"

Christopher shrugged, his eyes sliding away, then answered, "In my grandma's SUV."

CHAPTER 7

The fire scene in Chester was becoming quite a busy place. It was swarming with people: firefighters trying to do their jobs, investigators trying to do their jobs, and the medical emergency people all trying to do their jobs. Much of the private speculation about how the fire had started and rumors about Christopher Pittman's disappearance had reached the ears of the community quickly, and there were a lot of curious people, rubberneckers, and newshounds trying to sneak on the scene. Television cameras were coming out of the woodwork, attempting to get a shot of anything and everything that would qualify for good headliner news. It was becoming a media frenzy.

Coroner Carter Wright had spoken with forensic pathologist Dr. Joel Sexton, who had asked if the bodies could be loaded and transported in the same position they had been found. It was helpful, he was told, to Dr. Sexton's investigation if the crime scene could be kept as pristine as possible and none of the evidence be contaminated or tampered with. So as to prevent an "accidental disturbance" of the crime scene, severe restrictions were placed on anyone crossing beyond a certain point near the Pittmans' driveway. The last thing they needed was somebody tromping over the crime scene and stumbling over two dead bodies. It had happened before, and it could happen again.

Sheriff Benson and Major McNeil were still in charge of the crime scene and were holding their cards close to their chests. They were not about to give up any information concerning how the Pittmans died or the condition of their bodies to the press. And when they spotted a news helicopter flying overhead taking pictures of the scene, they knew they had to come up with an alternate plan for transporting the victims' bodies without the press knowing.

Normally, the rescue squads in Chester County transport bodies in one of their emergency vehicles to the medical examiner's office for autopsies. But this time, McNeil phoned local businessman Joe Stevens, who owned a towing service, and asked that he bring one of his big flatbed trucks normally used for transporting large loads and automobiles, to the scene. The plan was to use the orange and white vehicle as a decoy, while the flatbed truck was used to carry and transport the bodies to Dr. Sexton.

With the rescue squad's vehicles in plain view of the press at the top of the hill, the flatbed truck was pulled onto the scene and near the bodies. After photographing the bodies a second time, the agents covered them with tarps, sealed them down with duct tape, then lifted the bodies on the back of the flatbed with the front-end loader.

Benson and McNeil believed the press would pay close attention to any emergency vehicles coming or going out of the fire scene, but would never suspect the bodies were underneath the tarps on the flatbed truck. Their plan worked perfectly. As hoped, the newsmen took the bait and followed the decoy emergency vehicle away from the fire scene and into town.

Earlier in the day, McNeil had asked that one of his own detectives, Lucinda McKellar, join his forces at the fire scene. McKellar was in her fourth year at the Chester

County Sheriff's Department and currently served as a law enforcement victim advocate. But it was while working in child abuse cases that she had carved out her own niche. A tall, full-figured woman, with short dark hair and big brown eyes, McKellar's demeanor was that of an elementary-school teacher. Her peers were impressed with how children warmed up to her as comfortably as they would to Big Bird or Kermit the Frog. McKellar especially had demonstrated excellent rapport with children who were victims and was very skilled in obtaining their statements. McNeil already had it in the back of his mind that she would interview Christopher Pittman once he was located.

Upon arriving at the crime scene, McKellar was instructed by Major McNeil to keep in touch with 911. If any new information came in on the case, he wanted to know immediately. McKellar spent most of the morning beside her police vehicle, alternating between her radio and her cell phone. The call they had been waiting on came through at approximately 10:00 A.M.

"We've got a number for you," the emergency operator related to McKellar. "Investigator Darrell Duncan, from Cherokee County, reports a little boy has been found, who says a black male kidnapped him and killed his grandparents. They are holding him at the Corinth Fire Department in Gaffney. He says his name is Christopher Pittman."

"That's our boy," McKellar shouted into her radio.

McKellar conferred with Benson and McNeil. Lieutenant Tom Davis, SLED's arson section supervisor for Chester County, was also on the scene and was helping coordinate services. Davis had received a call from Dewitt "Spike" McGraw, of Cherokee County, also inquiring about the fire and the lost boy from Chester County. The three men debated for a few minutes, then decided they needed to send a group of officers to Cherokee County.

McNeil called McKellar over to the side. He had seen her in action many times and had great confidence in her skills, especially when she dealt with juveniles. She had developed a rapport with some of the most resistant children and obtained statements from them when he knew nobody else could have.

"Lucinda, I need you to go and talk with that boy," McNeil said, without having to think twice about it. "You'll pair up with Agent Williams and the both of you will respond to the location where the boy and his vehicle were found."

McNeil, crime scene investigator David Black, arson agent Andy Weir, and SLED's lieutenant Davis would follow them to Cherokee County. Cherokee County was about sixty miles northwest of Chester, a little more than an hour's drive.

Finally all the missing pieces were starting to fall in place.

CHAPTER 8

Chester County law enforcement officers were strangers to Cherokee County. After making a phone call for directions, they stopped on Highway 211 and pulled off at an old store. Sheriff Bill Blanton was waiting for them there.

"We've got all our personnel in the woods trying to find this black guy that supposedly abducted this young boy," Blanton advised. "The two hunters who found the boy said he told them this guy killed his grandparents and burned their house down. Then he kidnapped him and brought him out here."

"Where's his car now?" McNeil asked.

"It's a couple of miles down the road," Blanton said. "He got it stuck in the woods. We're waiting for Officer Joe Hill. I don't know exactly where the site is located, so he'll have to come and escort us."

A few minutes later, Deputy Hill arrived and led the other officers into the desolate area at the hunting club. Cherokee County's SERT team was already there, searching the woods with their K-9 team and SLED's helicopters. The two hunters who had found Christopher were there also, guiding them through the woods and explaining in detail what had happened earlier. Agent Williams decided he would stay at the site where the vehicle had been found and that Detective McKellar should ride over with Sheriff Blanton to the Corinth Fire Department and talk with the victim.

As Detective McKellar was leaving the Smokey Ridge Road site, she heard several helicopters flying over the area and asked if they belonged to SLED.

"Yes, that's our people looking for the kidnapper," Blanton confirmed. "We've been searching for about an hour now, but we've seen nothing as of yet."

While the cavalry was combing the woods for the suspect, Officer Darrell Duncan and Tammy Bright, a Cherokee County female detective, had sat with Christopher in the office. They had assisted him with any needs he had and passed on to their superiors any information he could give them that would have aided in the search.

For all pretenses and circumstances, Christopher Pittman was the victim of a horrible crime. He was a kidnap victim, as well as a witness to a double homicide, and that was how he was being treated. He napped off and on, and had no problems eating his lunch. He was never placed into custody, nor did he appear to be in any great trauma, so there was no use of restraints in any way. Although Christopher was relatively useless when it came to providing information about his kidnapper, he looked as if he were satisfied a search was being conducted.

When Detective McKellar arrived at the fire department sometime around 11:15 A.M., she went inside the office and found Christopher lying on the couch asleep. While she and Detective Duncan talked, he slept with his face turned inward against the back cushions of the couch. After Duncan filled her in on what Christopher had told the hunters, she woke him from his slumber.

"Christopher, wake up," McKellar said softly. She shook the boy a few times before he woke up.

Christopher sat up and stared at the tall, dark-haired woman, with doelike eyes, sitting in front of him. He listened as she told him her name and where she worked.

"Sometimes children have a hard time pronouncing my name Lucinda, so it's okay by me if you call me 'Lucy.'" She smiled.

The corner of Christopher's mouth flipped upward.

"I've just come from Chester County," McKellar continued, "and, because you're such an important person, I need to talk with you about what happened to your grandparents."

Christopher still looked at her with a lopsided grin.

McKellar wanted Christopher to know she viewed him as a victim and a possible witness to a crime. And that it was her job to gather information and get a statement from him as to what happened.

Christopher was very calm and polite. Calling McKellar "Lucy" a few times, he responded appropriately to all her questions and concerns. While he was being interviewed, Detective Duncan sat in the office and listened.

McKellar's experience with children had convinced her that oftentimes in child cases, adults don't always want to believe everything children say, simply because they are children. As part of her training, she was taught to do everything she could to prove even the most minute thing a child told her, so as to lend credence to their statements. Christopher's grandparents had been murdered. As a process of elimination, she thought it was best to administer a gunshot residue kit.

"When was the last time you shot a gun?" McKellar asked as she swabbed Christopher's hands.

"Uh-hum, I think it was yesterday." Christopher seemed caught off-guard by the question. "I was target practicing with my grandfather. We were shooting at Pepsi bottles. You know, the green ones."

McKellar assumed he was referring to the green Sprite bottles.

So as not to lead Christopher and put words into his mouth, McKellar asked him open-ended questions. In past experiences, some of her younger victims had gotten distraught as they told their story. She always found it best to write while they talked. Writing on a SLED-approved voluntary statement form, she asked, "Can you tell me exactly what happened?"

"Me and my grandfather were target practicing. It was about four o'clock yesterday. We were in the back of the house over the creek at the end of the property. We were in the condo. Granddad calls it a condo. It's like a tree house, kind of, but it's [really] a hunting tree stand. We were shooting at Coca-Cola bottles. [They were] a green-ish kind, like a Sprite bottle, but it didn't have a label. We shot for about thirty minutes. We were squirrel hunting, but I couldn't hit anything, so my granddad said I needed a little more practice, so we shot at the bottle."

"And what happened next?" McKellar interjected.

"We got back on the four-wheeler and rode back to the house. Then we went to Pizza Hut at five o'clock. We [then] went to choir practice. We got home a little after seven o'clock, or maybe a little after. Grandmother was talking at church. We got in about seven-ten probably. I didn't get on the computer until eight o'clock, [I guess that time] because I had a school project. I had to do that nasty homework. I had to write a letter. We had to write about the poem we [had] read. It's called 'I'm Nobody.' [It's about a] lady who stayed in her room for twenty-six years until she died of old age. That [time period] was back in eighteen-something."

"You're doing fine, Christopher." McKellar smiled. "But I need you to slow down so I can catch up with you." She waved her hand beside her, as if to cool it off.

Christopher nodded, then started up again.

"I'm on Zoloft. That makes me real sleepy. The doctor put me on it. I went to bed at nine o'clock. I usually go to bed at eight o'clock or eight-thirty. It was about eleven-thirty. I heard footsteps on the porch outside. I went in the bathroom. There's two doors. You can get in from my bedroom and the kitchen.

"When I was in the bathroom, I saw him come in the back door. I couldn't see him good at first. I heard my shotgun rattle. It was on the sofa. I didn't have room for it in the safe. I wasn't going to put it up until the next morning. I usually keep [it] in the cabinet by the gun safe. I had a box of my shotgun shells by the gun on the couch. I ran out [of the house] and went outside. I hid behind the four-wheeler trailer. I heard somebody yelling, but couldn't tell what they were saying. I heard four gunshots. It didn't sound like a high-powered rifle. It sounded more like a shotgun. I started crying."

McKellar felt sorry for Christopher. She half-expected him to cry as they talked, but he didn't. There was a bit of desperation in his eyes when he looked at her, as if he were in search of someone to believe him.

Christopher continued.

"Then I stayed outside for a little bit. He (the black guy) came out. I didn't know what he looked like. It was dark. He saw me and walked over to me. He pointed a shotgun at me. He said, 'Do you have any way of trans-portation?' I said, 'Yes, my grandpa's truck.' He said, 'Go get the keys.' The keys were in the kitchen. He walked around for a minute and said, 'What is in there?' I said, 'My granddad's guns.'

"[The black guy] started grabbing guns and ammuni-tion. We went down to the truck. On our way to the truck, we grabbed a gas can for my four-wheeler. We got in the truck. My dog, Chrisdee, was growling at him. I was sitting in the passenger seat. We just drove until we got there. We slept on some road. It looked like a place where people go dump their trash. There were knocked-down trees and stuff. I slept. I don't know if he slept or not."

McKellar shifted in her seat, then asked, "Okay, this black guy has kidnapped you, so what'd you do then?"

"When I woke up, we started hitting bumps and stuff. I woke up. We were at the hunting place. We drove all the way down there and got stuck. Then he got out and was looking at the tires. I got out and ran. He shot at me once. I got a little further, and he shot at me again. He didn't say anything. I think he put the gun back in the truck when he threw the keys. I don't know if he had any more guns with him."

"Then what happened?" McKellar asked.

"I followed the creek down a little bit; then I went back to the truck. I got my forty-five and some bullets, and I got some money he took from my grandparents. I started walking, trying to find a main road. That's when I saw the man in the deer stand. [That's when] the hunter saw my dog. I got a glimpse of the dog, [but] I don't know how my dog followed me down here."

McKellar did not give Christopher the third degree or challenge his story. Instead, she informed him he was not under arrest, nor was he being detained for any criminal offenses concerning the events he had made known to her. She asked him to sign a paper stating this and verify that he was free to walk away without saying anything.

Christopher's interview had lasted thirty minutes. As he provided the details, McKellar wrote them down. She was convinced he had understood all the questions and responded appropriately. After the statement was written, she handed it to him for review. He was asked to read it and make sure that she didn't make any mistakes, then sign his name at the bottom of each page.

"And would you initial the beginning and end of each paragraph," McKellar further instructed him. "It locks your words in so that nobody can change them."

Christopher took the pen from McKellar. He did as he was instructed.

McKellar then changed direction. "Sometimes I have a hard time understanding things," she told Christopher. "Just so I can get in my mind what happened, can you draw me a map of your grandparents' house?"

Christopher took the paper McKellar gave him and sketched out a layout of the house, then labeled the different locations. Among other things, he drew out a top floor, pointing out, "That's where the loft was. My grandparents slept there." With the aid of another, larger, two-dimensional drawing he had made, he walked McKellar through the bottom floor. "That's the gun cabinet and the back door, where that guy came through the house," he indicated.

McKellar remembered the layout of the house from the fire scene, and everything matched up with what he had told her. Impressed that he had drawn the sketch two-dimensional, she asked, "Would you date it and sign it, so people will know you were the one that drew that picture?"

Christopher dated and signed the drawing.

"And would you draw that place you told me earlier where you hid from the black guy?" McKellar asked of him. "I want to make sure I understand it correctly."

Christopher sketched an aerial view of his grandparents' house and yard, including a firewood shed and his grandparents' parked motor home. He drew an arrow to one side of the house and labeled it "SIDE OF THE HOUSE," then drew a circle near the woodshed, with a line drawn to the word "HID."

"Right there," he emphasized, pointing at the circle on his map, "is where I hid from the black guy. That is where I was hiding from this man that kidnapped me and killed my grandparents."

Christopher sat back in his chair and relaxed.

CHAPTER 9

Earlier in the day, Agent Spike McGraw had interviewed hunter Roland Pennington back at the hunting club. While they were walking in the direction of Pennington's hunting tripod, they found a .22 rifle lying on the side of a four-wheeler trail. Pennington looked at the gun and told McGraw it was consistent with the shot he had heard that morning in the woods.

McGraw asked Pennington if he believed there ever was a black guy who shot at the young boy in the woods.

"I don't think so," Pennington answered.

McGraw didn't think so, either.

Later, when the Cherokee County K-9 Team were let out at the vehicle in the woods, the only scents they sniffed out was that of the two hunters and Christopher. Their conclusion was that only three people had been in the woods that day. And that there was never a fourth man.

Every stick has two ends, but it looked as if Christopher had given them the wrong end.

McGraw had teamed up with Agent David Black and they were eager to search the Pittmans' black Pathfinder Christopher had gotten stuck in an area near the swamp. Chomping at the bit, McGraw had already secured and executed a search warrant, so he and Black had the legal right to open the door and look inside. Because the vehicle was locked, they gained entry by breaking one of the windows.

When the investigators opened the front door of the vehicle, they discovered there were even more contradictions to Christopher's story. The first thing they noticed about the inside of the vehicle was that the floorboard gearshift was in the reverse position and the driver's seat was pulled all the way up toward the front. The front seat was pulled up so far, it almost went under the steering wheel.

"Who was driving this car?" McGraw joked. "A midget?"

The information Christopher had given about the incident and his description of the suspect certainly did not jibe with what was seen in his car. On the passenger's floorboard was a five-gallon container of gasoline. Half-full. The backseat of the SUV had been laid down and contained a number of firearms—enough firepower, that somebody could have started their own private war.

So, if the black man was driving, where did Christopher sit?

McGraw and Black were also very interested in a .410 pump shotgun found in the backseat of the vehicle. Since spent shells for a similar gun had been found back at the crime scene, it was likely there was a connection between the two. When they pulled the Remington .410 outside the vehicle to render it safe, they found a shell already in the chamber and two additional ones in the two magazines underneath the barrel.

Black called out a list of weapons and ammunition found in the SUV: A Ruger .10/22 rifle and a box of .45-caliber ammunition. A box of .22 short ammunition. An Old Timer's knife and sheath. A box of .410 ammunition and another box of .45-caliber ammunition.

Where did this kid think he was going? To join a revolution?

McGraw had seen the little boy, earlier, at the fire station. He looked just like any other normal twelve-year-old child.

He was fairly calm and didn't look too upset. He certainly didn't look like the type who would make up an elaborate story like this.

Major McNeil had been waiting at the fire station all this time, just in case the media got out of hand and started thinking there was nothing better Christopher enjoyed than having his picture splattered across the evening news. Christopher had just eaten lunch, and while the two investigators talked, the boy took another nap. While Christopher was asleep, McNeil shared the latest information on his case with McKellar.

"I don't believe the boy's been telling us the truth," McNeil revealed. "I'll know more after they process the car, but so far his story isn't checking out. But, until we have further evidence, we'll still treat him as a victim, even though it looks like his role could suddenly change to that of a suspect."

McKellar knew if all of this was true about Christopher, then it wouldn't take the press long to get wind of it. Her suspicions were right on target. When she looked outside, there were several reporters with their cameras pressed against the windows, trying to capture an image of Christopher through the glass.

Christopher was still asleep on the couch.

"Wake up, Christopher," McKellar whispered. "There's some media activity going on outside the building and we need to go upstairs."

For two hours, McKellar and Christopher stayed upstairs in the firemen's recreational area. Christopher watched television, took a nap, and played cards with McKellar.

McKellar felt sorry for Christopher and wanted to talk to him about the loss of his grandparents, but she didn't know how he would react to that. *If I'm going to talk with him about something that traumatic, then maybe it's best to wait until a family member is with him.* She remembered his father was supposed to be driving in today from Florida.

While Christopher watched television, he would take periodic breaks and talk with McKellar. At one point, he came to her like a child who had just memorized something interesting in Sunday school and wanted to share it with her. Speaking very rapidly, he rattled off something that sounded like a Bible verse. At least, McKellar thought it sounded like something from the Bible. The only part she heard was a reference to "burning in the fires of Hell."

McKellar didn't understand the significance of the Bible verse and what it all meant to Christopher, but it certainly didn't seem like the kind of words that ought to be coming out of the mouth of a twelve-year-old.

CHAPTER 10

It was looking like a journalism convention at the Corinth fire station. When Major McNeil was told about the evidence found in Joy Pittman's SUV and how that stacked up against Christopher, he knew the press would have a field day.

"It's getting pretty congested around here," McNeil said to Sheriff Blanton. "Do you think we could use one of your offices at the law enforcement center?"

"Not a problem," Blanton assured him.

McNeil walked back inside the fire department and climbed the stairs to the second level. Christopher was sitting on the couch. That was the first time he had seen Christopher face-to-face. He motioned to McKellar with his index finger. "Want to step over here for a few seconds?" He didn't want the boy hearing what he had to say.

"We've finished processing the car and that's given us some new information," he said in a low voice. "Things have changed somewhat and Christopher needs to be transported to the Cherokee County Sheriff's Department. We're going to interview him again there."

McKellar knew from the sound of McNeil's voice that things had changed. And that they had changed for the worst. She didn't know what the new information was, but she began preparing Christopher for a quick escape through the back door.

"We're moving to the Cherokee County Sheriff's Office," she told him. "And, just like last time, there are a lot of people outside that are trying to take your picture. I want you to cover your face." She pointed to the hood on his jacket. "Keep this over your head and keep your head down. I'll help you down the stairs."

McKellar and McNeil led Christopher downstairs and into one of the bays, where Andy Weir was waiting in his white Crown Victoria. While McNeil held the car door open, McKellar guided Christopher out of the back door and into the backseat of the vehicle. As they whisked past the media, Christopher bent over and hid his face between his knees.

McKellar felt for the boy, knowing it had come down to this. One day, he's a twelve-year-old kid hunting in the woods with his grandfather, chasing squirrels and shooting at Coke bottles. The next day, he's a major suspect in a double homicide.

Throughout this entire ordeal, Christopher remained polite and calm. He never lost his temper, cursed, or presented a behavior problem with any of the officers. It was unimaginable to think he could have done something as horrible as shooting and killing his grandparents.

CHAPTER 11

The Reverend Chris Snelgrove had been at the fire scene nearly all morning. He had seen both the emergency medical vehicle and the flatbed truck enter into the crime scene, and then leave. He didn't know how Christopher was connected with the fire, but it was difficult for him to believe Christopher, in any way, was responsible for his grandparents' deaths.

"I had an idea if Christopher was in trouble, then he might come to my house, looking for help," Snelgrove told the detectives. "He and my son, Mitchell, are the same age. They consider themselves best friends. In the summer, when Christopher and his sister, Danielle, would visit their grandparents, they would always stop by our house and visit Mitchell."

Snelgrove was the Pittmans' pastor. He knew what went on in their home. Furthermore, he had firsthand knowledge that Joe and Joy Pittman loved their grandson dearly, and they were doing everything they could to set a Christian example for him. They had put a tremendous amount of love into raising Christopher and showered him with lots of attention and affection. Likewise, Christopher loved his grandparents. Even while they were in church, he always showed great affection to them.

"Christopher had a lot of physical contact with both Joe and Joy, and he was not afraid to show it," Snelgrove recalled. "I had never seen that before—a young man who was so dedicated and loving with his grandparents."

Earlier that morning, Snelgrove had driven home and waited on Christopher. As he rested in his recliner, he felt his whole body stiffen. Strung so tightly, he could almost feel himself vibrating. He closed his eyes and tried to think. How was he going to break the news of the Pittmans' deaths to his wife and children? What would he say to the members of his congregation who would be looking to him for answers? It was difficult enough for him to understand all that had happened that morning, but so hard to imagine explaining to others not only how it had happened, but why.

Several hours later, when Snelgrove was notified that Christopher had been found in Cherokee County, he cleaned up, changed into a fresh set of clothes, and drove back to the fire scene. As he walked up the Pittmans' driveway, he saw their two sons, Barry and Joe Jr., standing near the roped-off area, their faces twisted masks of emotion. He knew it had to be a frantic time for the boys, especially Joe Jr.

Snelgrove took a deep breath. He walked over to where Barry and Joe Jr. were standing. They both looked as if their hearts had already joined their Adam's apples. Slowly he recalled the events of the fire and told them what little he knew of the investigation. It was obvious the CCSD had dropped everything else and had turned their full attention to this case.

The Pittman brothers stood with mouths and eyes wide open, like they'd been hit with an electrical shock. Shaking their heads uncomprehendingly, they stared silently at Snelgrove and listened to what he was saying. After they talked about what had happened, Snelgrove walked them over and introduced them to the sheriff and the coroner. It was an awkward meeting.

"I'm sorry to have to tell you this," Sheriff Benson told

Christopher's father, deliberately phrasing his response so that it was impossible to miss that which he was referring to. "The information our detectives are giving us doesn't add up with your son's story. That's got us all thinking that perhaps he started the fire at your parents' home."

Joe Jr. looked stunned, as if that were the last thing in all the world he expected to hear. Trying not to show his frustration, he drew in a quick breath, then blew it out again. Before he could reply, the sheriff went on to say he had reason to suspect Christopher had deliberately set the fire, and he had evidence to validate those suspicions. When he asked about the evidence investigators had uncovered, he was told about the blood on his parents' bodies, the .410 shotgun shells found inside the house and in the yard, and the search of his mother's SUV in Cherokee County.

Sheriff Benson's words sounded too harsh to be anything but a dream. As the facts became more alarming, Joe Jr. fought back a loud groan. The words hit him like a numbing explosion.

Joe Jr. blinked his eyes. A sense of total helplessness swept over him, and he began to panic.

This was no dream. This was a nightmare.

CHAPTER 12

The spacious conference room at the Cherokee County
Sheriff's Department had the one thing Christopher enjoyed the most: a wide-screen television. It didn't take him
any time to find the remote and figure out how to oper-
ate the controls. Sitting at the polished mahogany table,
he held the volume button on the remote control until
the noise was unbearable. Then, for reasons known only
to him, he got up from the table, took his jacket off, and
started walking around the table. With a hint of wariness,
he stared at McKellar the entire time, walking around the
left side of the table.

McKellar was seeing a different child flitting around
the table. She had not told Christopher there was new
information, but, obviously, he sensed something had
changed. At least, he feared it enough to make his demeanor change.

McKellar was prepared for a verbal standoff, and said
in a stern manner, "Christopher, why don't you hand me
that remote. We need to have an adult talk, so please sit
down."

Christopher first appeared surprised that McKellar
was telling him to sit down, then looked suspicious of
what she wanted to ask him. Eyes sliding away, he

shrugged, handed her the remote, and sat back down in his seat.

McKellar adjusted the volume on the television to its lowest decimal. She turned to Christopher and said, "I have a lot of questions that I need to ask you, but before I ask you those, I need to go through a form with you." From a juvenile-intended written form, she read him his rights and his Miranda warning. So that he could see it, she turned the page around and let him follow along as she read. "Now, do you understand all your rights, before I start asking you any questions?"

Christopher spoke without looking at her, looked over at the television, as if that interested him more.

McKellar got his attention, intent on keeping him as cooperative as possible. "I need to make sure that you understand everything on this form, okay?"

He nodded. When asked to initial the form, he did that as well.

McKellar read all the information in as childlike a fashion as she could and explained it to him in age-appropriate language. Based on her observation and investigative training, he appeared to understand everything she was saying.

"What it means is that anything you say to me can be used against you in court." She hoped he picked up on the serious tone of her voice. "And that the questions I am was going to ask you could get you in trouble if you were to come to court."

"Yeah, I know that."

"And do you know a courtroom is a big room where you will be asked to come and talk to a judge and tell your side of the story."

"Yeah." He grunted, then signed the papers.

"You also have the right to have your parents or guardian with you during questioning. I know earlier in the day I learned your father is driving up from Florida. Do you want your father present with you?"

Christopher straightened up in his chair. He squinted his eyes at McKellar, then abruptly told her no. "I don't want my father. I don't want a lawyer. I don't want nobody."

"Christopher, do you know how important a lawyer is?"

"I don't care. I said I didn't want one."

McKellar stressed to Christopher that at any time he didn't want to answer any more of her questions, he could stop her and get a lawyer. She was about to review the waiver of rights, when Agent Scott Williams walked into the room. Williams's supervisor had asked him to join McKellar in the interview.

McKellar paused, then introduced the agent. "This is my friend, Agent Williams. He's also a police officer."

Christopher stared quizzically at Williams. He had talked with him earlier that day at the fire department, but he didn't remember their conversation.

The interview was about to take a nasty turn, so McKellar wanted to give Christopher the benefit of every doubt. She read the Miranda rights to him a second time, telling him, "Just to make sure, I am going to go through your rights again and explain those to you a second time so that Agent Williams can also witness that they were explained before you sign and acknowledge that you did hear me read your rights."

Christopher nodded the affirmative, acknowledging a second time that he understood his rights, then signed the form and dated it.

McKellar decided on another track. She purposely had avoided telling Christopher his grandparents were dead, hoping a family member would be with him when she broke the news. But since he was now a suspect in their murder, this was information she thought he needed to know.

"Christopher, you know your grandparents are dead," she said, suggesting the evidence didn't look good for him.

Christopher put his head down as if he were going to cry. For the first time, he looked as if he were overcome by emotion, but there were no tears. Then, as quickly as he was struck by emotion, he recovered. When he raised his head, his eyes were drier than a burned bush.

McKellar remembered Christopher had been at church with his grandparents the night before their deaths and guessed that was probably where he had heard the Bible verse referencing "burning in the fires of Hell." She confronted him, asking him to tell her what was so significant about this verse.

Before Christopher got a chance to respond, Agent Williams interjected, "Are you religious?"

Christopher sighed. He said that he was religious.

"Do you think your grandparents would want you to tell the truth?" Williams asked, revealing to Christopher that he already knew far more about him than he realized.

Christopher nodded, then answered, "Yes."

McKellar stopped her line of questioning and backed off. Basic detective school had taught her that if there are two investigators, then one should write and one should ask questions so as not to bombard that person. At that point, she allowed Agent Williams to take over as lead interviewer. He would ask the questions and she would write Christopher's responses, verbatim. She had no problem with that.

Christopher still appeared calm and relaxed. He wasn't slurring his words, nor was he hard to understand. At different times during the interview, he would lower his head, then lift his head and start talking again. He had no difficulty in responding to Williams's questions. In dribs and drabs, he gave the detectives details that were drastically different from his initial story.

"There are a few things that we need to clear up, Christopher." Williams's line of questioning had to have been hitting Christopher like a violent wave coming ashore. Sounding more clear-cut, now that he had all the facts, he spelled out the inconsistencies in Christopher's story.

"First, we've had a helicopter up in the air over the

hunting club for some time and the dog team has been on the ground looking for your suspect, but they haven't found anyone yet.

"Secondly, there are also some issues dealing with your grandparents' vehicle. The seat was pulled up to match someone more of your stature as opposed to this six-foot-two-inch black male you said kidnapped you.

"And thirdly, it is highly unusual that someone would kidnap both you and your dog."

Christopher offered no response to any of the agent's accusations.

Williams pushed further. No time to dillydally now. "Why don't you go ahead and tell me the truth about what happened."

Christopher shrugged. Williams was not the kind of man you could easily say no to. Christopher's arms fell limp by his side, as if all the starch had been taken out of him. He then lowered his head, looked up, and started talking.

"I called my grandparents yesterday to come to the school. I called them because the vice principal said he wanted to talk to them. Because the day before, that boy on the school bus said I choked him.

"It was about one o'clock or something. [The vice principal] talked to my grandparents. He wanted to know why I choked [the boy on the bus]. Because he was messing with me, that's why. He told my grandparents to take me home."

"And what happened then?" Williams asked, bearing down on him.

"We got home about two o'clock or two-thirty. We talked for about an hour. They told me they [were] going to lock me in my room. They locked me in there after we talked, until about eleven-thirty. My grandpa said if I came out, he was going to beat me with the paddle. I came out at about ten o'clock or something. I was going to get something to drink. My granddaddy got the paddle. I tried to get my shotgun. He hit me on my back and my butt. Then he said if I came out anymore, he would hit me across the head with it. He had beat me back into my room. He hit me five or six times. That [paddle] is what my dad used to hit me with."

Williams was confident Christopher was finally telling the truth. "So what did you do next?"

"When they went to bed, I waited about ten minutes. I got the shotgun out of the cabinet. I took it in my room and loaded it. I took a box of shells from the cabinet. I put three in it. Jacked one and put another one in. I went in their room. I just aimed at the bed. I shot four times. I turned the light on. I didn't really care then. My granddad's feet were hanging over the bed. My granddad's face was to the side. My grandmother was facing the closet. Her legs were in the bed. I didn't care then. I picked up the shell casings. I threw them in the door of my room.

"Then I got some candles from the bathroom closet. I got about three. I lit them. I put one under my bed, one on my floor. I put the other one in the living room on the floor.

"Then I got some guns. I got a Ruger twenty-two from the gun safe. I got the four-ten out of the gun safe closet; I had laid it on the sofa. I got 2 twenty-two rifles and my forty-five. Then I loaded up my dog, Chrisdee, and I put him in the passenger's seat.

"I got the gas can from the side of the woodshed. I put the gas can in the floorboard. It's red. It was about half-full. I was going to stick a rag in it and blow it up.

"I backed out where the black Pathfinder was. Then I turned the lights on.

"I got the keys from the side of the washing machine. I got thirty-three dollars out of my grandmother's purse. It was in the dining room. I got some rolls of coins from off the top of the gun cabinet. I drove about thirty minutes.

I stopped in Union. (Christopher did not realize he had driven to Gaffney, instead of Union, South Carolina.)

"It was this old trail that goes out to an open place. I slept until about five-thirty in the morning. Then I drove to where the truck is now. I stayed there and slept until six o'clock. Then I went a little further and got stuck. I got out and closed the door, then went to the passenger's side. I let my dog out. I got the forty-five rifle. Then I shut the door. I loaded it outside the truck. I put three in. There was an empty shell in the chamber. I didn't feel like taking it out. I told my dog to stay by the truck. I locked the truck. I buried the keys by the back of the truck under some pine straw. I shot at the squirrel with my twenty-two. I shot at it once."

"And where did you go then?" Williams asked.

"Then I was just walking and that guy saw me. Then I started yelling for help. I told them a black guy was shooting at me. I told him a black guy killed my grandparents."

"Are you sorry for what you've done?" Williams asked incredulously.

Christopher shook his head from side to side. "No, I'm not sorry. They deserved it. They hit me with the paddle. My daddy used to beat me with that paddle. I stayed with my grandparents when they lived in Florida. I stayed with them six years when my dad was in the military. I don't know if I would do it again." He lowered his head, then mumbled, "Everybody hates me. I'm useless. My dad sits there while me and my sister do the chores."

Williams gave Christopher a little time to breathe, before asking him to describe how he had started the fire.

"The house was on fire when I left. I put paper around the candle by my bed. I put paper around the one in the living room. I poured cigarette lighter refiller in my bedroom by the fire. I went out the back door. I didn't lock the door."

"Why did you make up the story about the black man?" Williams asked.

"I made up the story about the black man because if I get in trouble, you are going to send me back to my dad. I'm just going to run away again. I hate my dad. I ran fifteen miles before they found me. (Christopher was referring to a first attempt at running away from home.) My grandparents beat me once while I was here."

"Christopher, do you remember the shell you used in the four-ten shotgun?"

"Yeah, the four-ten shell was a number-six shell, about ten pellets. A two-inch shell."

By now, Christopher knew the drill pretty well. He waited for McKellar to present her handwritten summary of his statement, then read it and corrected any mistakes. As before, he initialed all the pages and signed and dated the statement. He also verified that the statement was prepared for him by Lucinda McKellar, voluntarily, and of his own free will.

After Christopher signed and initialed his paperwork, he got up from the table and lay on the floor to watch television. *Walker, Texas Ranger* held his interest for a short time; then he fell asleep.

At 5:13 P.M., Agent Williams stepped outside the conference room and informed Major McNeil and Lieutenant Tom Davis that Christopher had confessed to the murders of his grandparents. He was told that Christopher would be transferred back to Chester.

Detective McKellar let Christopher sleep on the floor until Agent Andy Weir had driven his vehicle to the back of the building. When she woke him, he was the same polite Christopher. "There are people here trying to take your picture. You will want to put your hood back on your head. Put your head down, like before, until we get into the car. You will be sitting behind Major McNeil, and I will sit next to you."

The plan had been to try and keep the media from

taking any photographs of Christopher, but somehow they figured out he was in Weir's vehicle and started putting their cameras up in the windows. Christopher was told to keep his head down and look at McKellar.

Christopher slept most of the way during the sixty-minute drive from the Cherokee County Sheriff's Department to the Chester County Sheriff's Department. Upon arrival, he met with Rick Westsinger, an employee with the Department of Juvenile Justice (DJJ), and Investigator Burly McDaniels. McDaniels helped him undress, checked him for any bruises or marks on his body, and collected his clothes for evidence. Christopher was issued the standard DJJ jumpsuit.

Sheriff Robby Benson watched from his office window as the officers gathered Christopher Pittman out of the car and escorted him across the parking lot into the building. It was an eerie sight.

"I first saw Christopher Pittman and what looked like a little kid wrapped in oversized chains. I said to myself, 'He doesn't look like the kind of person that would do that type of thing.' Of course, it's hard to think someone that young and small could do something that bad. We tend to think that murderers look like some heinous criminal, but that isn't always the case. Murderers come in all different sizes and all different ages. Christopher looked just like the twelve-year-old kid he was. He didn't look like a cold-blooded murderer.

"But I guess I realized Christopher must have been cut from a different [cloth] when I watched him interact with his father in my office," Benson said, only minutes after Christopher was transported to the DJJ facility in Columbia. "After just confessing an hour ago that he had committed this heinous, cold-blooded act of killing his grandparents, burning the very house they lived in to the ground, and trying to blame it on someone else, there he stood face-to-face with his *father*. His *father*—of all people, the *son* of the two people Christopher had brutally murdered—reached out and hugged him, then told him he loved him.

"But Christopher never reacted. He never once hugged his father. He just stood there, arms locked by his side, with absolutely no emotion. He never offered a word of apology for what he had done, nor did he grieve for his and his father's loss."

Benson guessed that was probably the most heartless act he had seen in a long time.

PART II
THE PITTMANS

CHAPTER 13

Those who lived in Chester County, South Carolina, always said Joe Frank Pittman could have been a model for Geritol. With his crown of white hair and winsome smile, he was easy to look at. An outdoorsman with mountainous shoulders, he had the kind of face you'd see in a bait and tackle shop. He was like some guy you'd seen hundreds of times before, standing over by the cricket bin, drinking his coffee out of a Styrofoam cup, waiting patiently for the man behind the counter to retrieve a box of blue worms and two dozen minnows.

Joe had beautiful brown eyes that peered out of his sun-painted face with surprising gentleness and amusement. Maybe English or German. Maybe a little bit of both. He had named his youngest son Joseph Dolphus, so he might have favored his German blood.

There was one thing about Joe Pittman everyone knew: he never tired of talking about his birthplace. A story so fascinating you'd swear he'd torn it from the pages of a John Steinbeck novel. The way he told it, he was born the son of a Carolina mill hand on January 23, 1935. He lived just for a short while in northeastern Chester County, where his father, James "Jim" Frank Pittman, labored at the Manetta Mills in Lando—a small village named after the town "Landeau" in Germany.

The mill was a thriving operation, one of the last of its kind to survive before closing in 1976.

Like thousands of other Southern textile workers in the 1930s, Joe's family was totally dependent on the mill for its livelihood. The Pittmans lived in one of the small four-room houses within walking distance of the mill. Each month, the rent was deducted from their paychecks and they were issued aluminum tokens for the purchase of food and clothing from the company-owned store. The owners of the Manetta Mills were fairly generous with their employees up until the Great Depression. But when it was obvious the number of people who needed jobs far outweighed the number of jobs available, Joe's father and other mill hands were forced to work longer hours for lower wages. Those who had run five looms in 1927 were asked to run ten looms in 1933. Their breaks were shortened to the absolute minimum. Employees were even asked to relieve themselves in a nearby bucket so as not to lose production time.

Working conditions in the mill became deplorable. Any employee who complained about it would be evicted from their company-owned homes and a new family moved in the next day. President Franklin Roosevelt's rhetoric about the forgotten man and the promise of a New Deal offered little hope for the textile workers.

Joe's father worked twelve hours a day, six days a week, just to keep his family fed and clothed. The summer prior to Joe's birth in 1935, the Great Depression eased and the National Recovery Administration brought about talk of a partnership between management and labor at the Manetta Mills. Workers nationwide asking for higher pay and better conditions had inspired employees of the Southern mills to organize and press for the same benefits. But the Manetta Mill owners had absolutely no interest in improving their employees' working conditions. When their workers threatened to join the uprising in September 1934, management closed the mill in response to a prostrike vote by the local union.

Later in the fall, a handful of mills, including Manetta, reopened, but the promised wage increases and production adjustments never happened. In fact, most strikers were blackballed in the industry and were forced to leave the area. The uprising of '34 failed to unite mill hands against the owners and only served to point out the weaknesses of the mill hands. They were nothing more than indentured servants and totally dependent on the owners. And not just for a job, but for shelter and food as well. Life itself was given and taken freely by the mill owners.

The debauchery in Lando became as painful to Jim Pittman as a poke in the eye with a sharp stick. Two weeks after Joe was born, his wife, Annie Bell, died, leaving Jim heartbroken, penniless, and the single parent of eight children. He had no choice but ask family members from Florida to help him take care of his children, especially little Joe, until he could get back on his feet. It took two years before Jim could finally reunite his family.

"I was little then, but I still remember what it was like to go through the hard times," Joe would recall in his adult life. "I know what it was like to go to bed with an empty stomach the night before and wonder if there'd be anything frying in the skillet the next morning."

Joe remembered a particular hard time in his father's life and a memorable one in his young life, and he would write about it in his book of memories.

"When I was about seven or eight, my sister Clara Lou moved from Florida and came to live with us. She was a beautiful girl, not as adventurous as the rest of us—she wouldn't go rambling through the woods, explore caves, or swim in the old Land Mill Pond—but a real angel.

"We lived in a large old-type Southern home by then that was unpainted and the boards had weathered and rotted by the time winter arrived. There was no electricity so we made due with a fireplace that was built even with the floor. The first thing we did every morning was hop out of bed and run to the living room and get warm by the fire.

"This morning was different. It was cold as usual, but my brother Harry was already standing in front of the fire when I got there. As you stood at the fire, you alternated sides so you wouldn't get skewed like a hog. We often pushed and aggravated each other by pulling on the already too-hot trouser leg.

"Clara Lou came in, wearing a rayon gown, and backed near the fire. We looked up and saw her gown hem was being drawn toward the fire, but she was in no position to break the flames. Before we could warn her, the gown exploded in flames.

"My father had just returned from fetching a bucket of water at the well. When he walked in and saw Clara Lou on fire, running around the room, he caught up with her and dumped the whole bucket of water on her face and head. He followed in behind her, tearing at her clothes until he had torn the hot coals off her body. Both his arms and hands were burned in the process.

"Clara Lou stayed in the hospital for a long time. She was in the seventh grade when it happened, and was always self-conscious of her scars. She used her clothes to hide them until she finally received grafts from her arms to all the bad burns on her legs. My father had saved her face and hair from burning, when he doused her in water."

At the end of the page in Joe's book of memories, he wrote: "I give thanks to God for my sister Clara Lou Pittman and pray for her every day."

Jim Pittman was still young enough to romance an attractive woman who didn't mind being saddled with nine kids. Apparently, it wasn't too much of a burden for his new wife, "Miss Omie." A few years later, they added a couple more children to his already full quill.

Eventually, when times got worse in South Carolina, Jim Pittman, Miss Omie, and their new family moved to

Florida to farm. And why shouldn't they farm? They had all the free labor they needed. But Jim found farming was a lot harder than everyone said it was, even with the help of his kids. With the help of some aid available through the WPA and other federal programs, the Pittmans got by, survived the depression of the 1930s and the so-called New Deal, or the "Raw Deal," as Jim Pittman and many Americans termed it.

Joe was in the seventh grade at Summerfield High School, doing okay for a tall, lanky farmer's kid. It was here that he first laid eyes on a skinny little girl with long pigtails and a beautiful smile. Joe checked her out, inspecting her much like a horse at an auction. On Joy Roberts's high-cheekboned face, he could see her permanent teeth in the front had already come in, but one was already broken and damaged. Still, she was not letting this stop her from flashing that big old smile.

"I'd never seen or met a person that had that name," Joe would record in his book of memories. "It was so indescribable to a personality like hers. The very first time I saw her, I knew that 'there is a special little girl.'"

"Joy's older brother, Eddie, was in the same grade as me, and we became friends," Joe said, finishing his own story. "I'm four-and-a-half years older than Joy, so the thought of me dating her never crossed my mind. She was always Eddie's little sister.

"After I graduated from high school, I started working for the Seaboard Airline Railroad and bought a 1951 Ford Sedan. I was now dating different girls from different parts of the state. I didn't realize it at the time, but I was looking for a special girl.

"In the meantime, this little skinny girl is not so skinny anymore. She still has that big joyful smile, but she's all grown-up. One night, I stopped at a popular drive-in restaurant, and parked next to me was none other than this beautiful young lady with her date. I was overwhelmed with her beauty and the fact that she was dating. I knew in my heart that this was the person that I wanted to spend the rest of my life with.

"It was just a few days later, when I was with Eddie, that we went to Legion's Beach at Weirsdale. I didn't know it until I arrived that Joy was there. She was dressed in this darling pair of shorts with a bib and straps, and, boy, did she make those shorts look good. I know my eyes had to be sparkling, for I felt radiant as I drew near to her. I started a conversation with her and I liked the vibes I was getting. It was clear that I was attracted to Joy.

"I knew Eddie was going back to college in Gainesville, so I asked Joy for a date and she accepted. I'm on cloud nine. Finally the big night comes for our first date and I get to her house and here comes Eddie to meet me. He says to me, 'Where are we going?' and gets into the front seat. Of course, I don't know what's going on, I thought I had a date with Joy and here's her brother instead.

"It was not until the next weekend did I have a chance to call Joy and find out what happened. Eddie had come home unexpectedly from college, just as Joy was getting dressed for our date. Eddie had said to her, 'Why are you getting all dressed up?' and she replied she had a date with me, Joe Frank. 'You can't be serious,' he says, 'Joe Frank doesn't want to go out with you, he's just being nice to you.'

"So Eddie had let all the air out of Joy's balloon. He told her she was making a fool of herself, so she told me she didn't want to make a fool of herself so she didn't finish dressing for our date.

"I did get a first date about two weeks later, finally, when Eddie was away at college. I will never forget that first date, for I got the first opportunity to get my first Joy kiss. It was short, soft, and received with as much love and feelings as it was given."

Joe told this story to his children, grandchildren, and anyone else who would listen. He would hold up a child-hood photograph of Joy, showing the long, braided pigtails and a broad smile revealing a broken front tooth. "My favorite picture of your mother," Joe used to say. "That is the way she looked the first day I saw her."

Joe Pittman would always end the story with the same words. Turning to his wife, Joy, he would smile and say, "I thank God for that kind of love!" Then they would kiss.

The rest of Joe Pittman's story was much like others that had been told: he and his lovely lady got married and started having babies. Shortly after their first child was born, Joe got drafted by the U.S. Army and was assigned to a demolitions unit. Joe always loved mixing chemicals and working with gunpowders and explosives. He was good at it—but he wasn't looking for a career. He already had one as a husband and a father. Joe came back home and returned to his job at the railroad.

After the fire, Melinda Pittman Rector and her siblings were sifting through the ashes of what was left of their parents' home. Near her parents' bedroom, they found the original handwritten copy of her father's book of memories. The sides of the manuscript had been scorched, but amazingly, the contents were unscathed.

"Growing up with my parents was a real treat," Melinda Pittman Rector would say to the press after the fire. "All the kids especially loved my dad. And he genuinely loved making kids laugh. He read to them, took them out in the woods and taught them all about nature. Everyone called him 'Uncle Joe' or 'Pop Pop'."

Melinda believed no one told how much Joe Pittman loved kids better than Joe Pittman. In his book of memories, Joe wrote about the joy of entertaining children.

"In 1960, I owned a 4x4 Willy wagon, that I used for work and for hunting and fishing. The children loved for me to take them riding in it. I would load up a group of children and with no destination in mind but to have fun with the kids.

"During these outings, I would often drive to the Ocala

National Forest. I would carry a small cooler and I would stop and fill it with Pepsi-Cola and ice. I would buy some saltine crackers and sardines—I often kept a few cans of sardines and Vienna sausage under the seat of the truck.

"I would drive all the back rut roads, the rougher the better. Late midday, the children would be thirsty and hungry. I would stop and get them a Pepsi, then pull out the saltines and sardines. Barry and Melinda didn't want any at first. I would use my pocketknife to put the sardines on a cracker and wash it down with my Pepsi, saying, 'Oh, boy, is that good!' By the time we stopped the next time to eat, y'all would be real hungry and learned to like what I ate.

"On one occasion I remember so well, we ended up at 'Brinson's Prairie,' just out on 466, east of Wildwood. This was before it was fenced in. All the children—my brothers and sisters and their children—were visiting at the time, and they were so excited and full of energy.

"And I took it upon myself to entertain them. I dropped the tailgate of my Willy down and invited about four of the older ones to sit on it. I don't remember the exact number of children, but there was about nine or ten.

"I'm driving around this pond through some water and I notice a cow pasture with plenty of fresh cowpatties. Then I look and see a boat under a large oak tree. It is an old three-seater cypress boat. It's got a big hole in the bottom, but other than that, it is in pretty sturdy shape.

"The children are all yelling for more excitement, so I come up with an idea. I asked all the children to stretch their legs, then chained the front of the boat to the back of my truck and took it around the pond for a trial run. With all the children and their parents watching, I waited until I was convinced the old boat was safe, then invited them aboard. 'Look out for the smaller ones and keep your feet clear of the hole,' I kept reminding everyone.

"And then the fun began!

"I eased out, pulling the now-loaded boat. I'm watching the children carefully, as I slowly pick up speed. At first, I drove in a large circle. When I see all is going well, I increased the speed until I start seeing the boat fishtailing. The children are exuberant, but then I start hitting the cowpatties and they start flying through the hole in the bottom of the boat. The ones sitting on the seat, directly behind the hole, were something to see before it was all over.

"Never have I seen a group of children have so much enjoyment, paying no attention to the amount of cow manure on them. They were pointing at each other and laughing, saying how funny they looked."

As in other entries from his manuscript, Joe added a footnote to his story: "I hope that all you children will remember the boat ride at Brinson's Prairie with the same heartfelt love that I do! I thank you, God, for all these wonderful memories, more than one man could ever deserve."

CHAPTER 14

There was no question Joe Pittman was very much a disciplinarian. And he could be stubborn, too. But he believed in discipline and that a child should respect God, his parents, his teachers, and the police.

Joe wrote in his book of memories about an incident where he had to discipline his youngest son, Joe Jr.

"There is this tree that Joe likes to climb. He often used it to avoid having to answer to his mother. It was his great escape. His castle. His fortress.

"When I call for him, he answers from up here in the tree. He states that the only way that he will come down is for me to promise that I will not spank him. I told him that I could not make such a promise and that he must come down from the tree now.

"He said, 'No, I'm not coming down, even if I have to stay up here all night.'

"I saw no reason to argue with him, so I went and got my chain saw, cranked it up, and started revving the engine. I walked to the full bottom of the tree. I had full intentions of cutting down the tree, Jo-Jo and all."

With a hint of sarcasm, Joe added, "Joe is really a loving and intelligent child, for he decided in a heartbeat that daddy meant business. To this day, Joe D. and myself lovingly speak about this, with him saying he knew that as sure as God made green apples, I would have cut that tree down."

At the bottom of the page, Joe scribbled, "God bless you, Joe Dolphus Pittman." On another page, he penned, "We've had a lot of fun talking about what we did together. I hope Joe will remember it, as I will, for the rest of his life."

Joe Pittman loved his children dearly and enjoyed telling stories about them. One of his favorite stories was about his daughter, Melinda.

"Melinda was always a daddy's girl and demanded that special love between a little girl and her father that is missing, so often on account of me being a railroad father.

"I remember her as a loving yet strong-willed child. She always wanted to do things for herself. She could climb before she could walk.

"We lived in a small mobile home when she was born. Joy had to take down her crib when she was nine months old, on account she would climb over the top and go splat on the floor. We were afraid that she would get hurt.

"Joy would always dress her up in little-girl clothes. We were living in a trailer park in Wildwood. The neighbors would take bets on how long it would take Melinda to transform into a little ragamuffin. It didn't take long, and she had fun doing it.

"Melinda never liked taking naps, and she would get mad at her brother Barry because he did. One day, after Joy had put you two children [down] for your naps, your mother heard Barry cry out in pain. Joy rushed in and found Barry sitting by his bed, crying and holding his hand over his nose.

"What happened was Melinda had tired of her mother saying, 'Why can't you be good like your brother and take a nap?' So she looked over at her brother, sleeping, and decided to get even with him for making her look bad for not taking a nap when she was supposed to,

"Melinda was a happy little girl that always wanted to please other people. She was very enthusiastic in her endeavors. One Christmas season, we had been shopping and Joy had let them in on a secret about a gift that she had gotten for me. She explained to Melinda and you other kids that it was a surprise and under no circumstances could they tell me what it was.

"When I got home, and after dinner that night, I got in my recliner chair. Here comes Melinda. I lift her up and she settles on my lap. I asked her what they had done today. She tells me, 'We went shopping, and we bought you a present, but I can't tell you because Ma will get mad if I tell you.'

"'That's right, sweetie,' Joy chimed in, 'You better not tell him about the secret because it's a surprise.'

"No sooner than Joy left the room, I decided to have some fun. I could tell Melinda was about to bust at the seams to tell me. I said to her, 'So, you know what the surprise is, but you can't tell, right?'"

"Melinda shook her head. 'No', she whispered, 'if I tell you, Mama will get mad.' Then she moved in closer and put her little hand on my face. She rubs the cheek and starts saying, 'Buzz, buzz, hum, hum, hum . . .'

"I asked her, 'Is it an electric razor?' and she beamed all over the room. I had guessed what it was without her having actually said the word 'electric razor.' I had to assure her mom that I had just made a lucky guess."

Joe wrote at the bottom of the page in his manuscript, "Sugar and spice and everything nice, that's what little girls are made of."

CHAPTER 15

Joe Pittman's childhood in Lando, South Carolina, had a profound effect upon him, and he would spend a lot of his adult life trying to reconnect. For some reason, he had felt safe in Lando, and as an adult, he longed for a chance to return. He and Joy frequently traveled in their motor home to visit Joe's sisters in Chester County. They would spend their weekends sharing memories and talking about past relatives, the long-disappeared textile industry, and the town it had once harbored.

"When a person grows old, he starts to realize he's got only so much gas left in his tank," Joe once said. "Then he starts thinking back. You do that more and more until you start missing the people you've never missed before. It makes you want to go back to the times from your childhood that are as fresh as if you were standing there."

Despite not having lived in Chester County since he was an infant, it was a place Joe Pittman still called home. One day, Joe promised, he and Joy were going to build a dream home there. In July 1997, he made it official. After he retired from the railroad and Joy from the Sumter County School District in Florida, they packed up their things and moved to Chester County. What they found after moving there was that they could live out their last days in a small country town where everyone tended to their own business, treated you like family, and the biggest event of any given week was going to supper at the Fish Camp on Highway 9. It was Joe's kind of life.

Joe was satisfied he and Joy had made a good choice in their new home. His sisters advised them that the people of Chester County were similar to any other Southern small-town population. There were a lot of hardworking folks, quite a few poor folks, and a lot of young folks who graduate from high school, packed their cars, and headed off to college, and only returned to visit on holidays.

It was odd, but the days Joe and Joy visited Chester, life seemed calm and appeared more serene. The surrounding towns of Charlotte, Columbia, and Rock Hill were all too busy and demanding for them. They were attracted to a simple, uncomplicated life, where people were more attentive to family and church, and moved at a slower pace. Chester's old-fashioned, rural ambience, suited them well.

Joe loved fishing, hunting, and all things outdoors. Joy enjoyed shopping, arts and crafts, and volunteering at the hospital. A twenty-acre hamlet off Slick Rock Road was just the slice of life they'd been looking for. While living in their motor home at the Chester County State Park, they started building their home. They kept at it, one board at a time, one brick at a time, and one nail at a time, until their dream finally became reality.

Wanting to connect spiritually with their community in Chester, Joe and Joy began their search for a home church. Their journey led them to the front door of New Hope United Methodist Church.

"Hi, I'm Joe Pittman," Joe said to the preacher, the Reverend Chris Snelgrove, before the morning service.

Snelgrove smiled, nodded, and extended his hand.

Joe leaned forward and with both hands clasped the preacher's between his, then gestured to a well-dressed woman standing next to him. "And this is my beautiful wife, Joy."

Snelgrove was immediately drawn to the gregarious couple. Just watching them, he said, was infectious. They were one of those couples he was instantly attracted to. Though they had been married for forty-four years, they still kissed and hugged, and held hands like newlyweds. He could see their love for each other was immense. The minute the Pittmans walked through the door, the ninety-eight-member congregation warmed up to the newcomers and welcomed them as if they were family.

And why shouldn't they? The Pittmans were not just your ordinary, common garden-variety flowers—these were two talented and spiritual people. Joy was an accomplished musician—a perfectionist who refused to play a piece of music until she mastered it. After they got settled in, she'd volunteer to play the church organ. Joe could sing, and promised to join the church choir, but he spent more of his time entertaining the congregation with stories about riding the lines on a Southern railroad and wrestling alligators. He had an anecdote for nearly every occasion, and wherever he went, he made friends.

Making people laugh was a real God-given talent. And whenever Joe was around, his friends would slap their knees, grin, and joke, "I don't know what Joe's drinking, but I'll have some of the same."

Joe's good nature was contagious.

CHAPTER 16

According to Christopher Pittman's family, the troubles in his life actually began with his parents, Joe Dolphus Pittman and Hazel Jones Pittman. A family member called the relationship "doomed from the beginning." The two amorous teenagers met in 1986 at Wildwood High School in Central Florida and quickly fell in love. Joe was a sophomore, and Hazel a freshman. Their daughter, Danielle, was born the next year. Hazel was just sixteen at the time. Joe graduated the following year from high school and joined the U.S. Army. He began boot camp at Alabama's Fort McClellan on May 11, 1988. Eleven weeks later, he and Hazel were married.

Joe Jr.'s marriage to Hazel Jones would be the first in a string of failed marriages.

On April 9, 1989, the young couple's second child, Christopher Frank Pittman, was born in Huntsville, Alabama. Six weeks later, he'd experience the first of a half-dozen family splits, divorces, and separations when Hazel left Joe and returned to Florida. By October 1990, Hazel had given birth to another son by another man and Joe was deployed as part of Operation Desert Storm. Hazel left the family while Joe was away, leaving the children with her mother, Delnora Duprey. It'd be a decade before the children would see their mother again.

"They had no relationship with their mother, and that was her choice," Duprey would admit. She adopted Hazel's third child, Christopher's half brother, and raised him as her own son. "My daughter left them when they were born, basically."

Joe returned from the Middle East in March 1992, and moved with the children back to Alabama, where he was stationed. When he was discharged that December, they moved in with his parents in Oxford, Florida.

Joe remarried in 1992, but was separated again a year later. He and the children moved back in with Nana and Pop Pop. Pop Pop would become Christopher's strongest role model.

"My mom and dad were really their parents," Joe confessed. Joy cooked for the family and washed the children's clothes. She drove Danielle forty miles round-trip to dance lessons in Ocala, Florida. And every morning, she took Christopher to North Sumter Primary School, where he went to class and she worked as a receptionist.

Around the house, the kids played on the five-acre property, swimming in the pool or taking rides with their grandfather on his Allis Chalmers tractor. Joe and the kids eventually got their own place a few miles away, but the children still saw their grandparents daily.

Christopher and his grandfather were especially close. They not only shared a middle name, Frank, but many of the same passions, including hunting, fishing, and taking things apart.

In 1997, Joe and Joy moved to South Carolina, building a house in rural Chester County. The move devastated the grandchildren they'd helped raise. Christopher, then eight, took their departure especially hard.

"I was devastated, too, to be honest," his father said.

A maintenance worker with the Sumter County, Florida, school district, Joe Jr., then thirty-five, did all he could to give his children normal lives. Christopher liked playing video games and played center field for his youth baseball teams. He was nicknamed "Bug" because of his love for insects. Described as quiet and reserved, Christopher was whippet-thin, but tough.

"My father was a single parent because my mother left when I was three," Danielle Pittman, Christopher's sister, remembered. "And he got help from both sides of the family, from my Nana and Pop Pop and my grandmother. My father fought in the Persian Gulf War. He was away about eight months. That time of life was pretty much a blur for me. I was about four, and all I remember is that my grandparents helped raise me.

"My father was strict. If we did something wrong, he would discipline us with a belt. He would spank us and leave a mark. Sometimes he would miss and it would go up and hit like our lower backs or right underneath on our upper legs, but he would try to spank us on the butt with it. We had a chore list that would take us probably thirty to forty-five minutes to do, if we did them altogether at the same time.

"My brother, Christopher, and I both had this thing where we would procrastinate and it would seem like the chore list took forever to get done. What we would be doing when my dad would tell me to clean my room, I usually spent that time playing in my room versus cleaning it.

"I remember growing up in Central Florida around the Oxford area and around Wildwood. It was a very rural area. There's nothing to do there. You would be lucky if you find two stoplights in it. Very small and racially mixed. The population for African American would be probably seventy-five percent. We had a number of black friends, who would then come over and spend the night. We were raised not to ever make any distinctions about somebody's color.

"What Christopher and I did for fun, we would go outside and play baseball and would take trees and we would make them landmarks or bricks or whatever we could find. And we would have one person pitch and one person bat. And since there were only two of us, if I was batting, he would pitch the ball to me and I would hit it, and as far as it would go, I would start running around the bases. If I didn't get all of the way around the base, then I would have to go back and bat again, and then, if I hit the ball, I would run back to the base that I was at and finish going all of the way around. So there was really no point to it, we just did it to say we were playing.

"Christopher and I spent a lot of time together growing up and became close friends. He is my best friend. My first name was Danielle and my middle name being Deanne, my grandmother derived the nickname Deedee for me. My brother couldn't say Danielle, so he called me 'Deedee'. And, actually, even though I don't care of him to call me that, he still calls me that today.

"Everybody just started calling him 'Kissipher.' I called him that because I knew it made him mad. I still call him that.

"When we were growing up, my brother and I were completely inseparable. We moved around a lot to different houses. And no matter what house we went to, no matter where we were, my brother and I were always together. He was always there for me. And even though he is my little brother and now I have to look up to him to look at him in the face, I still have a tremendous respect for him.

"Christopher has always been really quiet. And when I was younger, I used to get in trouble a lot because I would try to mother him. And he had a speech problem when he was younger and he went to speech therapy for this and people couldn't understand what he was saying because he couldn't pronounce his syllables correctly. And I would tell people what he was saying and what he was thinking. And I wouldn't let him speak up for himself because I wanted to protect my baby brother. And I always did that for him.

"We were taught to be polite. If we didn't say 'yes, ma'am,' 'no, ma'am,' 'no, sir,' 'yes, sir,' then we would get into trouble. That was a respect that we were taught that anybody even a year older than us would get. We were taught to respect our elders.

"Christopher never talked out against his elders. If somebody was disciplining him, he wouldn't speak and argue with them about that. He would usually just take the punishment and suck it up. He was about six and in the first grade when he got into trouble. I was there [on the bus], sitting next to him. He was using the seat as something to draw on and he had a few pieces of paper stuck up there. And he was drawing on them with a pencil and the pencil was very sharp. And when he did, he poked it. And he poked it, I believe, three times. I'm not sure, it could have been less or more. But a kid behind him saw it after he pulled down the paper. Christopher and I looked at each other like, 'Oh, my gosh.' He saw that he had poked it through, he had done it. And a kid behind him, an older one, went up and decided that she was going to tell on Christopher. And I think all that happened was that Christopher had to be able to pay to have the holes patched on the bus, which was like ten dollars or something like that. He helped his Pop Pop around the house and earned the money to help pay for the damage on the bus seat.

"We had been playing baseball once like we were doing, as I described earlier, and we got tired of doing that. It started getting dark as we went inside. And I said something and we started wrestling. We were playing, and I accidentally took my elbow and I hit him up in the nose. And it really was hurt. I hit him hard. And the baseball bat was right there, being that we were outside playing, and it was closest to him, so he picked it up and started chasing me. I was like, 'Oh, my gosh.' So I start running to the room and I closed the door and locked it. And he was pounding on the door saying, 'Don't do that again, that hurt.' And as I opened that door, I stuck my tongue out at him and closed the door again and listened to some music for a little bit. Then I came out and we watched television and we were fine.

"One time, we were at my ex-stepmom's parents' house in Ocala. And Christopher would go down to this big sandpit out there. So he would find a stick, golf club, whatever he could find, and he would hit the golf ball around with it. And he had this thing about golf balls, he was obsessed with golf balls. He would go and he would pick them up and keep as many in his pockets as he could. He liked trying to find the different-color ones, not just the white ones, but the orange ones and pink ones and everything. And he had some in his pocket and I said something to him and made him mad. And he threw the golf ball at me and hit me in my stomach and I was like, 'Oh, that really hurt.'

"So, I got mad and went into the kitchen and got the biggest cast-iron pot I could find. And he was turning around and I was like, 'Hey, Christopher,' and he turned around and I hit him upside the head with it and he slumped down on the floor and he just sort of gave me this look. He goes, he was like, 'That really hurt.' But I mean, he was being theatrical about it and everything like that. I was scared and I thought I killed him. He was like, 'Why did you do that, I didn't mean to hurt you. I was aiming at your feet.' I was like, 'Well, you don't do pitching when you play baseball.' He never did it again. When he fell backward, he was being dramatic about it, but he was okay. He said he was dizzy.

"Nana would come in and she would read stories at night. And Christopher would get in there and he and I would cook. I was closer to Nana than Christopher was. I mean, we were both very close to both of our grandparents, but I bonded more with Nana. We would visit them as much as we could, and they felt bad for moving and leaving us because they realized they were our stability. And they would make it a point to come down and visit us and see us, and we would go and spend summers with them. And we would go and visit them, sometimes they would come down and get us and drive back up to Chester.

"My dad would take us up there and spend a few days and then have to go back early. Christopher was always with Pop Pop. If I tried to spend time with Pop Pop and get him to myself, Christopher would get jealous. And he would try to come over there and be right there with us and everything. Christopher was Pop Pop's shadow. There were people that would come over and make comments if Christopher wasn't right there on top of him, like, 'Well, Joe, where's your shadow today?' He would be like, 'Oh, he's over there doing something.'

"When we visited Pop Pop in Chester, we would go out and take the BB guns and go practice shooting toward a target that my grandpa would have set up. We would have a contest to see who would get closer to the bull's-eye. My grandpa always won.

"We went camping or fishing all the time. We'd get rides on the tractor, a really big one that my grandpa would use to mow the field out in Florida. When they moved, he left it here and he had the four-wheeler, as the four-wheeler just kind of took the place of the tractor for us. We would take turns, one of us would be up front helping him drive and the other one would be on the back holding on to the little handle that we had back there to hang on to.

"In Chester, my grandpa had a friend everybody calls 'Red' and my grandpa and Christopher and Red would all go on fishing trips out to a little pond. And they would have contests to see who would catch the biggest fish, and then come home and talk about the ten-foot fish they caught earlier that day, but it got away and all that kind of stuff.

"Christopher spent a lot of time with his grandparents, sometimes a month or even six weeks at a time, one time we spent almost the entire summer with them. Actually, when they would discipline us, they wouldn't spank us, they wouldn't even touch us. My grandpa would sit down and he would talk to us and he would tell us what we did wrong and that he was disappointed and he would have us promise if we could, that we wouldn't do it again.

"My nana, the only way she would discipline us, she did the same thing my grandpa did. But if we were sitting at the table and there was company there—and sometimes even if it was just Nana, Pop Pop, Chris, and I sitting at the table—and we did something that she didn't like, she would reach under the table, get the inside of our thigh, and she would pinch you and give you this look. We called it the 'evil Nana look.' We would just kind of sit up and start behaving.

"But when Pop Pop disciplined us, he would sit down and he would let you know that you did something wrong. He would tell you that he didn't want you to do it again.

"I can honestly say that in my entire life growing up with them, I cannot recall one single time Nana and Pop Pop had ever spanked us, either one of us. They never spanked us with a paddle. Pop Pop would give us a big hug and tell us he loved us every time. I never remember any time that he didn't do that. After you indicated you understood and you weren't supposed to do it again, everything was okay."

Danielle swore Christopher had never acted out aggressively against their Pop Pop.

"If Pop Pop got on Christopher, it would crush my brother because he didn't want to do anything that would make Pop Pop sad. He absolutely worshipped the ground my grandfather walked on. It would literally kill him if he knew he did something to hurt Pop Pop.

"The paddle is something that my dad made to scare us. He had been talking about how the principals used to have paddles at the schools he attended, and he was like, 'I'm going to do something like that, too.' He got the paddle and went and drilled holes in it. He said that if he spanked us with that, it would really hurt, and he used it as an instrument to scare us with, basically, so that we wouldn't be bad. He made the paddle about a month before all of this happened. When Nana and Pop Pop came down to get Christopher, I believe he mentioned something to them about the paddle or it had come up. And Nana and Pop Pop took the paddle and put it in the back of their car, and said they were going to take it up there. I was back there with Nana and I saw it in there, and I said, 'Why is that in there?' She was like, 'Well, we found out about this and we don't want it. We don't think it's right for your dad to even scare you.'

"They didn't want Dad to scare us with the paddle. It was bad enough that he [had it, but] never used it, but they didn't like the fact he was even saying he was going to."

Danielle remembered how much her brother loved animals.

"Chance was a dog that we had found when were driving through the woods with my father. And it just ran out underneath the road, so we got it. And my granddad ended up with it because he fell in love with Chance. And Chance ended up getting off his little suspension thing he had. He had a cord that was running between two trees and then he had a leash that could come off as he could get around. He had gotten off of that and my grandfather was heartsick about it, so I had a performance in Ocala that I did, ballet and stuff life that, and we were out there and it was around a fair. And they had had this dog that looked exactly like Chance, except it was a female, so we bought it for my granddad. And my Nana came up with the name 'Chrisdee,' because she took 'Chris' off Chris's name and 'Dee' off of Deedee and decided to call it Chrisdee.

"Chrisdee is a dog that we got for my grandparents, but Christopher loved that dog. My grandmother ended up finding Chance a few days afterward. He was at the Humane Society or something like that. He had gotten into one of the neighbors' fields and was chasing the horses or something like that. And we got the dog back, so we kept Chrisdee after my grandparents moved to South Carolina.

"Rather than giving Chrisdee to Pop Pop, we kept him because Pop Pop still had Chance. So Christopher was responsible and took over the chores of feeding Chrisdee and walking Chrisdee. Christopher would go out and play with the dog, and I observed on more than one occasion he would be out there, down on the ground with Chrisdee, just sitting there petting her and grooming her.

"Christopher took Chrisdee to South Carolina when he went to stay with our grandparents. After the fire and everything that happened, Chrisdee ended up coming back to Florida and staying with my dad and I. She finally ended up dying from cancer."

Danielle explained about an incident when Christopher had gotten in trouble with the police. She said that a bull named Brownie lived to the right of them in a neighbor's yard.

"We had palmettos in Florida. They are a lot like palm trees, except the tops of them are on the ground. The cow was eating those because it was so hungry, but these things are so sharp. Christopher and I didn't see how the cow could eat those. My grandpa would get his pocketknife and he would cut up sprigs of grass and he would go over and feed it to the cow, and we would take it carrots and stuff like that.

"So it became an everyday thing. If we were outside and the cow was over there in that part of the fence where we could feed him, would go over and pick some grass or in the house and get some apples or something from inside and go out and feed the cow.

"Brownie is an animal that a friend of Christopher's threw the dart at. Christopher jumped across the fence and tried to get the dart out of Brownie, but the cow charged him. He ran and jumped back over the fence. Christopher was never violent toward animals.

"Even through all the times when Dad remarried and

we were being pushed around from home to home, Christopher and I stayed together. When I didn't want my brother to get into trouble, I would take up for him and he would do the same. There were times when I wanted to strangle him. There were other times when he was not so playful, as far as some fighting going on. He had shot a BB gun at someone's vehicle and the mobile home.

"Also, I was aware that Christopher had attacked another boy at school in Florida. It was a day when my dad let him wear my father's fatigues to school. He said to Christopher, 'Now, don't you lose any of it.' And he made Christopher promise that he could come back with every piece that my dad let him take to school. And for us, when we make a promise, that is as good as gold in our family.

"Christopher was also worried that he would get in trouble with our father. He was wearing dad's hat when a kid snatched it away from him and they were doing the monkey-in-the-middle thing and Christopher ran after him and tried to get it back and attacked the boy.

"As the oldest, I was doing a lot of babysitting. There was two-and-a-half years difference between Christopher and me. On one occasion, I had to lock myself in my room that time after the baseball incident so Christopher would leave me alone. Actually, so that everybody would leave me alone, not necessarily just my brother.

"During holidays, Christmas, Easter, and spring break, we would go see my grandparents. But, normally, they would come see us. I was with them in Chester during the month of June 2001. We would play it by ear; we would go and say that we were only staying for three weeks, and three weeks really meant like a month and a half. But we knew we always would eventually be returning to Florida and our father's house. It was like a little minivacation, a fun time to be around my grandparents. More fun than your regular parents."

Danielle described an incident she thought was particularly traumatic for Christopher.

"In August 2001, my biological mother came back. My brother had always asked about his real mother. He always wanted his real mother and she finally came back. She got a mobile home and she was staying in that. And Christopher and I were over there every day visiting her, trying to catch up. And about a month after she had been there, she told us that—she met us at the door and told us—we weren't allowed to get out of the car and we were never allowed to come back in the house or see her again.

"That was quite devastating the day we pulled up at my mother's house and she wouldn't see us. I felt worse for my brother because he had never known her before and I felt like I should have protected him and not allowed her to come back into our life. And I realize now that I had no choice, that that was just something that happened. It was beyond my control, but my brother was upset because he thought everything would be the exact way he wanted it, that we would have a perfect family like he always dreamed about having.

"And then she left, but I was used to the fact that she was gone. She had left me before and I was old enough to remember it. She was in and out. She would write letters sometimes and I would write, but I wouldn't get a response back. And I was used to that, he wasn't. A month-and-a-half later, Christopher was still quite upset about the incident with our mother leaving and ran away. He said he was going to South Carolina to live with our grandparents because he felt like he belonged there.

"The same day Christopher talked about running away, he came home with a bad grade and got into trouble with our father. Dad said Christopher had to buckle up on the studying and he was not going to be allowed to play his Nintendo anymore.

"Christopher had mentioned something a few days before about running away. He said he was going to see his Nana and Pop Pop or going up and staying with them. But he did that a lot. He talked about missing them and wanting to go up and see them. I didn't think he would do it.

"Every morning, the alarm would go off and I would go wake my brother up to get ready for school and then I would wake my dad up and get him up. I was in charge of waking everybody up. When I woke up the next morning and I saw Christopher was gone, I was like, 'Oh, my God, he really did it.' And so I went and woke up my dad and I was like, 'Dad, Christopher is gone.'

"Dad called the police. One of the officers had said something about if we knew he had any money. 'We can judge how far he can get if he were to get the bus fare,' the officer said. And I went and looked in my jewelry box and I then found out he had taken seventy dollars from me. But I had told him that he could take it whenever he wanted to. I had change in the drawer underneath it and that was still there. I had a jewelry box where the top lid opened and I had the money there. That was the bills, and I had coins and stuff in a drawer right beneath it, that was still in my jewelry box. I had earned that money from babysitting services I did for about four or five months.

"Christopher was found in Marion Hills at a store that had an RV and a little travel center hooked together. It looked like a truck stop, kind of like where there was a convenience store, and then they had a fast-food restaurant in the side.

"It took police a day to find Christopher. He was probably fifteen to twenty miles away from our house. He was playing video games when they found him. His Nintendo had just been taken away, and now he was caught playing video games. Me and my dad went and got him. Our stepmother at the time, she came over to the house to help us when we found out that Christopher had run away. She came over there to support us and everything like that and be there for us.

"Christopher was real, real mad, but I wasn't scared of

him. I was scared that he was going to hurt himself, but he never threatened to hurt me. It was in the evening, almost into the night, when Christopher came home and I talked with him. I was in the kitchen. He said he was mad at me because I didn't stick up for him when we were talking to the police officer [and the DSS] about some of the accusations he had made against our father. (Christopher had said Dad was abusing him.) I was trying to protect myself because I knew that I was going to be living with my father. And he was mad at me about that because he had always depended on me to stick up for him. And this particular time, I did not stick up for him. And we got home and my father wanted to see what he would say when he wasn't around. My father wanted to know what Christopher would say to me while he was gone. So he said he was going to the store and he instructed me that he would be sitting outside the window, that if I needed him, to call him.

"So Christopher and I were in the house, and he was mad at me because I didn't stick up for him. And he was there at the kitchen and I said something really mean to him. I don't even remember what I said, but there was a sheath hunting knife there and he picked up the hunting knife and he said, 'You know what, forget this.' He was like, 'I would rather die than live in this house with you and Dad.' And he held it up to his stomach like he was going to kill himself. And I screamed. I was like, 'He's going to kill himself.' I was like, 'Dad, come in the house because I'm scared he's going to hurt himself.'

"Dad came in and said, 'Christopher, give me the knife.'

"Christopher just handed Dad the knife and went over and sat on the couch and crossed his arms. He was mad. He never threatened me or Dad, but he was mad at us both.

"I never had any fear that he was going to come at me with the knife, but I called Dad because I was scared he might hurt himself. I knew our family had a lot of love for each other, but like most families there were some problems, especially between Christopher and my father.

"My dad pretty much gave Christopher a choice. He was like, 'If you want to keep giving these accusations about me and everything like that, then the police could take you and put you in another home. Do you want to go live with somebody else or you can cool it and you can stay here with me and your sister?'

"Christopher was still mad at this point. And all he wanted was not to be staying there in the house with Dad and I, so he told Dad, 'Well, I'll go with them then.' So he went with the police and they ended up putting him in a treatment center called Lifestream.

"Actually, Dad had to arrange for him to go to Lifestream. Dad called Nana and Pop Pop when he was in Lifestream and talked to them about Christopher. My grandparents came down from Chester to take him back up there with them. Christopher was having some difficulty, obviously, and wanted to run away, and they wanted to help him with that. They knew his mom had left and Dad was now separated from [Chris's] stepmom, and that they had my two little sisters, Haley and Gabriel, who were very young. Gabriel was still just a little baby.

"There was just a lot of things like that that probably hurt Christopher at that time. And, plus, Nana and Pop Pop had moved away from us a few years ago. Christopher didn't feel stable. He wanted them to be there as [his] stability.

"My grandparents said, 'If he's depressed, then he needs to go with us.'

"I wanted to go to South Carolina with Christopher and my grandparents, too. Who wouldn't? And I was jealous that Christopher was getting to go up there. But I felt like I had to stay and take care of my dad.

"I was fourteen at the time. If I was home by myself I was scared of the dark, and scared of being in the house by myself. And I thought my dad would be scared of being by himself at night, too. So, I decided to stay with him."

CHAPTER 17

Red and Lucy Weir had met Joe and Joy Pittman their first Sunday at New Hope Methodist Church. The two couples bonded quickly. Joe trusted Red so much that he gave him a key to his house so he could make sure everything was okay when he and Joy were out of town. Lucy and Joy spent a lot of time shopping and traveling to Charlotte or Rock Hill. Lucy sang in the church choir and Joy played the organ, so they saw each other quite a bit.

Over the years, the Weirs had met Christopher when he had visited his grandparents during summers and holidays. Red and Joe had taken him fishing a few times and they always saw him at church. They'd also seen him driving the family car up and down the long dirt driveway at his grandparents' home—something they say was odd, even though his grandfather didn't think so.

One night, while the Weirs were having dinner with Joe and Joy at Clarendon's Fish House, Christopher became the topic of their conversation. It all started when Joe's face showed great concern. He leaned forward, folded his hands on the table, and told the Weirs that Christopher was in serious trouble and he didn't know what to do about it.

Red and Lucy listened intently, their faces sympathetic.

When he finished, Lucy asked him, "What you gonna do, Joe?"

"I don't know." Joe was on the verge of tears. "We've been told he's not been feeling real well and has been admitted to a hospital."

"I know he's your grandson," Lucy acknowledged, "and you want to do all you can do to help him, but are you thinking about asking the boy to come live with you?"

Joe shook his head very slowly. "I just don't know." Then he wept. It was a deep and terrible weeping, coming from the cellar of his soul.

The next day, Joe did what anyone would do who feels as lost as a rubber ball in high weeds. He asked for help from a source greater than himself. Standing before the congregation at the church, he requested prayer and support from the church family.

"My grandson needs us," he began as he poured out another piece of his heart. The congregation listened intently, their faces empathetic. Joe sat down beside his wife in the first pew and buried his head in his hands.

Reverend Snelgrove stood up and beseeched everyone not just to pray, but to pray *earnestly* for Joe and his family. The Pittmans were sailing through some troubled waters and they needed guidance for future navigation.

Joe stood up, choked back his tears, and spoke again. "I want to ask Christopher to come and live with us, but I'm not sure that is the best thing. I just pray I am making the right decision."

At this time, no one knew much about Christopher. Only that he had had problems at home and had come to spend some time with his grandparents. "Please" and "Thank you" were all part of his politeness, and he was under his grandfather's feet constantly.

The Weirs remembered Christopher didn't talk a whole lot about his home life. They'd heard he thought his father was a hard and difficult man. He had had three unhappy marriages, and no doubt was a lonely man. An ex-solider who was accustomed to having what he said become law, demanding respect from his children, and making it clear he was the master inside his home. Although they believed Joe Jr. never meant for that to happen, it may have come off as sour, obstinate, and hot-tempered. If he was—as his son perceived him to be—a tyrant at heart; he had fashioned the pattern for the boy's view of life.

Joe and Joy Pittman knew there had been a continuous battle between their grandson and his father. If Christopher spoke back, he felt the sting of his father's belt. Sometimes, according to Christopher, it was the sting of a paddle. The boy told his grandparents he was afraid to live inside his father's house. Sometimes he reacted violently. Sometimes he ran away. Christopher and his father were two fierce, unbending wills in conflict, and the chemistry between him and his father was volatile.

Christopher was very thin when his grandparents came to pick him up in Florida. Hair closely cropped, he had a solemn, pale face, and large, staring eyes. Most of the time, he looked downward, laughed a little, but they could see he worried too much.

Joe and Joy immediately recognized there was something different about their grandson, from the last time they had seen him. Around adults, he was still polite, but in places like Pizza Hut and Food Lion, his face was always turned down as if there were something on the floor more deserving of his attention. He had visited them often in the past and made friends with other boys in the area, and they were hoping that this would help him snap out of whatever it was that made him feel so sad.

The Pittmans were devout Christians and were deeply concerned about Christopher and the dramatic challenges they faced in trying to reel him in. They would try and help him master his life, teaching him God's ways of finding a positive path of development. They were aware that being a parent in twenty-first-century America was anything but simple. Dealing with a temperamentally complex child like Christopher, it would require a lot of patience. He had had to deal with in his parent's separation and divorce, with his dad's remarriage—coupled with the day-to-day exposure to media violence and commercialism that poison's children's minds and spirits—all these were not easy matters to understand and to deal with.

But it was Joe Pittman, the grandfather, who had always had a soft spot for Christopher. The connection may have been that both had lost their mothers at an early age. An insight into Joe's frame of mind can be found in his memory book.

"I was two weeks old when my mother died. I never thought about having a mother, but as I grew up and hung around other children, I noticed they all had a mother. I had wanted one, too. So I tried calling my sister Edna, 'Mama,' and when she left, Thelma became Mama. Of course, it was particularly embarrassing for them, especially around young men or older boys.

"The reason that I make such an issue of this sixty-six years later is I just realized why I never called my stepmother 'Mama.' I always called her 'Miss Omie.' I loved her and respected her, for she was good to me, but I couldn't bring myself enough courage to call her 'Mama.' I suppose I was afraid she would say, 'Boy, I'm not your mama.'"

Christopher was ecstatic when he heard his grandparents were coming to get him. Their home was friendlier and warmer than his. It held no bad memories. He could enroll at Chester Middle School and attend New Hope Methodist Church, where he had friends. Yes, he could feel comfortable about living there and never have to doubt the love he was receiving.

"When Christopher left here, he was thrilled," Delnora Duprey said. "He was on cloud nine. He was going to live with his Nana and Pop Pop."

Whatever was bothering Christopher, Joe and Joy Pittman wanted to help. Dr. Eric Naumann was their family physician in Chester and he had agreed to examine Christopher.

On Christopher's first visit, November 5, 2001, Dr. Naumann talked with Christopher and his grandmother about his running away from home and treatment at Lifestream. Christopher was assessed and diagnosed with a low-grade depression known as dysthymia. In his treatment plan, Naumann saw he had been given Paxil at Lifestream, but switched him to a starter pack of Zoloft.

"Mrs. Pittman, I don't have any Paxil," Naumann told Joy, "but I'm going to give you another antidepressant that will work just as good. I want Christopher on twenty milligrams for the first seven days, then increase it to fifty milligrams on the second and third weeks."

Naumann explained to Joy and Christopher that the color of the pills changed with the strength, so they shouldn't have any problems determining what was 25 mg, as opposed to 50 mg. Christopher was asked to return in three weeks and told to seek help—first from his school counselor and then an outside counselor.

One of the reasons Dr. Naumann had given Christopher a Zoloft starter pack was because he saw on their statement that they were paying out of pocket. It had been Naumann's experience that a lot of people in rural Chester County, with no insurance and who take antidepressants, can't afford the medication and quit within the first week or two. In order for antidepressants to take effect, it normally takes four to six weeks. He didn't want Christopher stopping the medication and then in a month's time be right back where they started. He would rather put something in Christopher's hand that he knew he was going to take, because it was there.

But those who knew Christopher best said they could see a big change in Christopher's demeanor, once he started taking the medication. It was as if his life had turned as sour as a green apple.

"Christopher was always well-rounded and well-liked," Reverend Snelgrove said. "He was as normal and carefree of a little boy as there was. But when he came to live with his grandparents, it was clear the boy had changed from prior visits. He'd become withdrawn and depressed. It was a noticeable difference that everyone could see."

Family members in Florida also noticed a change, though in a different way. When Christopher and his grandparents visited Florida for the Thanksgiving holidays, he appeared happy, but very hyperactive. There was something that was out of character for him, they remembered.

"I saw Christopher at Thanksgiving," Danielle said. "I was at my house with my father. Nana and Pop Pop and Christopher were there, too. They came down on Thanksgiving, which was on a Thursday, and they stayed until Saturday. My grandmother said she had an appointment for Christopher that Monday with the doctor and that she had to get back to that. I begged them to stay longer, because I missed my brother and he missed me.

"I remember telling someone that was the happiest Christopher had been in quite some time. I remember he was weird, but, at least, he was happy. But all the time he was home, he was completely different than anything I had ever seen him before in my entire life. He was completely opposite of what he had been in the past. He would sit there and you would be talking to him, and he would be sitting there fidgeting with his hands the whole time. And he would start a sentence and then he would immediately change midsentence into another sentence. And he would do this five, six, seven, or eight times. He never finished one of the sentences that he started in the first place. He was continually up and down, in and out of the house. He was just crazy. He wasn't quiet, he was talkative. You couldn't get him to shut up. And that was unusual for Chris.

"At some point, if you got him to where you could get him to be still long enough, he would be sitting there next to Pop Pop and he would be happy; then he would get up and he would run out of the room and do something. He was all over the place. Then he would change, and a few minutes later, he would be upset about something. And then, a few minutes later, he would be over that and in tears about something else.

"I knew Christopher was taking medication because I was sitting at the counter; we had a counter and two bar stools that we were sitting at. I was sitting at the left-hand side and I was playing with my nana's rings. I would do that a lot, put them on my fingers and look at them and take them off. There was a ziplock bag that had a little packet of stuff in it. And I asked Christopher, 'What's this?' He said, 'That's the medicine that I'm taking.' It was in a little packet. It wasn't in a prescription bottle. They had them in this ziplock, packed so that all the packets would stay together. It was one of those like a bubble pack, where you pop the pills through the bottom.

"I saw Christopher take his medication. My grandmother faithfully handed the medication to him in the morning with breakfast and at night with dinner. Morning and evening. We were eating our Thanksgiving dinner—and we had it all out on the table—and Nana got up, and she was like, 'I have to get Christopher's medicine.' She got up and she went and got the pill and she handed Christopher the pill and said, 'You need to take your medicine again.' Christopher just kind of rolled his eyes and took it.

"I said something to Nana about him being weird and she said, 'Yes, I know, we have an appointment on Monday and we're going to talk to the doctor about it.'

Melinda, Christopher's aunt, said that Chris had complained to her about the pills he was taking: "He says, 'Aunt Mindy, I don't like taking them. I feel like my skin is like crawling, and I feel like I'm just on fire!"

Maternal grandmother Delnora Duprey observed Christopher's behavior was different as well. "He never did anything in tenth gear. He was always so laid-back, until he started taking his medication."

Joe Pittman Jr. said it was his oldest daughter, Danielle,

who first noticed the changes in Christopher, but didn't think much of it because he was so happy. Joe remembered his son couldn't wait to take his medicine.

"He was almost like a drug addict," Joe said. "I thought it was odd, but I assumed he was trying to be responsible."

Christopher saw Dr. Naumann again on November 26, at 3:30 P.M. Naumann had a conversation with Christopher's grandmother, who told him that Christopher was going to start seeing a school counselor that week. Christopher was taking the Zoloft, fifty milligrams per day, as ordered, and appeared to be doing very well. His appetite was good—he had gained three pounds—and he reported having lots of energy. Christopher told the doctor he had a girlfriend at school.

The only red flag Dr. Naumann noted was that Christopher had seen his father for three days and knew there had been bad blood between them in the past. After administering the Zung Self-Report Depression Scale, an assessment of twenty questions, to see if Christopher was depressed or not, Naumann recorded his test results showed minimal to mild depression. Even though Christopher looked great and seemed great, the assessment indicated he was still depressed.

"Maybe Christopher has an adjustment disorder," Naumann said to Joy. "If the situation changes you are in, then that could trigger depression. Let's keep him on the medicine and not take him off it. If he is going to start counseling at school, let's keep him on the Zoloft. He can return in six weeks. If he doesn't need it, then we can take him off of it. He's already been on it three weeks, and he looks as if he is doing well."

Naumann gave Joy enough samples of Zoloft to last six weeks. He put the medication in a brown paper bag and wrote the directions across the front: Zoloft, 50 mg, one time per day. He figured the samples would save Christopher's grandparents at least $90 per month.

CHAPTER 18

On the way home from Chester Middle School on November 27, 2001, Christopher Pittman began picking on a smaller, younger boy, according to another child who was on the bus. Near the end of the forty-five-minute ride, Christopher pinned the nine-year-old boy's head against the window and choked him, using two fingers.

"It began by him playing around," the boy said, pointing to Christopher, who was still standing at the bus stop.

The younger boy had begun crying, and the third boy said he tried to break it up. When they had gotten off the bus, Christopher told the boy he'd kill him if he told anyone. The boy dismissed it as nothing.

The next day, the parents of the boy who was choked reported the incident. School officials called the Pittmans, who set up an appointment the next day to speak with Assistant Principal John Rodgers about the matter.

Rodgers's office was a bare rectangle in the Chester County School Administration Building. Christopher was just in his third week at school, and already in trouble. He didn't understand it. Back home in Florida, he and his sister never got into trouble. Earlier that year, he had made such good grades he was chosen to participate in a Florida program that would provide four years of college after graduation.

Christopher sat against a blank wall, several feet from John Rodgers, the vice principal at Chester Middle School, and across from his grandparents. Rodgers, a fortyish mediator with a salt-and-pepper beard, horn-rimmed glasses, and a quizzical expression, had investigated the incident thoroughly.

The vice principal summarized what had happened.

"I had a visit yesterday from two parents, who said their son had been attacked on the school bus." Rodgers turned in his chair to face them. "Their child was a second grader, but the attacker was a middle-school student. They said they thought his name was Christopher Pittman."

Rodgers paused, gazing from the boy to his grandparents.

"This was the first I had heard about an incident on the school bus, but I promised the parents I would look into it. When I called Christopher to talk to him, he said [he] had slipped and barely touched the other student. He said another student would verify that story."

Christopher lowered his head.

"Well, I called that student; he said Christopher had choked the second grader. The boy verified the parents' story and that is why I called you and left a message."

In a tone suggesting it was obvious who was at fault here, Rodgers told the grandparents he would have to ban Christopher from using the bus until they could settle the issue.

Christopher had tried to explain that was not how it happened. He leaned toward his grandparents and interjected, "One kid threw a piece of paper at the second grader, but he thought it was me. I tried to explain to him it wasn't me, but he didn't listen. He's got a sister, who said she was gonna bring a knife to school and cut me." He paused, then lowered his head again, hoping they would all get the message.

Rodgers arched an eyebrow.

"I checked into that," he said, facing Christopher's grandparents, all the while gauging their response to their grandson, who was breathing deep and staring at the floor. "There was a threat, but that came after the choking. I also checked the second grader's neck and it was still showing some marks as if it had been grabbed." He suggested they take Christopher home as some type of school suspension.

Christopher's grandparents rose from their seats in hurt and disappointment. In a voice that grew stronger as he spoke, his grandfather assured Rodgers they would handle the matter at home. He turned to his wife for affirmation, and she nodded her approval.

Rodgers's tone was cautionary. What Christopher definitely needed was a firm message. His grandfather met his eyes, letting a confident smile play across his mouth. He assured him their grandson would get the message.

Christopher and his grandmother stepped outside Rodgers's office, but his grandfather stayed behind. In tears, he attempted to explain Christopher's situation and why he had moved from Florida and was living with them.

"We've taken him in and are trying to help him work through all of that," Joe said in a voice barely above a whisper. "Please keep us in your prayers."

Rodgers nodded and thanked him for his willingness to cooperate.

There had been a quick handshake, a neutral word of encouragement, and the Pittmans were out to the car and on their way home. But Christopher wasn't off the hook so easily. His grandparents were old-fashioned and believed in immediate discipline for doing something wrong. They believed in today's world there was "too much talk" and "too little discipline." Joy had seen a lot of that in her job at the school. The child does something wrong, he or she gets sent to the principal's office, who calls Mom or Dad, and then everyone sits around and dribbles about the "problem" for a few weeks before anything is ever done. It was sending a confusing message to the child.

Using Christopher Pittman's own testimony, CCSD investigators speculated that the Pittmans left the schoolhouse and arrived home somewhere between 2:00 and 2:30 P.M. It is believed they talked for about an hour, Christopher insisting all the while he hadn't done anything wrong but try and protect himself. They must have told him he would be disciplined immediately for his wrongdoings.

Joe Frank Pittman believed in tough love. More than likely, he had assessed the situation as follows: *Whatever it takes, Christopher needs discipline in his life.* Christopher said his grandfather's solution was to confine him to his room for the rest of the night. If Christopher cried for ninety minutes, he still was to remain in his room. If he came out of his room, he would get his marching orders and be asked to return. His grandfather was adamant that he remain in his room.

Investigators were convinced Joe Pittman laid the law down for his grandson. If Christopher wanted to live with his grandparents, he would learn to play by the rules. Not by his rules, but their rules. And as long as he understood that, he was welcome to live in their home.

"You will write a letter of apology to the boy and his family," his grandfather probably told him in no uncertain terms. "You will take it to school and give it to Mr. Rodgers. If anything like this happens again, we'll pack your things up and send you back to your father in Florida."

According to eyewitnesses, the couple attended rehearsal at church that night. Christopher went with them. At one point during the rehearsal, church members said they remembered Christopher was kicking the back of the pianist's stool repeatedly. When Joe Pittman saw what was happening, he walked Christopher outside and had a word of prayer with him. They left somewhere around 8:00 P.M., saying they were going home early to help Christopher with his homework. But everything seemed fine.

Two days later, on November 30, 2001, Dr. Eric Naumann heard about the murders on the radio. That morning, he was at the front of the office signing a chart when two officers from the sheriff's office came in front.

"We have a patient of yours incarcerated that needs his medication," the officers informed Naumann. "His name is Christopher Frank Pittman. We are here to ask if you could write him a prescription to continue him on that same medicine."

Naumann stopped what he was doing, then wrote out the prescription. "I hope this can be of some help to him," he told the officers, handing them a script for "Zoloft, 50 mg, once per day, 30 pills and three refills."

CHAPTER 19

With Christopher Pittman safely tucked away in "juvee jail," Chester County homicide investigators were busy trying to figure just what had happened. Good investigators can take bits of information that appear unconnected and incompatible, then somehow fit them together into a plausible and logical order that all makes sense. This requires an agile mind, an investigative mind capable of seeing situations and faces from several different points of view. It requires a mind that is capable of interpreting those situations and viewing facts objectively.

But this is the bread and butter of what investigative officers do. They are charged with the responsibility of discovering who committed a crime and uncovering enough evidence to prove that person's guilt. CCSD detectives concurred that the Pittman case was like nothing they'd seen before. They had to consider certain possibilities that had seemed unthinkable—especially that of a twelve-year-old literally blowing away two people he loved most in the world and then burning their house down on top of them. But, as they gathered their evidence, it all clearly pointed directly at Christopher.

CCSD investigators acknowledged that there are many challenges all parents face in raising children in today's society. It is not so easy to find answers to those challenges that lead to a positive path. But sometimes a child will run aground and fight even those who love him the most and are trying to help him get his life together. They believed this was the situation with Christopher Pittman and his grandparents.

Melinda Pittman Rector knew her parents as well as anyone. The bitterness of losing them had come on the tail end of her life, just as she was getting to know her parents again. She was ambivalent in that she felt both overwhelmed and cheated at the same time.

"We were just beginning to work through all that adolescent stuff that so many of us go through. You know, 'Why they did so and so, and why I acted like I did; then one day everything tangible is gone and all that I have left are the memories.

"I will admit I was angry that my parents were cut down prematurely. I went through grief counseling, but all I got from that was a pat on the back and told, 'Just be thankful they were both Christians and are with Jesus now.'

"But that wasn't good enough for me. It wasn't like they were in the prime, like they had lived to be ninety and then they died. We were angry that somebody had killed them. But the only problem was this somebody that killed them was no stranger. It was my nephew Christopher—one of my own flesh and blood. He was a teenager from our family that we loved very much.

"Of course, I've gone over it so many times in my mind trying to figure out just how all this happened.

"I have two siblings, an older brother, Barry, and then my baby brother, Joe. Little Joe, to keep from being confused. I was the only daughter, the middle child. I still kept in contact with my parents on a regular basis after I graduated from high school. It was pretty easy at first, as I was only one hundred and three miles away from them. I joined the navy to see the world and got stationed one hundred and three miles away from home. How's that for luck?

"So, it was a couple of times a month, sometimes every

weekend, depending on what duties I had, that I would see my parents. And after that, basically, anytime I could get over there. My husband's career in the military did move us around a lot. He ended up retiring from the military and we visited my folks, whenever we got a chance, but thank goodness for telephones. It was, at least, twice a month, sometimes more, that I would call my parents. And we had some really good conversations.

"Joe Jr. and I were very close. There was eight years' difference between him and me. But I guess I was kind of like a surrogate mother at times, but we were very close. And as he started getting a little older and interested in girls, and everything else, we still remained close. Of course, I stayed close to my mother, because Joe Jr. was a handful.

"After Joe Jr. got married and Danielle was born, we still remained very close. Then he and his wife came to live with us for a while. They were trying to get on their feet financially, so it really didn't bother anybody in our family that they were living with us, because that happens a lot, with job changes and everything that goes on in the economy. If you got the room, and somebody needs the help, you bring them on in.

"When Christopher was born, he was cute as a button. Unfortunately, he was born at the time when things were getting pretty tough with his family. He spent a lot of time, as most of the grandchildren did, over at grandma's house because they'd lived there for so long.

"My mom and dad's house was like a central point for all of us. As the children grew and had grandchildren, it was always home. There were many times many of us had to move in or say, 'Mom, something is going on in my life, can you handle the kids for a while?' And she would take them in. She even took us back in a few times. She used to make jokes to me about it; she'd say, 'I pushed one out the front door and there's two slipping in the back.'

"But that Christopher, he was something else. That's all I can say. Danielle was so excited she got a baby brother. And she took over mothering him. Christopher wasn't a talkative child. But he had these eyes and he talked with his expression. He was very animated with his expressions. And my mother used to have to get on Danielle for speaking for him. It was like she knew what he was thinking.

"So we stayed around Christopher, my husband, my son, and I. My husband was deployed at the time overseas and I was staying with my mother; it was right after Christopher was born and up until a little after he was two years old.

"We called him Kissipher and we watched him grow. As Christopher grew up, he was very well-mannered and polite. He was very respectful toward his elders, which my parents tried to raise us all that way, to have respect for your elders whether you agreed with them or not. And Christopher was a unique young man in a lot of ways because he was so well-behaved, especially considering most of the peers that he was surrounded by.

"Christopher loved being outdoors. He loved fishing. My father had built him a fort, a tree fort, and he liked spending a lot of hours out there. Christopher, my own son, my niece, and other nieces came to visit, and they just had tree swings and just did a lot of things normal kids do.

"I never heard of Christopher being in trouble with the people at school or the police. I was my mother's daughter, and her only daughter, and we discussed a lot of things. We kept up what was going on in the family and what was best for the grandchildren and trying to make sure that they progressed into their adulthood with as much stability as possible.

"But my brother and his first wife, Hazel, were very young when they had Danielle. They were still pretty young when they had Christopher. When Christopher was born, he spent a lot of time at my mother's house and with his sister. Hazel left my nephew and my niece; she just abandoned them. My brother, some years la remarried again, but the situation didn't work out and, basically, the kids lost a second mom. My brother remarried a third time, which lasted a little bit longer, but she left, too, when Christopher was twelve. So, they've lost a lot of mothers.

"I always thought Christopher and his dad were pretty close. They had to be pretty close, because back then my brother was mother and father and trying to work and do everything else to raise his children. That's where my parents and I had tried to step in whenever we could, because we all knew that all they ever wanted was a mother. That's all they wanted, so we tried to put a lot of female influence in their lives.

"My dad was an outdoorsman. He grew up in a very large family and they hunted for their food. His father taught him how to live off the land, so to speak, and it was a way of life. My father shared his love of nature with all of us. He shared it with me and he shared it with my brothers while we were growing up; then he shared it with his grandkids. He shared it with his little fellow, Shadow.

"My father taught Christopher how to read. He would read stories with him, then let Christopher read it back to him. He taught him jokes, and little things, like tying a shoe. Whatever he needed, my father was there to help him.

"My mother was very crafty and very innovative, and seemed to hold her grandchildren's attention, who tried to figure out what she was doing. She taught crafts to all her grandchildren.

"I know my brother Joe disciplined Christopher. He would usually take something away. If they crossed the line into disrespect, then they would get a paddle on the rear.

01, we had a reunion, of some sorts. I got a
l from my brother—he was the first one to call
upset. Christopher had run away and didn't
he was. He had the police looking for him.

And then, of course, because my brother's upset, my mother had to call me and tell me all about what was going on, and then my other brother had to call me and tell me. So everybody was concerned.

"Christopher was found by a Florida state trooper at a truck stop off I-75. He had told a state trooper he was going to South Carolina, that he was going to hitchhike to my parents' house. Christopher was taken home, and when he tried to commit suicide, he was then transported to Lifestream.

"I did get to speak with my brother on the phone about Christopher. During this period of time, my family was discussing and making arrangements for him to live with our mom and dad in Chester. They were discussing and trying to decide what would be best for Christopher and how he could deal with his hurt over his mother abandoning him again. I was part of that discussion, too. It wasn't unanimous—my mother, myself, and my father had felt that it would be best for him to live in South Carolina for a while, have some time off. My brother didn't want to split him and his sister up again because Danielle had always been kind of Christopher's lifeline, inseparable, so to speak. But he finally agreed.

"When my parents were talking with my brother about Christopher coming to live with them, they said, 'You know, it's like we're not taking him away from you.' But we all knew that Christopher would be better off at that time living with my mom and dad in Chester.

"I spoke to my mom about the arrangements that she and Dad would have to make for Christopher to live with them. That included, for example, alterations of the home and fixing the home up in the area that would then be Christopher's bedroom. When my mom and dad agreed for Christopher to come live with them, that was not the first time they had one of their grandchildren come and live with them. And whenever a grandchild would come into her home, something that was important to my mother was making sure the child had familiar surroundings, things that they could call their own. We had one bedroom in her home that probably changed colors, curtains, and paneling, at least, eight times. Because whenever the grandkids would come in, she would set up a bedroom and let them pick out material and colors. They would help decorate the room to their own taste, so they felt like the room was theirs. And Mom did that every time she had one of her grandkids move in with her.

"My mom and dad drove to Lifestream in Florida, and then took Christopher back to Chester. Thanksgiving was in the middle of that event and there was a lot of visitation between my brother and my parents at that time. Around Thanksgiving, I found out from my mother that Christopher was on medication. I had called my mother several times after he was discharged from Lifestream and even during, and we were trying to make holiday plans. My son's birthday was coming up, so we spoke a lot, but my mother was sharing a few concerns about how restless Christopher was. I spoke to Christopher as well.

"Whenever any of my nephews or nieces were with my parents, I always started and went down the line, talking, until I ended up with my mom. Mom told me about Christopher's medication and how he said it made him sleepy. During that period of time, around the third week in November, I spoke with Christopher on two different occasions. One of the things that concerned me was when I spoke with him, he started speaking very fast on one occasion—he just rattled on. I couldn't really understand a word he was saying. I had never known him like that, so I was like, 'Okay, I don't know what's going on, you know, if he ate too much sugar or what.'

"And another time, I had a conversation with Christopher and he was the opposite. You know, I was like dragging every word out of him—I would just get like a reply from him that was almost like a grunt or two syllables. It was difficult to get him to start talking.

"Christopher and my mom both told me that he was

going to the doctor during the week of November twenty-sixth. I told Christopher that some of the things he related to me just didn't seem right. I'd been on various type of medications in the past and it hadn't done me that way. I told my nephew to be sure to tell Nana and Pop Pop how he felt and what was going on with the medication, so that they would be aware of it. I asked Christopher to put my mother back on the phone and told her the same thing. I said to her, 'You need to let his doctor know what's going on.' She said they had an appointment on Monday and would let the doctor know about Christopher's medication.

"During that conversation with Christopher, there was a lot that concerned me about his state of mind. He told me that the medication he was taking was making him sleepy. I was trying to ask him how he was feeling, because I noticed he wasn't speaking like he normally speaks to me.

"So, I said to him, 'Well, maybe you need to sleep.' He said, 'But I don't want to sleep because when I sleep, I have nightmares.' I asked him what kind of nightmares and he told me. But what he was telling me, I had to drag everything out of him.

"On Monday, when I called my mom, Christopher answered the phone and he was speaking fast again. And he pretty much said, 'Nana's not here.' He was fast talking, antsy, and, basically, lied to me about my mom not being home. He told me that he did not like taking the medication he was on, and he said it very adamantly. I asked him how it made him feel and he said that it was like his skin was crawling and he was burning underneath. And I asked him if he was burning, and he said, 'It's like I'm burning under my skin and I can't put it out.'

"I was concerned about what Christopher told me. When I called Mom on Tuesday, Christopher answered the phone and I told him to let me speak with my mother. Mom confirmed they had been at the doctor the day before, but the doctor seemed to think Christopher was fine and that he needed to stay on the same medication.

"I never had an opportunity to talk with her again. The next phone call I received from South Carolina was from Shirley Carter. I was told that my parents' house was burning. Shirley then called me on the phone and told me that my parents' bodies had been found in the fire.

"I was trying to make arrangements to go to South Carolina. We had an ice storm in Texas that night and no flights were going out, so I ended up driving. Before we arrived, we were trying to communicate with everybody on the cell phones on the way out to Chester. Just before we got there is when we found out about Christopher's confession that he had murdered my parents. We were horrified and disbelieving. We were never aware before this ever happened of Christopher ever being violent other than in a playful way toward another person. Christopher and my father got along with each other wonderfully, like two peas in a pod. It was like Christopher was glued to my father. They did a lot together and Christopher was always right behind him. If Christopher was around, you didn't see my dad without Christopher being right there. They were very close. He pretty much worshipped the ground my father walked on. Dad couldn't even cut the grass without Christopher being right there."

PART III

TRYING TO MAKE
SENSE OF IT ALL

CHAPTER 20

Although Christopher Pittman had confessed to murdering his grandparents, homicide investigators suspected he had left out many of the details. Crime scene investigators had remained at the fire scene the better part of the day, trying to fill in those missing pieces, discussing the many tasks they still had left to cover and interviewing neighbors and talking with family members.

In a small town, like Chester, South Carolina, where neighbors are very involved in the community, law enforcement has to be careful. People love to talk and will come up with all kinds of strange-story scenarios and even make up some wacky, off-the-wall conclusions to the parts they haven't figured out. CCSD investigators let the rumors fly. They believed it was good for business because it kept the people busy listening to rumors while the forensic investigators did their job.

Rock Hill Herald reporter Jason Cato was not looking for rumors when he contacted Sheriff Benson on November 29 about the Pittman fire. The twenty-nine-year-old Chester native never imagined he would be covering the daily beat, but a couple of months' work in an endocrinology lab at the Medical University of South Carolina—cleaning petri dishes and sanitizing before he even got close to joining in the fun of counting cells through a microscope—was enough to convince him he didn't want to be a scientist.

Cato had always enjoyed writing and had worked for the college newspaper. His father had started his career as a reporter/photographer with the *Chester News* before becoming the editor of the *Beaufort Gazette,* and advised him if he really wanted to be a journalist, then he should follow the same route. Cato was hoping to take a short leap into the big leagues, and the summer after graduation, he flew to London, England, where he landed a job with a magazine-publishing house. Nothing really glamorous about that job, for sure, as he basically delivered the mail and got paid less than the monkeys and elephants at the zoo.

It was the long end of Cato's short journey, and his father reminded him so. But he was determined to prove his father wrong, if for no other reason than sons are supposed to do that when seeking their own kingdoms. For several years, he played around with a couple of different careers as a freelance writer and copy editor, but none of those were his cup of tea, and ultimately he came back into the field where he said he would never go, newspapers. When the *Herald* offered him a full-time position in April, 2001, he took it.

On the day of the Pittman fire, Cato was scheduled to work a little feature in their paper called the "Cops Reporter." When he came in around 2:00 P.M., the newsroom was already abuzz. A twelve-year-old Rock Hill girl had been found raped and strangled to death in her bed that morning, and when big stories break, the entire newsroom comes alive. Cato could feel the energy, from the reporters to the editors to the copy desk. Most all the reporters were covering that story.

Cato was told about another case—two bodies had been found in a house fire in Chester County. It was a sad and tragic story, one that didn't seem terribly exciting. It was odd, though, that no one in Chester County wanted to answer his questions about the fire and kept referring him to Sheriff Robby Benson's cell phone. When Cato finally reached Benson, he kept cutting their conversation short and saying he'd have to call him back. Within the hour, Cato discovered why Benson was being tight-jawed and knew that he was onto something big.

Cato told his editor that twelve-year-old Christopher Pittman had just confessed to killing his grandparents before setting their house on fire. What was already a big day in the *Herald* newsroom just got a lot bigger. Without realizing it, Cato was starting the biggest story of his career, never imagining, at that moment, just how big it would become.

Cato made several phone calls, one in particular to Sixth Circuit deputy solicitor Michael Hemlepp, who said he had plans to file charges later that day against the boy. While not addressing his case specifically, Hemlepp said, "It is possible for juveniles to be charged as adults in South Carolina. There are many variables to consider in making that decision, but in the end, the decision would not be up to my office."

"When the time comes, who will make that decision?" Cato asked.

"This is a serious crime, but this is a really young kid," Hemlepp said. "Ultimately the decision of what happens to him will have to be made by a Family Court judge."

The idea of a twelve-year-old having to face a man's punishment in a court of law was intriguing.

On Friday, November 30, when the Pittman story broke, the *Herald* was the only newspaper that reported it. It was Cato's story that had put them out front and there was nothing he enjoyed more than beating his competition. The *Charlotte Observer* had a bureau in Rock Hill and he loved to get the scoop on them.

That same morning, Cato drove down to Chester for a follow-up story. He had written his piece from his office the day before, but he wanted to visit the fire scene and get a feel for what had happened. When he finally located the dirt driveway that led up to the Pittmans' burned home tucked back in the woods, Nicole All-shouse, a reporter with NBC 6 out of Charlotte, was already there. A short time later, a reporter he recognized from the *Charlotte Observer* arrived. In her face, Cato saw a tinge of journalistic shame at having been scooped. He was determined that it remained that way.

After gathering details and talking with a few people at the scene, Cato headed into town. He went by the sheriff's office, then over to eat lunch at Gene's, a meat-and-three-vegetable restaurant that serves country cooking cafeteria-style. As he walked through the line, he could hear a couple of people in front of him talking about insurance and wondering when they'd be able to see Christopher. As he thought about it, he realized they must be the Pittman family. He soon found out he was listening to conversations of Joe Pittman, his brother, Barry, and their family friend Shirley Carter. Cato followed the Pittmans in line, sitting a couple of tables away, but continued to face them. When Shirley Cater got up a few minutes later to get something, he approached her.

Shirley invited the polite reporter over to their table, introduced him to Joe and Barry, and helped him to get an interview. "Meet us at my house, around seven P.M., and the family will talk with you then."

Cato had learned a long time ago that reporters who willingly poke their noses into other people's business are quantitatively different from "normal" folks. Being a good reporter requires persistence and a passion for prying into the most intimate and private details of others. Reporters try to uncover and explore all the elementary aspects of the human condition. Hoping to create a logical and plausible narrative out of seemingly disparate facts, they get it all to their editors for proof and then out in the newspaper the next day.

Cato was very excited that his paper was going to have

something that no other paper would—an exclusive with the family—but a bit nervous at the same time.

That Friday night, Joe Pittman, Jr. Christopher's boyish thirty-three-year old father, sat in Shirley Carter's home and talked with Cato about his parents' death. Instead of wallowing in grief and remorse, he clung to the only things that he had left—a close-knit bond with his brother and sister and the immeasurable love they shared for their parents.

Seated next to Joe was his sister, Melinda Pittman Rector, and their older brother, Barry Pittman. The last time the three had been together was in December 2000, when the entire family celebrated Christmas at their parents' recently completed house. Now, a year later, they were back, sifting through the remains of their parents' lives.

Joe flipped through a stack of photographs and stopped on one of a two-story house covered in a blanket of snow. The house in the countryside looked like a Hallmark Christmas card. "That's what their house used to look like." He held up the photo of his parents' dream house they built in northwestern Chester County. "They were so proud of that house."

When Cato asked Joe to describe his parents, he said, "We all agree on one thing, our parents were the greatest people we ever knew. None of us would hesitate for a second to give our lives for them."

What a quandary this guy must be facing, Cato thought, knowing Joe Pittman was left with the tragic reality that his parents' lives had all brutally been ended by his twelve-year-old son. Cato asked Joe why his son had been living with his parents and what could have possibly gone wrong, but those were two questions Joe didn't want to address.

"There was nothing wrong, I will say that," Joe finally conceded. "He needed a break, and he wanted to come up here and live with his grandparents."

Still, as much as the siblings tried to avoid it, the

somber reminder of why they were all together in Shirley
Carter's home, talking with reporter Jason Cato, kept
creeping up, along with the unanswerable question of
why it happened.

"Right now, what keeps us going is that we love our
parents and miss them dearly," Barry Pittman said. "We
may never know what happened, but I know my parents
would forgive anyone for anything."

Joe Pittman said there was no question about him for-
giving his son.

"I want my son to find peace. I also want him to get
help. But most of all, I want my little boy back," he said,
choking back tears. "I still love him very much and I
would give my own life for my son without question.
That's the way we were raised."

Cato thanked the Pittmans for the interview. He had
gotten the information he needed for his story, and information generated stories and interesting stories sold
newspapers. It was as simple as that. Mostly, what he felt
for them was a kind of distanced sympathy, even pity, but
he had been plying the trade long enough to know not
to let his feelings get in the way of a good story.

After Cato's story ran that weekend, he received a
large number of phone messages and e-mails from
people around the country asking whether Christopher
Pittman was taking any antidepressants.

Dr. Ann Blake Tracy, director of the International
Coalition for Drug Awareness, in Salt Lake City, said she
had already heard about Christopher's case. Tracy, who
had worked on cases such as the school shootings at
Columbine High School and the murder/suicide of
actor Phil Hartman by his wife, told Cato that the incident was a "typical scenario." She said antidepressants,
such as Paxil and Zoloft, increase the amount of serotonin, a neurotransmitter, in the brain and that these
drugs were the closest thing to PCP or LSD.

"What they do is make you get up and act out your
own worst nightmare," Tracy said. "There are other

violent crimes committed by children on these types of
antidepressants that demonstrate their potential danger,
including a fifteen-year-old boy in California who
stabbed his grandmother sixty-one times five days after
being prescribed Paxil. Another fifteen-year-old boy in
California shot and killed his father before shooting his
mother and attacking her with a shovel ten days after
being prescribed Paxil."

Cato was very interested in what Tracy had to say, especially when she said, "There's no question that
antidepressants are a culprit in the Pittmans' deaths."

The following Sunday morning at 11:00 A.M., at the
New Hope Methodist Church, a memorial service was
held for Joe and Joy Pittman. Their pastor, Chris Snelgrove, presided over the services. As a tribute to Joe, the
choir sang, "Life Is Like a Mountain Railway."

Joe and Joy had no way of knowing, when they moved
to Chester in 1997, that their retirement would last only
four short but memorable years. They certainly didn't
know when they took in their grandson that their lives
would end five weeks later.

As expected, Christopher's fate was on everybody's
mind. The Pittman children emphasized it was their parents' spiritual connection that always led them to help
anyone they could, including Christopher. It also would
have made them strong enough to forgive him.

"Love makes everything right," Barry Pittman said to
the mournful crowd. "We may never know what happened, but I know my parents would forgive anyone for
anything."

Joe Dolphus Pittman was a broken man, struggling to
find an explanation for what his son had done. At the
same time, he remembered how much Christopher
loved his parents and how they loved Christopher. "For-
giving may have been their easiest task," he said, "but
knowing [Christopher] would have to spend the rest of
his life in jail would have been the end of them."

As Joe Pittman prepared to bury his parents in their

hometown of Summerfield, Florida, on Monday, he struggled with what his twelve-year-old son had admitted to. The normal outlets for a man whose parents had been brutally murdered—anger, revenge, and justice—weren't there for him. He was both the grieving son and a sorrowful father. As he spent time preparing final arrangements for his parents, he also was coping with trying to find a son trapped inside a boy he didn't recognize.

In trying to understand it all, Joe came to the only convenient conclusion—the belief that antidepressant medication led Christopher to kill his parents.

"I'm not a doctor," Pittman said to Jason Cato over the phone, "but I really think it was the medication. The medication he was on, I believe, pushed him over the edge."

Cato asked Joe why he believed the medication was responsible.

"You see, he's been diagnosed as clinically depressed and had been prescribed Paxil and Zoloft, both are powerful antidepressants used to treat depression and panic disorders. But they are not supposed to be prescribed to children." Joe said the more he thought about it, the more it all made sense. The more the medication and what Christopher did connected. He remembered Christopher becoming fidgety, and that he couldn't sit still. And Christopher had talked about his skin being on fire—signs of compulsive restlessness that some doctors had warned is a possible side effect of the medication.

After talking with Joe Jr., Cato began researching the drugs Paxil and Zoloft. They were both antidepressants, classified as selective serotonin reuptake inhibitors (SSRIs). Cato read on the National Library of Medicine Web site that the drugs were used to treat mental depression, obsessive-compulsive disorder, panic disorder, and post-traumatic stress disorder. And that these medicines were thought to work by increasing the activity of the chemical serotonin in the brain.

Cato was surprised to see the number of experts on

the Internet that claimed there had been a direct link between these types of drugs and extremely violent reactions by some of their patients.

Dr. Peter Breggin, a Washington-area psychiatrist and author of the *Antidepressant Fact Book,* told Cato in an e-mail there had been too many tragedies in recent years to ignore the drug's influence.

"This kind of bizarre violence is characteristic of these drugs," Breggin wrote. "I hear something like this every week, maybe twice a week. Often, but not always, these types of antidepressants produce mania and feelings of extreme irritability that lead to overreaction. Definitely, these drugs are not recommended for children under the age of eighteen."

Like the good reporter he was, Cato contacted Tim Daughtery, an associate professor of psychology at Winthrop University in Rock Hill. Daughtery stated that there was no credible scientific evidence that links antidepressants to violent behavior. But if such a link were discovered, Daughtery said he would not be shocked. He said there was some evidence out there that serotonin was implicated in some forms of violent behavior, but warned that the two were not directly linked.

"So how would this relate to someone like Chris Pittman?" Cato asked.

"The best thing to do now is look at the reason the twelve-year-old was on the medication in the first place," Daughterty said. "When a child taking one of these drugs acts out violently, the cause usually isn't the drug, but the cause is the mental illness. These are children with problems that make them act out in these ways."

Cato remembered in the weeks preceding Christopher's move to Chester and the killing of his grandparents, Christopher was caught in a whirlwind of behavior problems. He had been grounded after receiving a bad report card and trying to run away on October 23 to get to his grandparents' house in Chester. Christopher told officers in a neighboring county he had run away because his father was beating him, but his father denied the accusation.

Joe Pittman Jr. said he placed his son in a Florida treatment center for three or four days, then allowed his son to stay temporarily with his parents in Chester County on the advice of a counselor.

"He just needed a break," Joe Jr. said. "A psychiatrist thought it would be a good idea to give him a little breather."

On November 28, Christopher had been disciplined for getting into a fight on the school bus. He was to return to school the following day to receive a suspension sentence, but that meeting never took place. Instead, Christopher spent the day being questioned by the law enforcement officers about the death of his grandparents.

"Lack of emotion," Cato remembered Sheriff Robby Benson saying about Christopher. "I felt something was not quite right the first time I met the boy. He just looked me straight in the eyes and answered my questions without any emotion. It struck me as odd there was no fear, no remorse. I don't think he realized the consequences. I think he would have been more upset if he lost a football game."

Joe Jr. said he understood what the sheriff was talking about. He no longer recognized his own son. "That sparkle he had in his eyes is gone now. It's like an empty window. The night of November thirtieth, I put my arms around my son and told him that I love him, but he didn't say a word. He didn't show any signs of being upset. Any normal little boy you put your arms around and hug, he's going to cry. He didn't cry at all."

When Cato related Christopher's story to Dr. Ann Tracy, she said Christopher's behavior didn't surprise her, but she expected it to change in time.

"Once he comes out of it, he'll really regret it," Tracy said. "Until then, he'll still be in his delusional state where he tries to justify his actions."

Joe Jr. said he only wanted one thing out of all this: "I hope they can find my little boy and bring him back."

After talking with Tracy, Cato called Joe Pittman in Florida. He was intrigued again by what Pittman had to say about Christopher.

"My family and I have been over this thing and we believe it was the drugs Christopher was taking that made him do this," Joe said. "There's just nothing else that can explain what happened."

On December 9, 2001, Jason Cato revealed to the public Joe Pittman's theory and it became the first story published linking Christopher's homicidal behavior to the antidepressant he was taking. It would ultimately become the defense he'd eventually use at trial.

Like most people Cato had talked to, he was pretty skeptical about blaming it all on the antidepressant. But the more he thought about it and researched it, he sensed there had to be some truth to it. It was certainly an issue worth exploring.

"We weren't getting much out of the Pittman story at this point in terms of details," Cato recalled, "and this was a way to explore what might have happened. There were plenty of other stories out there about antidepressants, but most of them were suicides. But there were a lot of stories similar to Christopher's where their tragic behavior at the end was such a radical departure from how the person had normally been prior to taking antidepressants."

Reporters like Cato are, by nature, intensely curious people. They have a deep, abiding desire to know and understand the truth, and, in order to get there, they have to ask rude, nosy, interfering, and highly personal questions.

Cato was a master at getting people to open up. He had the innate ability of establishing a rapport with others and could communicate effectively. He learned early in his career that people are complex and sometimes are reluctant to reveal information. Sometimes a person has the information and isn't aware of it. And then sometimes a person has the information and is just waiting for the opportunity to deliver it.

Cato also had the advantage in that he was stubborn. He didn't give up easily and continued trying long after any other reasonable person would have given up. Part of this was, he supposed, his pride or arrogance, an unwillingness to let his competition get ahead. And part of it was experience. He knew that if he stayed with the Pittman story long enough, it would eventually come undone.

CHAPTER 21

The Department of Juvenile Justice Detention Center in Columbia, South Carolina, is a facility where kids are transferred when they were picked up off the street and charged with a crime. The juveniles remain there until they go to court or are discharged. The facility is as busy as Grand Central Station. Law enforcement vehicles are up and down the road and in and out of the facility twenty-four times seven, bringing in kids handcuffed and taking them back out handcuffed.

On any given day, DJJ will have from eight to fifteen new admissions coming, boys and girls. There is a lot of activity there, and a lot of anxiety. For many of these kids, they've never been handcuffed before. They've never been to jail before. At the time Christopher Pittman was transferred to DJJ, there were 144 juveniles in this facility, seventeen of them were girls. Their ages were from eleven to seventeen, and their charges ranged from sexual offenders to breaking and entering, assault and murder.

After Christopher Pittman had been escorted through the facility and told where he would sleep, he took a long look at his room. The accommodations for B-10 didn't quite suit him. It was a haunting little room, with a creepy little bed, so unlike the bed he enjoyed at his grandparents' home. As his watchful face changed into a cruel frown, he realized he would never sleep the same old sound sleep again.

After Christopher got settled into his room, he was sitting in the recreational area on the B pod and talking with a group of juveniles. One of the juveniles asked Christopher why he was at DJJ and he told them he had killed his grandparents and burned their house down.

Psychologist Julian Sharman preferred that Christopher tell him about his crimes, rather than to the other juveniles in the facility.

"I knew that Christopher was scared, like many other kids coming into the facility for the first time. For most of these kids, they've never been put in a police car or handcuffed before, and not only that, but they're driven quite a distance from their homes, so they're away from their families for the first time. They're frightened. Many of them have threatened suicide, recently or even on that day. A lot of kids will say if you send me to DJJ, I'll kill myself."

Every child coming into DJJ is required to have an assessment, primarily to ensure they had been placed in the appropriate wing. Sharman was the only psychologist on the clinical team and he knew how critical room assignments were in the detention center.

"Well, they're really cells," Sharman clarified. "They're not rooms. They have doors that shut electronically once the kids are in there. It is a detention center, so it's quite a shock for many kids coming in to be placed in a room and have the doors shut on these small cells."

On the second day at DJJ, Christopher was in his classroom looking through the *State* newspaper and noticed an article and a picture depicting his crimes. He cut the information out of the paper and carried it back to his cell. Holding a picture of his grandparents' burned home against the cell window, he started tapping on his cell window until he got the attention of the juveniles in the recreational room across from his cell. When they looked up to see what all the commotion was about, they saw Christopher pointing and laughing at the picture, as if he were mocking what he had done.

On November 30, 2001, two days after the murders of his grandparents, Dr. Sharman talked with Christopher. During the conversation, Christopher had no trouble talking with Sharman and understood his questions. He wasn't crying, nor was he upset. He was a little squirmy, but for the most part, he was fairly engaged. Christopher was so matter-of-fact that after he sat down and started chatting, the conversation seemed casual.

Christopher admitted shooting both grandparents. He told Sharman how he came to live with his grandparents and how he and his father were not getting along; that his father was both physically and verbally abusive, and he would make Christopher and his sister do all the chores while he just sat around. They also discussed his suicide threat, the three days in Lifestream, and his seventy-two hours on Paxil.

Then the conversation turned dark. Christopher told him about the murders.

"My grandparents came to Florida and took me to a house they had built three years ago in Chester. I got into trouble at school and my grandfather told me to stay in my room and not come out or else I'd suffer a beating with a homemade paddle. I came out to get a drink and my grandfather beat me back to my room. He hit me five times. I then thought about how to get rid of them."

Although a lot of Christopher's sentences were disjointed, he quickly got to the point of his story. He had planned the shooting and the fire, then waited until they were asleep and shot them four times.

"I aimed at the bed, then looked at them," Christopher said, lowering his head. "There were lots of blood."

Christopher said he sprayed lighter fluid around the house, put his dog in the truck, and drove to Gaffney and slept on the roadside; that was where the police had found him.

In all of Christopher's unceasing talk about his crimes, he stopped to mention that the .410 rifle he used in the shootings was given to him at Thanksgiving by his father for shooting squirrels. The .410 had been given by his grandfather to his father, who in turn gave it to Christopher.

"I actually bought the bullets myself and tried them out in the rifle." Christopher said he was angry at his grandparents and his father, and that was why he had shot them with those bullets. "They put me down. Called me a loser. They said I couldn't do anything right."

Sharman was shocked at Christopher having no remorse. As he told the story about shooting his grandparents, he appeared calm and quiet about the incident, and seemed to feel justified by what he had done. He was adamant about not seeing his father or living with him.

"While I was writing the assessment, Christopher moved in closer to me. He had a big smile on his face and seemed to want to connect in a boyish way. He wanted to tell stories, and talk about his dog. He said he had bought it for eighty-six dollars when it was just a puppy."

On December 4, 2001, Sharman saw Christopher again. In his notes, he wrote, "He's a quiet, shy boy. Sometimes shakes. Eye contact sporadic, depending on the subject. Regarding his grandparents, I asked, 'Christopher, do you feel upset about what happened?' And he responded, 'Kinda.' That has become his word."

"Did you love or hate them?" Sharman asked.

"I loved them and sometimes I hated them."

"Do you feel they deserved what happened?"

"They asked for it."

"Was there anything they might have done to prevent this incident?"

"They could have sat me down and talked with me more."

"How about your father—do you love or hate him?"

"I hate him."

Fifteen minutes into the interview and Sharman still

saw no sign of remorse from Christopher. Not only did Christopher feel justified in what he did, but he didn't seem to care much about what happened to him.

"Christopher seems like a normal twelve-year-old," Sharman scribbled in his notes. "A little immature, but nothing remarkable. It's difficult to comprehend his actions, but mostly difficult to comprehend why he's not traumatized at all by the horrific nature of the incident. In comparison with other kids he has talked with in similar circumstances, he is not forthcoming with information and doesn't need to talk about it, as would someone who feels guilty or needs assurance that they are okay. There have been some who came in with family murder charges who have reacted very similar to Christopher, and some come in very traumatized and very upset. But this doesn't seem to apply to him."

Although Christopher was placed in a room by himself, he would always buddy up with someone. At five feet two inches and ninety-seven pounds, he was one of the smallest kids in the facility, easy prey for the older teenagers, who were very aggressive and very dangerous. Christopher got into a lot of fights. The first week he was there, he got kicked in the mouth and got his tooth chipped.

Earlier that week, Christopher had appeared before Family Court judge Walter Brown Jr. He was represented by Chester County public defender Yale Zamore, who had asked Judge Brown Jr. for the psychiatric evaluation.

"Your Honor, with what appears to be a mental-health history in this case, it is not in the child's best interest that the evaluation be released until we know more about it," Zamore said in an even voice.

Not looking dangerous at all, Christopher swiveled around in his chair as the judge and his lawyer talked. He was just a kid wearing an oversized suit, looking thin and out of place in a court of law.

Sixth Circuit John Justice was no neophyte when it came to prosecuting juvenile suspects. Justice asked for

Christopher to remain in custody and continued confinement during his evaluation. His office had thirty days from the previous Friday to ask Family Court to move the case to Criminal Court.

"We probably won't make that decision until the end of the month," Justice told Jason Cato in an interview. "We want all the facts in the case before making a decision. The case right now is still in the investigation and analysis stage. I can tell you we will not be seeking the death penalty. As you know, in 1988, the U.S. Supreme Court set sixteen as the minimum age for capital punishment. Due to the boy's age, this case would not qualify."

Christopher listened. When the judge announced he was being charged with two counts of murder and a charge of first-degree arson, his fleshy lips—oddly large lips for such a small boy—suddenly tightened and trembled.

On the way out of the courtroom, Christopher suddenly started laughing. Even though it was probably the laugh of a scared child, dressed in chains and being escorted to a police car, he saw something funny. It was a disturbing moment.

CHAPTER 22

On December 5, 2001, Christopher Pittman was transferred to the William S. Hall Psychiatric Center for a two-week observation visit. He was to be interviewed by South Carolina Department of Mental Health (SCDMH) forensic psychiatrist Dr. Pamela Crawford. Crawford was licensed and board-certified both in general psychiatry and in forensic psychiatry, and was the director of the forensic division at Hall Institute, a division of DMH that dealt with psychiatry and child psychiatry. As director, she was responsible for the supervision of the evaluations related to competence and criminal responsibility. She was also in charge of the units that took care of the well over one hundred patients who were there for various reasons. Crawford had been forwarded a court order, requesting an evaluation of Christopher Frank Pittman.

The court order required that two evaluators complete an evaluation of Christopher Pittman. Because his case involved a homicide, he had been admitted to the residential-care facility, where he could be observed. Dr. Crawford and Dr. Mia Delaw, a child forensic psychiatrist, were assigned to complete the evaluation on Christopher. Dr. Darryl Meyers, an evaluating psychologist, was also asked to treat him.

The purpose of the evaluation was to gather information

about Christopher. As part of the evaluation, Crawford consulted a neurologist, who evaluated Christopher for any neurological problems, examined him, completed an EEG and MRI of his head, and then assessed his brain wave patterns.

The thrust of Crawford's evaluation was to determine if Christopher was competent to stand trial. She wanted to know if there was a mental disease or defect at the time of the murders that made it impossible for Christopher to differentiate between legal or moral right and legal or moral wrong, or was he unable to appreciate the wrongfulness of the actions. A competency evaluation would reveal if Christopher was able to assist his attorney in his defense, and whether there was evidence of a mental disorder or problem that would hinder his ability to understand the legal proceedings.

Christopher was first interviewed by Dr. Crawford and Dr. Delaw on December 12, 2001. Christopher appeared calm, pleasant, and cooperative. He understood the questions and answered them appropriately. Crawford read him his Miranda rights aloud and asked him to describe them back to her. It was clear to her that he understood what they were talking about.

When Christopher discussed the murders, he told the psychiatrists he had gotten into trouble at school and that his grandfather was very angry with him. He said that when he got home in the evening, his grandfather had beaten him with a paddle, that he took the paddle and hit him several times, then sent him to his room.

"When my grandfather started hitting me, I heard a voice," Christopher said. "At first, I heard a voice coming from all around me. Then I started thinking it was my own thoughts about killing my grandfather that came to me as he was hitting me. Afterward, I went to my room and that's when I decided to kill my grandparents. I planned on killing them after they went to sleep."

Christopher admitted that after his grandparents went to sleep, he went to the gun cabinet and got the shotgun, then went into their room and he killed them. Crawford noted the details. For a forensic psychiatrist, everything he said was significant. In particular, when he told her he went into his room and waited for his grandparents to go to sleep, that indicated some type of planning to her. One of the symptoms of someone acting impulsively, or that they are driven by other forces, is they're not typically able to sit and plan and wait. Christopher showed, at the very least, that he had some clear thought about what he wanted to do and he waited until his plan could be executed. He was able to delay this thought about killing them, until they were asleep and in bed.

The two psychiatrists were of the opinion that Christopher was calm, clear, and organized. When asked if he regretted what he had done, Christopher said he knew it was wrong and he regretted it, but he still felt his grandparents had deserved it.

"Part of the time, I regret it," Christopher admitted, "but part of the time, I feel like they deserved it."

"Why is [it] that you think they deserve it?" Crawford asked.

"They shouldn't have hit me," Christopher said hoarsely.

"But why specifically do you feel like your grandmother deserved it?"

Christopher let his eyes settle upon Dr. Crawford. It was a question, no doubt, he had pondered for some time. Finally he said, "She didn't stop my grandfather from hitting me. That's why she deserved it."

Christopher said later during the interview that he had mixed feelings about what he had done; that at times he had some regret about it and thought his grandparents didn't deserve to die.

The fact that Christopher told Dr. Crawford two weeks after the murders occurred that he knew what he had done was wrong indicated to her that he knew right from wrong. In relation to criminal responsibility, his saying that to her was significant in terms of his having awareness of the crime he had committed. In that same interview, Christopher told how he had used lighter fluid and candles to set his grandparents' house on fire.

"I set the fire to get some lead time." Christopher looked pleased with himself, as if he had some naughty little secret he hadn't told anyone. "I knew the fire would distract people from what had happened and get me some lead time. I thought, too, that people would originally think I had died in the fire and that would give [me] some more time to get away."

Christopher talked about how he had stolen money from his grandmother's purse and had taken her truck when he left. Specific to his criminal responsibility and knowing right from wrong, his answers were noteworthy and provided great insight into his behavior.

"It shows not only that he knew it was wrong," Crawford would later testify in court, "but that he knew that it was legally wrong to do this. He knew there would be some consequence for his actions. It also goes to show some planning, some organization in terms of how he is going to get away and cover the crime. I have evaluated numerous people and people who have been not guilty by reason of insanity. Trying to plan it in this way and to leave in this way would not be consistent with someone who is so disorganized they don't know right from wrong. So the fact that he actually left the scene and escaped and had a plan to escape was very significant."

At the time of the murders, it wasn't entirely clear to Dr. Crawford if Christopher was hearing voices, and if these were the voices he said he could not resist. She believed he had the capacity to resist the voices, that he had the capacity to conform his actions, and he had the capacity to resist the actions he took that night in his grandparents' bedroom.

Crawford questioned Christopher about his dosage of Zoloft at the time of the shootings. "He said he was initially taking twenty-five milligrams; then that was increased to fifty milligrams in the morning, and then it shifted to the evening time. Christopher also told Doctor Greg Landy, a psychopharmacologist, Doctor Bonnie Ramsey and the nursing staff at the facility, that he was on fifty milligrams. This was two weeks after he killed his grandparents. And in the review of the records from DJJ, he also told them he was on fifty milligrams and even described the color of the tablets to them. So on numerous times to numerous different people he was in contact with, Christopher said he was taking fifty milligrams. But never once did he say he was taking one-hundred milligrams or two-hundred milligrams of Zoloft.

"After the December fourteenth interview, I spoke with Christopher's attorney Yale Zamore and wrote a consult letter to Doctor Greg Landy, who was actually my supervisor and the director of Hall Institute at the time. Zamore had mentioned that Zoloft might be an issue in the defense of this case, so I consulted with Doctor Landy, then responded to the request of patient and attorney report that Zoloft was significant to patient's killing of his grandparents. I put in my report there was no evidence to support that the medication had influenced his behavior at this time."

Crawford was aware of the medication issue in relation to Christopher's case, and felt it incumbent not only to get Dr. Landy involved, but to learn as much as she could about the medications. Because she was a treating psychiatrist and not a psychopharmacologist, on December 18, she called the distributors of Paxil and Zoloft and asked them to send her literature on the latest information they had on these medications. She also completed an independent Internet search and got additional information on the drugs from Dr. Landy.

With the information about the side effects of these antidepressants in hand, Dr. Crawford prepared a list of questions not only for Christopher Pittman, but for family members, schoolteachers, and law enforcement agencies. She wanted to see if any of the signs or symptoms that Christopher exhibited the week of the killings would come up as a side effect of Paxil or Zoloft, that would be significant in this case.

Crawford began by gleaning her opinion from Christopher's records. When she reviewed his statement to the hunters, she concluded he had developed and told a story that was obviously self-serving. His fabrication of a black man that kidnapped him and killed his grandparents demonstrated his knowledge of wrongfulness, that he was aware of the legal consequences to what he did.

Crawford then interviewed Detective Lucinda McKellar and Special Agent Scott Williams. As she researched the side effects of Zoloft, one of the overpowering symptoms was that the medication induced a manic state. In her conversation with the two officers, she asked them if there was evidence of any psychiatric difficulties the day Christopher had confessed to murdering his grandparents. Using her checklist as a guide, Crawford went through all the symptoms of mania: his ability to concentrate, whether he was hyper, verbal, speaking rapidly, distractible, or anxious. She wanted to get the information about Christopher from the officers and then look at it from a psychiatrist's perspective to help determine his state of mind at the time of the murders.

What Crawford found out from the officers was that Christopher was calm, organized, not irritable, and definitely not distracted on the day he confessed to murdering his grandparents. That day, he was able to engage in playing a game of cards and watching television. According to the officers, there was no evidence, as far as they could see, of any symptoms of psychosis, and that he had maintained a stable mood when he talked with them.

Crawford reviewed Christopher's drawings of the house, constructed at the time he was interviewed by Lucinda McKellar. To Crawford, it showed a degree of organization, that he was able to give specific information about where things were in the layout of his grandparents' house. It showed attention to detail, so much so that his state of mind at the time of the interview was that he could provide new detail.

"My granddad's feet were falling over the bed," Christopher had said. During the interview, he had been able to describe the melee in his grandparents' bedroom. "My granddad's face was to the side. My grandmother was facing the closet. Her legs were in the bed."

Crawford believed Christopher clearly showed he had remembered details of the murder scene. It was her experience in evaluating people who are insane at the time of a murder, there is not that level of organization. People who are insane do not have the ability to recall things as specifically as Christopher had.

"I picked up the shell casings," he had confessed. "I threw them in the door of my room. Then I got some candles from the bathroom closet. I got about three. I lit them. I put one under my bed, one on my floor. I put the other one in the living room on the floor. Then I got some guns. I got a Ruger twenty-two from the gun safe. I got the four-ten out of the gun safe. I took 2 twenty-two rifles and my forty-five. Then I loaded up my dog [and left]."

In her medical opinion, Crawford believed Christopher's actions translated into a very detailed plan of escape. She thought it was all part of his organized plan: the delayed fire in his grandparents' home, taking money from his grandmother's purse, stealing an arsenal of weapons from his grandfather's gun chest, stealing his grandmother's car, carrying his dog, Chrisdee, with him, and then getting the hell out of Dodge before he got caught. Although Christopher got his wires crossed on where he intended to go on the night of the murders, he had given lots of thought to what he was going to take with him and how he would avoid the consequences of what he had done once his grandparents' bodies had been discovered.

"At the time Christopher gave the statement, he was not sorry about what he had done," Crawford concluded. "He didn't have remorse at that time. He knew what he had done was wrong. He said they deserved it. He had justifications for his actions. He has been consistent in saying, 'I did this because I was angry about being paddled. I did that in response to having been paddled' is essentially what he was saying."

Dr. Crawford and her associates would complete the complicated process after reviewing all the medical records from William S. Hall, the medical records from Dr. Howard Smith at the Lifestream Behavioral Center in Florida, the medical records from Dr. Eric Naumann, the school records from North Sumter Primary School and South Sumter Middle School in Florida, and Christopher's Florida Comprehensive Test scores. In addition, she examined the voluntary statements he had made to Chester County law enforcement agents, SLED's investigative notes, and a statement from his father, Joe Pittman Jr., to the Chester County Sheriff's Department.

Crawford's team of evaluators also reviewed Dr. Meyers's psychological evaluation of Christopher while he was in the facility from December 6 to December 11, 2001. They compared this to the DJJ psychological services notes, his MRI and EEG report, and the neurological consultation.

Due to the issue that had arisen from Christopher's family and his attorney relating to the effect of his medications, Dr. Crawford continually consulted psychopharmacologist Dr. Greg Landy. She also reviewed the statements of all law enforcement officers involved in his arrest, the autopsy reports on Joe and Joy Pittman, as well as the pathologist's report, and Dr. Smith from Lifestream. She drove to Chester and interviewed as many of his teachers as she could talk to, as well as interviewed members of Christopher's family, Reverent Chris Snelgrove, and Kimberly Pittman, one of Christopher's former stepmothers. In addition, Crawford interviewed Christopher a total of four times during December, and once again in February 2002.

The results of the evaluation by Crawford and her associates were that Christopher Pittman was competent to stand trial and he had the capacity to understand his legal rights and assist in his defense. She found him coherent and quite forthcoming in his recounting of the night of the murders. In consultation with the two child psychiatrists and the child psychologist, Dr. Crawford diagnosed Christopher as suffering from a conduct disorder.

"The question still in our minds, though, was confirming the diagnosis of Christopher's conduct disorder," Crawford added. "I think it had been pretty well established that he did have a conduct disorder. But I thought that it was important to establish further those kinds of behaviors in talking with family members and his associates. On January 26, 2002, I talked with his aunt Mindy, and asked her about general issues as related to Christopher. One of the symptoms we see in conduct disorders is violence toward animals, so I asked her had any of that ever taken place."

Melinda related to Crawford a story about, a dog she owned. She said that the dog had always been afraid of Christopher and that on one occasion, after they were having dinner, he was missing from the table. She heard a noise in the other room and it was her dog. Christopher had taken an ink pen of some sort and was attempting to shove it up the dog's nose.

Also, during that same event, Christopher was kicking the dog very hard and cursing. Melinda said he was hurting the dog, and that he looked like he was enjoying it too much. Christopher was grounded for two weeks after that as a result of the assault on the animal.

Crawford noted the significance of the event, in that one of the elements in diagnosing conduct disorder is cruelty to animals. When Crawford asked what would happen to Christopher when he was punished, Melinda stated he would be angry, that anytime he was punished, he resented it.

On January 26, Crawford talked with Christopher's

most recent stepmother, Kim Pittman, to whom, she had heard, Christopher and Danielle were very close. Kim said that Christopher had always been a very angry young man, as long as she had known him. When asked for specific information in terms of how he treated other family members, Kim said Christopher would jump on Danielle, tackle her, and pin her to the ground. She said all of this was not in a playful, lovey-dovey manner between brother and sister. All this happened, she added, before Christopher was admitted to Lifestream.

In an interview by phone, Crawford was told by Joe Pittman Jr. that he thought Christopher's problems all began when he was entering adolescence, about a year before his twelfth birthday. Joe said he remembered Christopher had started misbehaving after his half sister had been born. He said that Christopher lost his temper easily and that he had a hard time controlling his son. Joe specifically talked about the incident prior to going to Lifestream. He said that his son was angry because he had come home with a bad grade, and Joe had taken his Nintendo and television away. Christopher was very, very angry about that.

Dr. Crawford was still looking for any evidence about the effects of Christopher's medications on his behavior. Because his attorney was proposing that Zoloft had caused him to murder his grandparents, she asked his father specifically about what happened at Thanksgiving. Joe responded that Christopher was doing well at Thanksgiving, that he was his normal self.

Just to make certain she and Christopher's father were on the same sheet of music, Crawford went through a list of behaviors that would be indicative of mania. Joe said Christopher was not hyper-verbal, not speaking rapidly, not fighting, nor was he getting into any arguments. He said Christopher was as normal as he gets; that he was not talking rapidly, he had no trouble sleeping, and his ideas weren't jumping around.

Crawford asked Joe about Christopher's behavior. She

was searching for specific evidence of mania or akathisia, but didn't find any evidence of that when talking with Joe Pittman Jr.

When Crawford interviewed Danielle Pittman, she questioned her about the records from Lifestream that indicated there had been violence exhibited toward her from Christopher in a form of a golf club and baseball bat. Danielle said that Christopher, on at least one occasion, had thrown golf balls at her and caused bruising. And that on five or six occasions, when she would be left to babysit for him, he would get angry and would come at her with a baseball bat or a golf club. Danielle admitted she was afraid of Christopher during those incidents.

In trying to confirm Christopher's conduct disorder, Crawford also talked with Dr. Howard Smith at Lifestream. During his brief stay at the treatment center in Florida, Christopher had been diagnosed with oppositional defiant disorder, which is a milder version of conduct disorder. Smith talked about the incidents involving Christopher attacking his sister, his behavior on the unit, and whether there was evidence of mania. In Smith's opinion, there was no evidence of mania and Christopher's behavior on the unit was consistent with the oppositional defiant disorder.

Crawford asked Smith about Christopher running away from home and was told that the incident was a result of his anger at his father. Smith described a very dysfunctional relationship between Christopher and his father.

Crawford thought it was also crucial to talk with those persons who didn't have a particularly vested interest in the case, in terms of family members and friends, and to get a sense of how he was behaving right before this happened. So she visited the school and interviewed those persons who were familiar with Christopher's behavior before November 28, 2001.

Assistant principal Deborah Johnson told Crawford that Christopher was essentially a normal kid who was kind of flippant, meaning he was not as respectful of authority as one might think that some kids should be.

Christopher's math teacher, Daniel Edwards, said that he was an average student, quiet, and that he didn't cut up in class. According to Edwards, Christopher was his normal self the week before the murders. He was not speaking rapidly, not irritable, not angry, and not anxious.

Diane Coleman, Christopher's art teacher, said that she had one incident with him where he was making fun of her and mocking her. Coleman said that he was essentially a normal kid, and she saw nothing abnormal about him the week before the murders. He was not hyper, nor was he nervous. She said Christopher was disrespectful at the time, but was essentially a normal kid.

School counselor Stephen Cummings had dealings with Christopher also, and like the others, he said Christopher was a normal kid the week prior to the murders. Sometimes he was a little fidgety, sometimes he was a little hyper, but, mostly, he was real quiet. When Crawford asked Cummings if Christopher was within the normal behavior range for kids, Cummings said he was. Certainly, Christopher wasn't a perfect kid, and he had a bit of an attitude, but there was nothing abnormal about him.

Crawford also spoke with the Pittman's family practitioner, Dr. Eric Naumann, who told her that he gave Christopher twenty-five milligrams of Zoloft for a week and then increased it to fifty milligrams. Naumann said the last time he had seen Christopher was two days before the murders. Crawford understood that to be significant in that a physician, his family doctor, had seen and evaluated him.

During an interview with Christopher in early December, Crawford was alarmed when he rambled on about how he was making bombs within the facility. He was explaining to her how he could make something, some version of a bomb, in which he would take Styrofoam and mix it with gasoline. He then discussed how he had made other kinds of bombs with gasoline, with aluminum and other things, which he said he had blown up when he was angry.

Christopher also told Crawford he had tried LSD when he was there in Florida. Although any account of him taking drugs was not reflected in his school records, there were disregard for rules, notes out of class without permission, in-school suspension bus infraction, and warnings from the school counselor.

Crawford had been working in forensic psychiatry for nearly a decade. All of her work was basically grounded in the gathering of information. Her job was a bit like detective work in that the vast majority of information gathering involved social interaction—getting people to supply the information she needed. She was fortunate that she had the advantage in her official status where she could elicit a certain level of cooperation, but the fact is people like to talk, and especially to psychiatrists.

Over the years, Crawford had learned that even people who are shy and reserved will, if encouraged and given a sympathetic ear, often chatter like magpies. And when people talk, they reveal information, even if they don't mean to. They can't help it. Professionals like Crawford, who are trained counselors, psychologists, physicians, or psychiatrists, know what questions to ask and normally get the answers they are looking for. Sadly, the average person is accustomed to the fact that nobody is really paying attention when he talks, so when encouraged to talk freely, he often lets things slip unintentionally or lies.

All of what Crawford had heard from the family, detectives, and school officials would be utilized in helping her form her opinion. The information gathered from all these sources would not only be included in a written report to both the prosecuting and defense attorneys, but would reappear in the court trial during her testimony. Some of those who had talked freely to Crawford during the initial interview session in early December 2001 would, no doubt, hang their heads in embarrassment and deny most of what they had said, especially when they realized their words had come back to bite them in the butt. But once information from a verbal interview is entered as hard-core physical evidence, changing the contents and implications of what has been said is about as difficult as shoveling fog out of the Boston Harbor.

CHAPTER 23

On December 20, 2001, Christopher Pittman was transferred back to DJJ after his two-week stay at the William S. Hall Psychiatric Center. While he was being kept in state custody and undergoing a mental evaluation, proceedings continued in regard to his being tried as an adult. Even though the written psychiatric report from Dr. Pamela Crawford had not yet been issued, it did not deter solicitor John Justice from filing that motion on December 28, 2001.

"The motion asks that he be tried in criminal court under adult law rather than in Family Court," Justice presented his position to reporter Jason Cato at the *Herald.* "I don't have all the information in regard to the young man to make a final determination, but in order to preserve the deadline, I had to file the motion by today."

It was not unusual for the prosecution to ask that Christopher Pittman be tried in an adult court, given the type of allegation and type of crime he had committed. The admitted shooter was twelve, but he had confessed to shooting his grandparents four times. Although Christopher was a juvenile, his crimes were adult, and, most troubling, was the absence of any motive as to why he did what he did.

When it was announced that Christopher Pittman had joined the growing list of underage children who would be tried in an adult court system for the crime he/she had committed, there was a public outcry. There were other juveniles in the same boat as Christopher. Thirteen-year-old Nathaniel Brazill, had been convicted recently of second-degree murder for shooting his teacher. He was currently serving twenty-eight years in prison for his crime. Nathaniel Abraham also was convicted of second-degree murder for shooting a man when he was eleven years old. And then there was the infamous Lionel Tate, who, in 1999, killed his six-year-old family friend while imitating a professional wrestler's move. This defiant twelve-year-old became the poster boy for juvenile killers after being the youngest person in the United States sentenced to life without parole. After serving only three years, Tate was released on parole.

Christopher was trying hard not to join the infamous elite, but he was well on his way to becoming one of them. On January 8, 2002, he told Dr. Julian Sharman he was feeling depressed. Even Sharman noticed that he seemed quiet, less animated than their previous meetings.

"Why do you think you might be depressed?" Sharman asked.

Christopher looked downward. "I hate being here. I get picked on by everyone." He stated he was being verbally harassed by one of the officers again and he had been bitten on the finger by one of the other kids in the facility. Christopher also talked about his father and mother. "I never have liked my father," he said. "I have butterflies in my stomach whenever I am around him."

Christopher talked a lot about his father's abuse, his being whipped with a belt and a paddle. He said he just checked out as he grew older. He couldn't remember the exact incident that prompted him to run away from home, but he did recall he was found by police and brought back home to his father. After threatening that evening to stab himself, he was taken to Lifestream. He said he was very upset that his sister had lied to the Department of Social Services (DSS) in Florida and not admitted that their father had hit them.

When Sharman asked about the several weeks in Chester before the shooting, Christopher said, "The first week was okay. School was good." And when Sharman asked what it was that went downhill after that, Christopher added, "My grandfather began acting like my father."

Later that month, Sharman got a phone call from Joe Pittman about Christopher. He was concerned that Christopher had been prescribed the same medication, Paxil, that he was taking when he first went into Lifestream. He said that Christopher had had a bad reaction to Paxil. Sharman referred Christopher to the physician and he was taken off Paxil.

"The way it really happened," Joe Jr. related to Jason Cato, "was that a DJJ doctor called me in Florida and said Christopher was under a bed, telling people to leave him alone and stay away. The doctor told me he had been getting into fights with other juveniles and had cut marks all over his body. When we talked about what was happening with Christopher, I found out they had put him on Paxil again. I pleaded with the doctors to stop giving Christopher these antidepressants, and once they stopped, his behavior, attitude, and his grades improved. In fact, he was the only person on his wing to make the spring honor roll."

Melinda Pittman Rector had visited her nephew at DJJ and had noticed the changes in him once he had been taken off his medications.

"The first time I saw Christopher after the death of my parents was in Columbia at DJJ. I couldn't tell you what building he was in, but I just remember him being in an orange jumpsuit.

"I didn't recognize Christopher. I was standing there with my brothers and my husband, and I kept asking, 'Where's my nephew?' And they keep pointing, but I couldn't see him. And it took me a while to recognize him.

"But in just the way he looked physically, he didn't look like my nephew. What was different about him, this nephew that I thought I knew? He was aloof. He was very, very cold and dark. There was no life in him. Even his stance was different. His head was up, and he was almost defiant. He looked like somebody that had been running. My father would have said he had been run hard, like he had taken about a three-mile run. I just didn't recognize him.

"Christopher didn't talk to me. He didn't hug me. He didn't show any kind of emotion to me at all. That was unusual for him, for he has always talked with his eyes and been very expressive. But he was just cold and robotic. For the next several weeks, I returned to DJJ to see Christopher. The first couple of times I visited him, he was very withdrawn, fidgety. He really wasn't all there mentally. He had this thousand-mile stare, where he didn't look at you, but he looked through you. He also had a lot of marks on his body that concerned me. I wasn't sure what was going on, but I'm a curious person and wanted to know what was happening.

"In March 2002, after he had been taken off the Paxil, I visited him with Pastor Chris Snelgrove. When we got there, we noticed right away that Christopher didn't look like he had in the past. He looked better. His eyes were bright, and for the first time in months, he would look at me and not through me. He was actually talkative instead of just saying nothing, and we could finally get a response out of him, something that I wasn't able to get before.

"I will admit, I had been angry at Christopher. But I had been able to resolve that anger. I started asking questions and thinking about lots of the whys. I had always cooperated with the police's investigation fully, providing information, pictures, and diagrams to the solicitors when they requested it. I had told them Christopher was not a violent child, not impulsive, not aggressive, nor was he hostile. Those were all accurate descriptions of my nephew, of his life from the time I first saw him when he was born until he went to Chester to live with my mom and dad. And I never saw anything in him before October 2001 that concerned me or made me even suspect that he was a violent child.

"Before the shootings, I never asked what dosage of Paxil or Zoloft Christopher was on and he never told me. Mom never told me, either. I just know when I talked to him, he was having problems with his medications. I talked with my mother about it, and she said they had visited Dr. Naumann, but I don't think his medication was ever changed. After all I have read and heard, then witnessed at the detention center, though, it isn't hard for me to believe Christopher's medications had caused him to do what he did."

Danielle Pittman had only been able to visit her brother at DJJ three or four times. Because of her age, her visits were restricted. She, too, had struggled with what Christopher had done.

"When I heard about what happened to my grandparents, I felt it was all like a bad dream. I was surprised, and never, in a million years, imagined that would have happened. I just couldn't believe that my grandparents would be gone, because I always imagined them as being invincible. They were my superheroes. And knowing how my brother loved them, I didn't think he could do something like that.

"I was in complete disbelief for the first week. I was just numb. I didn't understand what was going on. I kept trying to call my grandparents' number and I just knew Nana and Pop Pop would answer and this was a bad dream. All I would get is a busy signal. I wanted to talk with Christopher the first week, and then after that, I was mad at him. I resolved that anger against Christopher.

"When we were burying my grandparents, it was the day before my fifteenth birthday. We all took handfuls of dirt. My family, my aunt Mindy, my uncle Barry, my dad and the grandchildren that were there, we all took handfuls of sand and put it in and said our last words to Nana and Pop Pop. And when I dropped a handful of sand, I went behind a tree that was there and I started crying. I don't even remember who came up to me and hugged me and was trying to comfort me. And I told them, when we buried Nana and Pop Pop today, we buried three people because I honestly didn't believe I would be able to see my brother have a chance at a normal life ever again.

"But then somebody started mentioning something about the medication. I said to them that would make sense because the thing about this whole situation was that it didn't make sense. And Christopher being influenced by the medication to shoot my grandparents was the only thing that had really made any kind of sense to me, so I hung on to that."

Those who knew and loved Christopher were still left bewildered when they tried to explain what had happened to the boy they thought they knew. How could Christopher, a seemingly normal, beloved little boy, turn out to be the monster police claimed him to be? Was it some genetic defect? Was it some kind of sickness he had? Did something just snap inside and he went crazy? Was it that he had a bad side that nobody saw? What did they call it? A bad seed? All these questions begged for answers, but there were none.

CHAPTER 24

While Christopher Pittman's family and friends were still trying to understand the unfathomable, Christopher was struggling to survive at the detention center. From the first day he was admitted at DJJ in 2001 until his court date in 2005, he would be written up at DJJ for a total of thirty-nine incidents. Thirty-two of those thirty-nine write-ups were in his first year, and the majority of those write-ups were for threatening staff, cursing and calling the staff "niggers," fighting, harboring contraband, and insubordination.

On January 19, 2002, Officer George Blackwell's job was working the security detail of the juveniles on the B wing. Blackwell was the acting main detective control operator. One of his coworkers learned that Christopher had a pencil in his room, and when he asked Christopher to give the pencil up, the youth refused. When Blackwell asked for the pencil, Christopher started cursing him and calling him names under his door.

"Fuck you, Mr. Blackwell," Christopher had yelled several times.

During that same month, Officer Frederica Lawson-Prince also had problems with Christopher. During Christopher's first months at DJJ, she had written him up for threatening staff and verbally abusing the staff. On

January 31, 2002, Christopher screamed at her, "You bitch, don't you know who the fuck you're dealing with? I will fuck you up. You wait and see. I'm going to show you. I'm going to fuck you up bad."

Things went from bad to worse for Christopher.

Clinton Grant, a juvenile correctional officer supervisor, knew that Christopher had gotten into a lot fights since being admitted to DJJ. Christopher was always verbally abusive to the staff. On October 17, 2002, Grant initiated a shakedown of Pod B during the third shift. When they got to room B-10, Christopher's room, they found a piece of aluminum fence line from the basketball court. The metal object had been sharpened down into a point and a little handle fashioned at the top. The homemade shank had been found under Christopher's bed and could have inflicted serious harm.

On October 3, 2002, during a routine search and shakedown, Christopher was found to be in violation for possession of drugs. The crushed yellow pills had been discovered in the light fixture of Christopher's room in a ziplock bag. On another occasion, Tylenol pills were found hidden in his state issued bo-bos (sneakers) and Christopher was cited for hoarding contraband.

On August 17, 2003, Billy Ray Warren also had an unpleasant encounter with Christopher, just two weeks after he started working at the detention center. On that particular day, Christopher didn't want to go into his room. He wanted to do his laundry, instead. In a calm manner, Warren told Christopher he had to go into his room, but he refused. Warren had to tell him a second and third time before he finally went back to his room. Christopher then unleashed a string of profanities on Warren, calling him everything from a faggot to a motherfucker. Even with the door closed, Christopher continued cursing and kicking the door.

When solicitor John Justice heard about Christopher's problems in DJJ, he was not surprised. The idea of Christopher being tried in an adult court was not unusual at all for Justice. He always believed Christopher had made a conscious decision to kill his grandparents, and had done so.

Christopher had been charged as a juvenile, but walked through a procedure called the "waiver hearing." In certain crimes—murder being one of them—Justice had the right to petition the Family Court judge to waive the defendant up to general sessions court. The solicitor had done this in Christopher's case and was successful in getting the court to treat this twelve-year-old as an adult. Justice had another reason for believing Christopher should be tried in an adult court. After murdering his grandparents in cold blood, Christopher made up a long and protracted story, deliberately led the police in a false direction, and consciously lied to law enforcement officials. His actions showed absolutely no mitigating factors in connection with the murders and compromised any thoughts of leniency that Justice would have cast in Christopher's direction.

Christopher's previous behavior also conveyed to Justice that he was making the right decision. His prior acts at home with a BB gun and putting darts into a bull was indicative of who he was. If the defense wanted to portray Christopher as a kind, wonderful, docile, and sweet kid, then Justice would trip them up in a rebuttal case with those things that had happened, as well as behavior in the juvenile detention center during the past three years. Juries didn't look favorably on juveniles who sharpened plastic spoons into weapons and attacked workers with racial slurs, threatening and calling them "niggers" and "motherfuckers."

As far as Justice was concerned, Christopher Pittman cared only about Christopher Pittman. He was always looking for somebody else to blame for his problems, and now he wanted to blame Zoloft.

But there were others who believed it was too easy to jump to the conclusion that Christopher was an evil person and needed to be put away for life. The fact that he sharpened a spoon in prison was no proof he was a cold-blooded killer. Ask anyone who has been in detention or prison, and they would tell you all about the abuse, mistreatment, and violence that go on inside. Maybe it would come out later that he was doing this to protect himself and had no intention of harming anyone. Christopher's supporters were confident he was not this monstrous killer the state claimed him to be.

As public defender Yale Zamore worked on Christopher's defense, not surprisingly, he saw things a lot differently than the prosecution did. From his perspective, he would present as much evidence in court as he could about how much this twelve-year-old boy loved his grandparents. Then he would present the scientific evidence and testimony from expert witnesses to present a reasonable likelihood that Zoloft had caused Christopher's adverse behavior. Once the jury heard how much Christopher depended on his grandparents, then it would not be a leap to show what he did was inconsistent with how much he loved and depended on them.

"This case is a legal minefield," Zamore said. "It must be handled exactly right. Our own expert psychiatrist will assess Christopher Pittman, making this his third evaluation."

Given the scientific evidence, Zamore believed the defense would fly. Could a jury believe this is such a cynical world we live in that this evil, malicious child decides to blow his grandparents' heads off, then burn their house down, go and get his dog, and drive away like nothing ever happened? Wouldn't they see that his medication had put him in this state?

Part of Zamore's strategy was that the Food and Drug Administration (FDA) had not approved Zoloft for juvenile depression. The way he understood it, Pfizer had already indicated people who took it may become manic, violent, or suicidal. Pfizer couldn't dismiss this, but if this company, a multibillion-dollar company, had said this, then a jury would have to believe that there's a possibility that taking a drug like Zoloft by a child—who shouldn't have been taking it in the first place—could have had this effect.

In the meantime, months and months dragged by and still the lawyers could not talk about a trial date, except to say that cases move forward in a courtroom only when psychological evaluations and investigative work are complete.

"This is a child," Zamore said. "Yes, it is difficult and slow-going. Yet he doesn't lose his constitutional rights because he is a kid."

Both sides had agreed to the psychological evaluation done by the state, but back in late December 2002, with a thirty-day procedural deadline looming, solicitor Justice had filed a motion asking that Christopher be tried as an adult for his crimes. That filing triggered another required competency evaluation to be done by DJJ and set the trial back even further.

The decision about whether Christopher would be tried in Family Court or an adult in Criminal Court would have great effects on potential penalties if Christopher was convicted. Although capital punishment was not an issue in Christopher's case, he still could be facing life imprisonment.

"My son didn't do it," Joe Pittman Jr. told anyone who was willing to listen. "I'm telling you he didn't do it." Joe was sorry that the incident ever happened and blamed himself. "What good is it going to do to punish my son for the rest of his life? I've already lost my parents. I don't want to lose my son in the process. I knew he wouldn't have done this, had he not been taking Zoloft."

Christopher's lawyer was now claiming he had acted in a fit of agitation and psychosis when he shot his grandparents, and it was all caused by the antidepressant he was taking. The antidepressant defense had been raised by at least one hundred different people accused of violence, but it wasn't an argument that Pfizer wanted to succeed, particularly now, when the FDA was under fire for withholding information about the dangerous side effects of antidepressants.

Finally, after nearly two years in legal limbo, it was rumored that Christopher Pittman's case would go to trial in the fall of 2003. John Justice planned on taking the case before a grand jury in October of that year, and if Christopher was indicted, his trial could begin by the end of the year, possibly in November.

"This is a very difficult case, and it's being handled very carefully on both sides," Zamore said. "All cases should be handled carefully. But with something as emotionally charged, as sensitive and as serious as this, you want to be extra careful."

After a Family Court hearing in June, Judge Brown had written in his court order: "Based on the evidence presented, it is the opinion of this court that it is not likely the defendant could be rehabilitated, offering the seriousness of the offenses. Because the alleged offenses are of a premeditated nature, the reasons for my decision are to protect the community."

Since that hearing, both sides had been awaiting a final report from the defense's psychiatrist, Dr. Lanette Atkins. Justice said he had received a copy of her report the prior week.

"For the first time, there's no legal reason not to move forward," Justice revealed to Jason Cato. "In Criminal Court, this boy faces the possibility of spending the rest of his life in adult prison." While the punishment in Christopher's case was interpreted as adult time for adult crimes, Justice said judges consistently had been handing down sentences of between thirty years and life.

Jason Cato called Joe Pittman Jr. and asked what he thought about Christopher's upcoming trial. Joe said he had not been kept up to date on the timetable of his son's case and that he was not aware of the impending grand jury proceedings or that the trial could begin later this year.

"Nobody tells me anything," Joe said from his home in Florida. "I'm now in the process of hiring a private attorney to help with my son's defense. I don't want to tick anybody off, but I want the best for my son."

In a radical move, Pittman told Cato he was pursuing additional legal help to make sure Christopher got the best defense he could, using the medication angle. Since the time of Christopher's incident, Cato had told him about how the British government had banned Paxil from use in children, due to increased tendencies of suicide and violence. In June, the U.S. Food and Drug Administration launched studies into the same issue in America, and even issued a warning to doctors reminding them these antidepressants were not approved for use in children. Cato was a mountain of information and kept Joe and his family up to date on the latest developments in psychopharmacology.

Finally the last legal hurdle before Christopher's trial date could be set was cleared on November 9, 2003. His case was one of about one hundred that was presented to a Chester County grand jury, which would determine if enough evidence existed for a trial.

Solicitor John Justice said, "Few cases are ever deemed insufficient to move forward, and I didn't expect the Pittman case to be among those. The standard for the grand jury is whether there is probable cause, and there is certainly probable cause in this case."

As expected, Christopher was indicted the next day for the murders of his grandparents. The action allowed the case to move forward to trial, which was anticipated to be as early as February 2004. "The boy was indicted on two counts of murder and one count of second-degree arson," Justice said. "Neither came as a surprise. Anything other would have been a surprise."

For each of the murder charges, Christopher faced between thirty years and life in prison. The arson charge could bring an additional thirty years.

Yale Zamore, Christopher's attorney, anticipated the case would be resolved by April 2004, either by going to trial or through a plea agreement. He said he and Justice had discussed the possibility of pleading the case.

"I do that with every case," Zamore said.

Justice said he hoped to take the case to trial, but he also could be persuaded to accept a plea agreement. "Seldom do we rule out making any accommodation to get a guilty plea, even in this case," Justice said.

Any such agreement, however, would need Christopher's approval, and that was something sources close to the case said he was not interested in. Now fourteen, he was the sole client in the case and suddenly had become interested and proactive in his defense.

At an FDA hearing on February 2, 2004, in Bethesda, Maryland, Christopher sent a letter to be read by his father. The FDA had been reviewing SSRIs since June, when a clinical study surfaced that linked the use of such drugs, specifically Paxil, to increased episodes of suicidal thinking or behavior. Several months before the hearing in October 2003, the FDA had reminded doctors these drugs must be used with caution and that labels for these drugs already carried cautions about the possibility of suicide in depressed patients. In their release, the FDA noted, "To date, that the data does not clearly establish an association between the use of drugs and increased suicidal thoughts or actions by pediatric patients. Nevertheless, it is not possible at this point to rule out an increased risk of these adverse events for any of these drugs."

At the FDA hearing in Maryland, Joe Pittman's hands shook as he read his son's confession to a roomful of strangers during the hearing. In the letter, Christopher described what had happened to his grandparents and how he felt while taking the antidepressant Zoloft. Because of his medication, he states, he had taken the lives of two people that he loved more than anything. He said the doctor was prescribing him large dosages of Zoloft. "The doctor gave me a sample pack of Zoloft. He told me to take fifty milligrams once in the morning and once at night. Then, after a week, he changed it to one hundred milligrams in the morning and one hundred milligrams in the morning and one hundred milligrams at night. I didn't notice a change in my behavior until I was completely off the mediation. It made me hate everyone."

Christopher wrote in his letter that everything just kept getting worse afterward, then he snapped and took it out on his grandparents. He claimed it was the voices echoing through his mind that told him to kill his grandparents. Christopher recalled that during the incident it was like watching his favorite TV show, where he knew something bad was going to happen to his favorite character, but no matter how much he tried to stop it, it was out of his hands.

"The only thing you can do is just watch it in fright," Christopher concluded in his letter. "You can't get up and turn it off because your just to shook to get up. Because of my own personal experience on the medication, I would not want anybody to go through what I have and am [going through]."

Jason Cato attended that same hearing and talked with other families who had also suffered from the side effects of antidepressant medication. Through an assortment of varied and poignant articles about Christopher's case and the possible effects of Zoloft on his behavior, Cato kept his story on the front line. Through long hours of research, he became somewhat of a local guru on SSRIs and their effects on juveniles. Cato interviewed a spokesperson for a nonprofit group, the International Coalition for Drug Awareness, who told him they were pushing for more investigations into the effects of antidepressants and children. In their latest news release, they had blasted the FDA for being too soft in its latest stance toward the use of antidepressants in children.

"The federal drug agency is sugarcoating the issue," Lisa Van Syckel, the group's New Jersey coordinator, told Cato in Bethesda. "After reviewing much of the same material as the FDA, the British government has banned certain antidepressants, including Paxil, from use in children."

When Cato asked if she thought any additional rulings would be made by the FDA on antidepressants before Christopher's trial, Van Syckel said she doubted it. "A major revelation, however, is expected out of Great Britain by then. It references a link between suicide and violence in adults being treated with these drugs, and it is expected to be made public by year's end. I'm hoping more breaking news will come out of the United Kingdom, because they are more honest and straightforward. They are not trying to hide anything in Great Britain."

Cato also had investigated a study released in March of that same year that questioned whether juveniles understood the adult criminal justice system enough to aid in their own defense. The study, Cato penned into one of his articles, was conducted by the private McArthur Foundation and concluded that understanding complex legal proceedings was as difficult for children under the age of sixteen as for adults deemed incompetent to stand trial. The study suggested further that a third of the juvenile defendants between the ages of eleven and thirteen, and one-fifth of those who were fourteen or fifteen do not understand the proceedings.

Public defender Zamore assured Cato there was only a remote possibility that Christopher's case could be sent back to Family Court. That would occur only if the solicitor requested the move and the judge approved, something Zamore called unlikely. "But, you never know. Sometimes something that happens at the last minute changes the entire picture," Zamore said. "Cases are like living creatures. And things change, sometimes from moment to moment."

Cato would remember later that never had truer words been spoken.

On January 10, 2004, South Carolina attorney Henry "Hank" Mims was hired by Christopher's father. Nine months later, Yale Zamore resigned, and Mims, along with Houston attorney Andy Vickery and a high-powered team of medical malpractice lawyers, signed on to defend Christopher Pittman.

In June 2004, Judge Paul Short Jr. removed himself from the Pittman case after it was discovered that his wife owned stock in Pfizer, the company that makes the antidepressant Zoloft, and circuit court judge Daniel Pieper, of Charleston, was appointed to replace him. Again the trial was postponed.

On August 30, 2004, John Justice announced, due to medical reasons, he was stepping down from the case and Fifth Circuit solicitor Barney Giese had agreed to take over.

And in a move favorable to Christopher's case, the FDA ruled on October 15, 2004, that all antidepressants would now come with "blackbox warnings" to alert doctors and patients about the possibility that drugs can cause some patients to become suicidal. The move was considered one step below a ban.

While attorneys and judges took their bows and exited, others scrambled to familiarize themselves with Christopher Pittman's case and how the FDA's new ruling would affect it. In the meantime, Christopher was planning a little vacation for himself and one of his classmates, Mario.

On January 16, 2004, Christopher and Mario's escape plot was uncovered and would become known as the "let's go to the dentist and let's escape plan." The two boys were about the same size, but because Christopher had been there long before Mario came, he knew his way around the detention center. He said he had written the plan down as Mario had explained it to him. They were going to Charlotte, that was where Mario was from, and then they would go to Florida, where Mario had family that he purported were in the Jamaican Mafia. Security staff at DJJ intercepted the letter. They recognized the letter was in Christopher's handwriting, but it sounded as if Mario had dictated the letter. Christopher's dentist appointment was canceled the next day and their fantasy escape plan fizzled out.

CHAPTER 25

Fifty-seven-year-old Andy Vickery was a well-known, Yale-educated, medical-malpractice lawyer specializing in suits against pharmaceutical companies. He had won a wrongful death suit in Wyoming, a landmark $8 million verdict, making it the first challenge an SSRI maker had lost in court. Though he had spent twenty-five years as a trial lawyer, the last eight had dealt heavily with suits against drug companies. Vickery said he had only considered handling two criminal cases involving antidepressants. The Pittman case was one of them.

There was no one more qualified to defend this technical and complicated case than Vickery and his team of lawyers. They had dedicated years of their lives to battling the drug companies and collected millions and millions of pages of documentation from their previous litigations. They wanted the world to know that this was Pfizer on trial and what came out of this case could have major ramifications for the drug industry. It would not only determine the future of Christopher Pittman, but of the $3 billion blockbuster drug that was in jeopardy.

"You have a drug that in some respects is very similar to LSD and cocaine, but it comes in a pill your doctor prescribes and the pharmacy fills," Vickery said of SSRIs in an interview with Jason Cato. "To convince a jury of that, however, often requires costly experts. The Pittman case desperately needs a defense that has enough money to hire experts not only with the expertise, but the flat-out courage to say it."

But the questions still lingered in the public's mind: How would the prospect of bringing a Zoloft defense into court and having civil attorneys help Christopher Pittman's case? Would the jury believe they were motivated by something of a bigger picture, other than the defense of this child? There was no question that they were also involved concurrently in other litigations in which they stood to win on behalf of their client a large contingency fee.

However, the perspective was what mattered to Christopher Pittman and his family. These attorneys and their experts were providing services in his case pro bono. They were not seeking a fee directly from him, and they were doing this because they felt Christopher would get a raw deal unless someone, like them, who had a very specialized knowledge of the industry, argued before the jury and brought a very visible defense. There were documents from Pfizer that had come to them in civil proceedings, documents that would be nearly impossible for a criminal lawyer to obtain. Christopher's life was on the line, and it was an advantage for him that they already had these documents.

On the prosecution's side, when Barney Giese took over the case from John Justice, he knew he was looking not at months of work to review, but at years of work to review. From all he had read about the case, he assumed there must be some frequent side effects of antidepressant medications, but it was as obvious as the nose on his face that this boy knew what he was doing when he killed his grandparents. Giese's predecessor had called Christopher "boy" so often, and with a carelessness that was far from complimentary, that Giese believed he was burrowing into something dark, something evil, when he read about the crimes. The boy had

hidden the evidence by burning down his grandparents'
home, then got into their car and left the scene of the
crime. And when he was caught, he furnished police
with this preposterous story about a black man coming
into the home and killing his grandparents. Now it was
Giese's understanding that usually when people are in
a state of intoxication, they don't have the capacity to do
that.

Giese would team up with deputy solicitors John
Meadors and Dolly Justice, John Justice's daughter.
While Giese had the nature and temperament of a country boy in the courtroom, Meadors would go after
witnesses like a pit bull. It was as if he were born to ferret
out all things that were hidden, and once he latched
onto something, he would not turn it loose. In the heat
of battle, his passions ran high and he would challenge
his adversaries, no matter who they were. Never one to
back down from an issue, Meadors would worry over it
like an old schoolmarm, turning it over and over, and
keep coming back to it, until he was satisfied that he had
discerned every facet of the truth.

The way the prosecution saw it, the state's case was
against Christopher Pittman, and not against Zoloft. It
was simple enough—if he knew right from wrong, then
he was guilty. There's no defense there. It didn't matter
if he had all kinds of mental problems, was on medication and hearing voices from Mother Mary herself, he
could have all that and still be legally sane. What he
did—the fire, the running, the lying—was all inconsistent with what they said was morally wrong. It was clear
enough for him. The state needed to stay away from
Zoloft and concentrate on a common-sense approach to
his guilt.

Granted, there would probably be great sympathy for
this child, and there would be those protesting that this
case never should have gone to trial. The cry would be
that the prosecution should have worked with the defense and the doctors and determined what was best for

the child. So how would putting Christopher Pittman away for thirty years, or more, make society any safer?

In relation to the boy's Zoloft-induced defense, the prosecution couldn't see there was any other explanation the defense had for the kid shooting his grandparents other than he had gone bad. A defense lawyer is not entitled to pick his cases and pick his facts of the case. He/she has to deal with the hand that's dealt. In this case, the Zoloft defense was the only option the defense had.

There were those following the case who weren't surprised to hear that Vickery and his legal eagles had agreed to defend Christopher Pittman. The general consensus was when you've got lawyers who have spent their entire life suing Pfizer and other drugs companies—and now they're dropping in like parachutes, wanting to be this kid's criminal defense lawyer—there's something more to it than meets the eye.

"Oh, what a surprise," one lawyer commented after reading about the case in the newspaper. "They're defending this kid for free. You just know if there's an acquittal, then they're going to try and parlay it into a whopper multimillion-dollar settlement."

PART IV
THE TRIAL

CHAPTER 26

Charleston, South Carolina, is famous for its "first shots being fired." It was perhaps appropriate that the first hearing in the matter of *State of South Carolina* v. *Christopher Pittman* was conducted inside the Charleston County Judicial Center (CCJC) intersection of Meeting and Broad Streets, in a section appropriately named the "Four Corners of Law." This civil area that houses county, state, federal, and ecclesiastical buildings on each corner is as sober and dignified, and intact architecturally, today as any time in Charleston's long history. It is impressive to stand on the fourth floor at the courthouse and gaze upon the old Charleston battery, where in 1861 a newly established Confederate army rolled their black cannons along the base of the harbor and blasted the daylights out of the Union-occupied Fort Sumter, thus beginning the Civil War.

There weren't many spectators attending the hearing, but those who did and who took time out from the courtroom during the day quickly recognized that Downtown Historic Charleston is unlike other communities that depend upon tourism to stay alive. Historic Charleston has no theme parks, no endless parade of festivals, no entertainment functions, and no trinket-selling or T-shirt shops.

Still existing as a working city, Downtown Charleston and the Four Corners of Law is as real as it has ever been.

The very large and modern 180,500-square-foot Charleston County Judicial Center is so snuggled behind its historic neighbors that most rookie lawyers have to stop and ask for directions. Constructed so that it does not dwarf the adjacent row of historic two-story Broad Street buildings, this massive steel, state-of-the-art building sits placidly like a huge ocean liner that has been swept dry by some hurricane and left to rest on the law corridor.

The people that had fought the brisk 2004 December day to be present at the trial were now inside the courtroom. They were watching the Honorable Daniel F. Pieper in action for the first time. Later in the day, they would probably would walk out and swear that Pieper stopped and rubbed the head of a 1700s William Pitt statue in the judicial center's entrance hall every day. And that Pieper took off his shoes, got on his knees, and bowed to a quotation carved in stone above Pitt's statue that read: "Where Law Ends, Tyranny Begins." And he did this, no less, than five times every day.

Make no mistake about it, Daniel Pieper bled law in black-and-white transcript form whenever he cut his arm. But that was not a problem, for the people who sat inside the courtroom were mostly lawyers, cops, and subpoenaed witnesses. The *Who's Who* list included: attorneys for the state, solicitors Barney Giese and deputy solicitors John B. Meadors and Dolly Justice; attorneys for the defense, Andy Vickery, Hank Mims, Paul Waldner, and Karen Barth-Menzies; and witnesses to the facts, Dr. Lanette Atkins, Christopher's maternal grandmother, Delnora Duprey, Detectives Darrell Duncan and Lucinda McKellar, and Pfizer attorney Craig May.

Regardless of what the press wrote, this hearing was more than a precursor to the trial. More important issues were at stake than "let's see what cards everybody has been holding in their hands." One of the major issues Judge Pieper would decide was if Christopher Pittman's case would be sent back to Family Court and taken out of general sessions court. Also, up for grabs were the issues related to whether Christopher had been denied his constitutional rights to a speedy trial. After all, he had been locked up for three years. And, finally, were the Pfizer documents ever going to be released to the defense? According to the defense, Pfizer had access to information that proved there was a high correlation between juvenile aggression and homicidal acts.

Without any fanfare, these highly skilled and knowledgeable people had a job to do. They not only were deciding the fate of a twelve-year-old boy who had committed double homicide at that age, but, in their decisions, they had the potential to change forever the way pharmaceutical companies sold drugs to juveniles and how doctors distributed them.

Christopher's lawyers had traveled over a thousand miles to argue that trying any minor under the age of fourteen in an adult court was unconstitutional. They were jacked and ready to go. With Andy Vickery leading the charge, they insisted the state had the responsibility to prove Christopher Pittman was a danger to society and that he was not capable of being rehabilitated, and they had not done that. To prove their point, they brought along one of their star witnesses, Dr. Lanette Atkins.

Andy Vickery drew first blood.

"Dr. Atkins's principal job is doing criminal competency examinations on children in the state of South Carolina. She is board-certified in both child psychiatry and forensic psychiatry, and she has spent more time with Christopher than all of the other professionals put together over the course of the last few years."

Vickery paused, letting the judge take it all in.

"Dr. Atkins has spent time with Christopher. And she has spent considerable time talking with his relatives and people who knew him, reviewing his care situation with the other **health** professionals that cared for him, both before **and after this** incident, and reviewing all of their records. So, **she has both** the expertise and the factual foundation **to look into** this matter torturously."

Vickery **explained that** his expert witness would testify that Christopher, **at the** time of this alleged offense on November 28, and 29, 2001, was a bright twelve-year-old, but was behind a couple of grades in school. And he was taking a psychoactive medication that produced a psychotic state, which in her opinion so controlled Christopher that he did not appreciate the difference between right from wrong on the day of these incidents, nor, indeed, did he have the capacity on the following day to give any statements to the police.

Vickery was confident Judge Pieper would consider this new information and reverse the court's decision to try Christopher as an adult. "I think on the two critical issues before the court: Dr. Atkins's testimony would be that there is no evidence that he presents any danger to the violence of South Carolina. He never had any problems with the law prior to this. And prior to this, the only instances of violence he had were a day or so before when he was also under the influence of Zoloft and had an encounter with a boy on the school bus.

"He has been at DJJ for three years now. I think that she will tell you that not only is he rehabilitatable [*sic*] but that he has made remarkable strides. Once he was fully cleared off of psychoactive drugs, which took some time, by the way, when he was in custody. But once that happened, he has been a model prisoner, and he has been a model student. He has caught up the grades he was behind. He always brings me, every time I come to see him, Judge, a stack of papers. And the lowest grade I can find is an eighty-eight and most of them are A's. He's doing well in his schoolwork.

"The mental-health professionals that treat him are impressed with him, with his attitude and with the prospects of his rehabilitation. So that's the testimony

that I would offer, but not from myself but from someone who is competent to give it, Dr. Atkins."

Dr. Atkins took the stand and recited for the judge her
involvement with Christopher since November 2002,
boasting there was no other mental-health professional
anywhere, other than perhaps Dr. Julian Sharman, who
treats Christopher in DJJ, who had spent the kind of
time with him that she had. She summarized Christopher's behavior before and after the murder of his
grandparents and assured the judge that he had made
tremendous progress in his environment.

"Every time I go into the department," Atkins added,
"I talk to them about how Christopher is doing. They will
say, 'He's just excellent.' Everybody tells me he's the type
of kid that doesn't belong in the Department of Juvenile
Justice."

Vickery asked Atkins if Christopher could be rehabilitated.

"Yes, he has made enormous strides in that regard,"
she stated. "In fact, he's caught up and is ahead academically. He could finish school early."

"Dr. Atkins, is there any reason to be concerned about
him posing any danger whatsoever to the citizens of
South Carolina if he were walking the streets as a free
young man today?"

Atkins was quick to offer her professional opinion.
"There would be no more danger than there might be
for somebody like me. I mean, we can't predict anybody
whether they are going to do something violent. But the
fact that this was a crime that happened against a family
member, the fact that he was not in touch with reality at
the time of the crime, the fact that he is stable now, even
if he had some problems with psychiatric illnesses in the
past. We know now what his potential problems were and
they can be caught early and medicated. He does not, in
my medical opinion, represent any danger to society.

"In fact, he is a child that I would feel comfortable
having in my own home. I know I can't take a child home,

but I mean he is one that I would not feel uncomfortable having around my seven-year-old daughter and I don't say that about many children that I see."

Vickery nodded, then returned a smile. "You mentioned being out of touch with reality. Do you believe that on November 28, 2001, he had a psychotic break?"

"I do."

"And do you believe it was Zoloft induced?"

"I do."

"And as a result of that, do you believe he was able to distinguish right from wrong?

"No."

"Do you believe the day after when he gave the two written statements to the police that he had the mental capacity to appreciate the consequence of what he was doing and to effectively waive his constitutional rights?"

Atkins leaned forward in her chair. "No, I mean, I wasn't able to evaluate him at that time, but we don't normally expect children to be competent until they are between the ages of eleven or twelve. He was a child that was behind some socially and academically. So, looking back, I would expect, based on what I saw later, that he would not be competent to understand the consequences of what he was doing when he waived his rights. I mean, we see juveniles every day, and you have to really rephrase rights so that they can understand them and go over them and repeat them to make sure that they really understand the gravity of what they're doing. And with this type charge that he had, no, it could be my opinion, at that time, he was not able to competently waive his rights."

"How about the drug-induced effects?" Vickery continued. "Do you believe that he still had either mania or psychosis on the day after?"

"Definitely. I mean, there was evidence in impulsivity. There was evidence in grandiosity. He said he didn't really recall specifically whether he had done it or not. He had a vague memory. He felt like things were a TV program. It was more like he felt like it was a dream. He

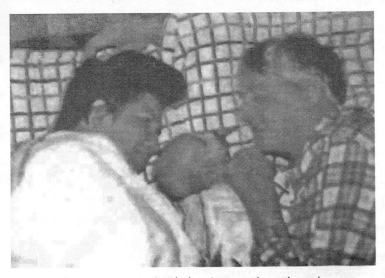

Joe and Joy Pittman were elated when their grandson, Christopher, was born on April 9, 1989. *(Photo courtesy of Melinda Pittman Rector)*

After Christopher's mother abandoned him when he was six weeks old, the Pittmans helped raise him. *(Photo courtesy of Melinda Pittman Rector)*

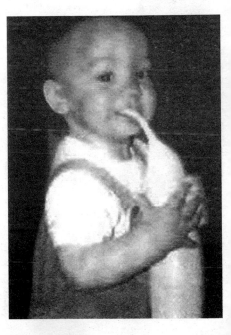

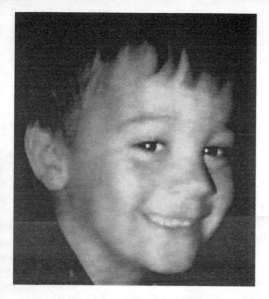

As Christopher grew older, he was described as a sweet, quiet, and laid-back child.
(Photo courtesy of Melinda Pittman Rector)

Christopher and his grandfather were especially close.
(Photo courtesy of Melinda Pittman Rector)

When Christopher was eight, his world fell apart when his grandparents moved to South Carolina. *(Yearbook photo)*

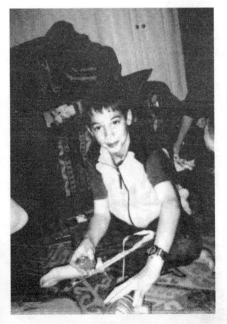

In 2001, at the age of 12, Christopher ran away and threatened suicide; he was hospitalized and prescribed an antidepressant medication. *(Photo courtesy of Melinda Pittman Rector)*

When the Pittmans heard Christopher was in trouble, they didn't hesitate to take him in. *(Photo courtesy of Melinda Pittman Rector)*

The Pittmans' dream home in Chester, South Carolina.
(Photo courtesy of Melinda Pittman Rector)

Christopher and his grandfather did everything together.
(Photo courtesy of Melinda Pittman Rector)

On the night of
November 28, 2001,
Christopher shot his
grandparents with a
.410 shotgun as they
slept and then set fire
to their home.
*(Photo courtesy of
Melinda Pittman Rector)*

By the time the West Chester Volunteer Fire Department arrived,
the Pittmans' home was already engulfed in flames.
(Photo courtesy of Ann Grant)

Joy's prized grand piano lay among the ruins.
(Photo courtesy of Melinda Pittman Rector)

For three years, Public Defender Yale Zamore *(above)* fought to keep Christopher's case in family court rather than in criminal court under adult law. *(Photos courtesy of Jim Stratakos, The Herald, Rock Hill, South Carolina)*

Joe Pittman, Jr. believed the antidepressant medication Zoloft had pushed his son over the edge and was responsible for his parents' death.
(Photo courtesy of Jim Stratakos, The Herald, *Rock Hill, South Carolina)*

Judge Paul Short, Jr.
(Photo courtesy of Jim Stratakos, The Herald, *Rock Hill, South Carolina)*

Solicitor John Justice.
(Photo courtesy of Jim Stratakos, The Herald, Rock Hill, South Carolina)

The defense's expert witness, psychiatrist Lanette Atkins.
(Photo courtesy of Jim Stratakos, The Herald, Rock Hill, South Carolina)

By age 14, Christopher had grown into a six-foot,
one-inch tall young man. *(Photo courtesy of Jim Stratakos,
The Herald, Rock Hill, South Carolina)*

Christopher replaced Yale Zamore with a team of lawyers that included
Andy Vickery and Karen Barth-Menzies. *(Photo courtesy of Jim Stratakos,
The Herald, Rock Hill, South Carolina)*

While defense attorney Hank Mims *(above)* worked overtime at getting Christopher out on bond, Jason Cato *(below)*, reporter for *The Herald* newspaper, worked equally hard at keeping his story in the public eye. *(Photo of Hank Mims courtesy of Jim Stratakos,* The Herald, *Rock Hill, South Carolina; photo of Jason Cato courtesy of* The Herald, *Rock Hill, South Carolina)*

Chester County Victim's Advocate Lucinda McKellar testified that Christopher told her a black man killed his grandparents and kidnapped him. *(Photo courtesy of Jim Stratakos, The Herald, Rock Hill, South Carolina)*

Along with McKellar, Special Agent Scott Williams heard Christopher later confess that he had killed his grandparents and set fire to their house. *(Photo courtesy of Jim Stratakos, The Herald, Rock Hill, South Carolina)*

On the first day of Christopher Pittman's trial, prosecuting attorney Barney Giese called the defendant "pure evil." *(AP Photo/Wade Spees)*

Prosecuting attorney John Meadors showed arson investigator Andy Weir a photograph of the Pittmans' burned home. *(AP Photo/Wade Spees)*

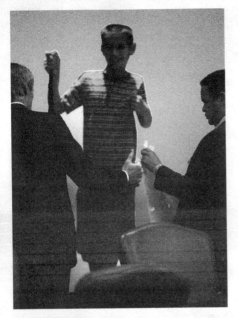

The jury was shown a poster of Christopher at age twelve.
(AP Photo/Wade Spees)

SLED firearms expert Ira Parnell demonstrated how Christopher deliberately shot his grandparents. (AP Photo/Mary Ann Chastain)

Circuit Court Judge Daniel Pieper ran his courtroom with an iron hand.
(AP Photo/Alan Hawes)

Defense Attorney Paul Waldner comforted Christopher after the judge
sentenced him to thirty years in prison. *(AP Photo/Alan Hawes)*

Danielle Pittman Finchum cried as she addressed reporters outside the courtroom. *(AP Photo/The Post and Courier, Alan Hawes)*

In spite of all that had happened, Christopher Pittman's family remembered how much he loved his grandparents and how much they loved him. *(Photo courtesy of Melinda Pittman Rector)*

wasn't sure if he had actually done anything to kill his grandparents, on the next day. So, definitely, he was still under the influence of the medications and I think for months afterward, not due to the direct effects of the medication, but due to the fact that it induced the manic episode, which is something we've known for over twenty years that any antidepressant can do."

Solicitor Meadors was not impressed with Dr. Atkins. He thought she was not only long-winded, but wishy-washy. On cross-examination, he asked her if she, all of a sudden, had an interest in Christopher Pittman's case, but didn't seem too interested when she had been asked to testify in Chester Family Court at the waiver hearings on April 8, 2004.

Atkins admitted she had had some struggles with this case for a long time. She said she had even told the defense attorney she wouldn't be able to help him with the case, but later changed her mind.

"I generally come down on the prosecutor's side. I find children to be competent and criminally responsible, unless there is some age that they are not old enough to understand or there's an MR issue or there's some kind of mental illness.

"So this is a very unusual stance for me to take. It took me a long time to really reach my decision because I had no doubt from the very beginning that this was a child that had mania induced by an antidepressant. He had clear symptoms from everybody that I talked with.

"My concerns were, was he able to appreciate right from wrong and that was my biggest struggle. And looking at the records, there were things that documented that he had not had hallucinations. And I was struggling with that because he had initially said that he had hallucinations, command hallucinations, but then he went back to say they were thought processes in the head. And so every time I would talk with this child, he would say, 'No, they are just my thoughts.' So, I really struggled and struggled and struggled with it. It just wasn't clicking and that's something that . . . it's not usual for me to spend that much time in a case.

"Finally I said, 'Kids don't know how to describe hallucinations.' And the normal process when we get to do competency evaluations is—when you ask people about hallucinations you say are you really, are these voices outside your head, inside your head, are you sure they are not thoughts? And I think at that point, Christopher didn't know how to describe them, so he went to the point of saying these are thoughts in my head. And when I actually said, 'Christopher, I don't want you to tell me what you thought was going on, I want you to interpret it for me. I want you to tell me exactly what happened,' he described it as echoes in his head, saying 'Kill, kill, kill,' which is not a normal thought process."

Meadors wanted to know how her opinion differed from the original waiver hearing.

"I was not at the waiver hearing," Atkins answered, "but was available, had Mr. Zamore decided to call me, or if the judge had asked me. I was surprised I wasn't called."

Meadors had a curious look on his face. He read for her solicitor Justice's question during an April hearing: "Let's get to the crux of this thing. Assuming you had to testify now, to what degree, if at all, would you testify to an opinion that based on your expert understanding from a medical standpoint that Christopher Pittman did not know legal right from legal wrong and could not appreciate the legal or moral wrongfulness of his conduct at the time that these incidents occurred?' Do you remember that question, Doctor?"

Atkins nodded.

"And your answer was, 'At this point, I don't feel comfortable testifying either way,'" Meadors reminded her.

"At that point, I didn't feel comfortable testifying either way," Atkins stated. "I felt like I needed to know what the new information was to make sure that my opinion did not change. I'm always open to my opinion being either way based on any further information that is obtained.

"After spending this two years of time interviewing Christopher and multiple members of the people involved, I haven't found the inconsistencies. But Yale Zamore was telling me there was significant inconsistencies that Dr. Ballenger [a psychiatrist hired by the solicitor] was reporting. And I thought that I did not need to render an opinion, at that point, without looking at what the problems were with the inconsistencies. I needed to talk to Dr. Ballenger and reexamined whether I could support that opinion to a degree of medical certainty.

"I did not know what Ballenger had said and that was my problem, because I had no idea what the inconsistences were with Ballenger's statement. 1 was told there were numerous inconsistencies. That was my biggest problem. Yale Zamore told there were numerous inconsistencies that Ballenger had reported, but he did not tell me any details about that. If he could have told me the details about them, then I could have resolved it there that day and felt comfortable with my opinion. I told all three of them that.

"Those people could have observed the demeanor and actions. Those things are documented, and I reviewed those carefully. His behavior was not good when he was first detained and when he was first at Hall Institute. But if you look at the behavior he had, it was aggressive, irritable behavior, which is consistent with mania. He was doing things like reporting that he was making multiple bombs and selling them for prices, which is grandiose delusions.

"Manic episodes generally don't resolve until six to nine months, you know, an average of six to nine months following the onset of a manic episode. It takes months after a manic episode, generally. If you look at the normal cycling, you take about six to nine months between cycles of depressive and manic episodes."

Meadors leaned against the lectern and shook his head. He had the look of "Okay, I'll let you dribble on for as long as you like," and Dr. Atkins took him up on it.

"When I first met with the family, as you would expect with any family, they were very angry. I mean, they lost their parents. Melinda Rector in particular expressed appropriate anger toward Chris during our initial interview. I think as they have been able to deal with their own grief and to look at all of the available literature about things and look at how inconsistent Christopher's behavior was with a child that they knew before and after, that their opinions have changed.

"But, initially they were very angry. And you would expect anybody to be angry if your parents were killed.

"I know from reading and from my education regarding forensics and child psychiatry, I do know that kids are not generally competent to stand trial until sometime between eleven and twelve. And so there is just for competency to stand trial, and then you have to look at the gravity of the situation. And if they were more extreme charges, then you're going to have to be even more careful to understand that they understand the gravity of what they are going through. Because you look at it in terms of what are the ramifications, make sure they understand the ramifications, and a child of his age would very unlikely be able to.

"Christopher was a child that was behind academically, that was behind socially when I met him a year later. So based on that, it's my opinion that he would have been unlikely to be able to be competent to make a decision to waive his rights.

"There was another particular kid that had similar crimes, that he had been talking to. I asked him—I described him as a friend—'How is your friend?' He said, 'I don't have any real friends here. My only friends are the staff and Dr. Sharman. People in here don't have the ability to be friends. They are not somebody you can trust to ask for any advice. They are not somebody that you can really talk to. I try to be nice to them, but you don't really have true friends within the Department of Juvenile Justice.' And I thought that was some great insight for him."

Christopher's maternal grandmother, Delnora Duprey, was the second witness to testify on his behalf. She described Christopher as an extremely quiet and shy child. As an example of how nonaggressive he was, she told the court she had adopted Christopher's half brother at birth and when the two little boys would play, the younger one would pick up a toy and literally hit Christopher on the head.

"But Christopher never even pushed him," Duprey stated. "He never laid a hand on him. He would just walk away and cry. Even back then, never. He was very nonaggressive."

Duprey admitted under cross-examination that the months preceding the murder of Christopher's grandparents, there were definitely some major family issues going on in his life. But she said she would not have hesitated if he were released from custody today to have him live under her roof in her home.

"I have always teased him [when] I visit him at DJJ," Duprey stated, "that if he could fit in my pocket, I would take him home with me."

In regard to Christopher's right to a speedy trial, Vickery told the judge the obligation to make sure that the speedy-trial rights are met is the government's. "As I read the South Carolina rules and statutes, there should have been a hearing every seven days. There should have been an order every seven days to retain custody over a juvenile, and that simply wasn't done. In August of this year, Mr. Zamore and I had a conversation. He filed a demand for a speedy trial, and then subsequently Mr. Mims and myself filed the motion to dismiss on speedy-trial grounds."

The judge reminded Vickery that was about the same time that solicitor Justice stepped down from the case.

Vickery's position was that when a young man stands before the court at a trial, and is not the same young man who was involved in the incident, then his case becomes prejudicial.

"Now, this young man right here"—Vickery asked Christopher to stand—"this young man is almost as tall as I am. He has got whiskers. We have a defense in this case about the impact of a psychoactive drug on a twelve-year-old.

"He looked different. He weighed different. And so the jury in the case, unless Mr. Pittman testifies, the only message they will get from him is observing him in the courtroom. And what we all know as trial lawyers and trial judges is probably seventy percent of the message that is received by jurors in the jury box is visual. So, even if he doesn't testify, they will receive information from him and about him by perceiving him. And the young man they perceive at age fifteen is a very different young man. And as the jury weighs the evidence about the impacts of a psychoactive drug on his mind, they are looking at a different young man, different size, different weight, et cetera."

Vickery had made a valid point.

"Your Honor, it would be disingenuous for me to suggest to you that he had not done very well in his environment. He has done well considering what his environment is. But my goodness, listen to the testimony that the court just heard this morning. We heard the specialist in child psychiatry and forensic psychiatry say this young man has no friends. He has no friends. He tries to be nice to people, but that his only friends in his environment currently are the staff because he can't trust the others.

"Well, that is not normal. That is anxious. That is prejudice to the defendant to be three years incarcerated in the situation where your only friends are not those your age, but who are the staff there.

"And then you heard his grandmother say that she

sort of kids with him every time she visits him that, 'Boy, if I could, I would just put you in my pocketbook and take you home.' It is evident that this young man has plans and thought about plans for the future and that I submit that he has been prejudiced.

"Now, I realize that speedy-trial motions are not often granted. And I realize every one is judged on a case-by-case basis. And I realize that one of the things that we wouldn't be human, as we look at them, if we didn't say, 'Well, wait a minute, you mean my only remedy is to dismiss the charges? How about if I just give him a speedy trial now?'

"The only problem with that is the United States Supreme Court said in *United States* versus *Barker* that where the court finds that the speedy-trial right has been violated, the only possible remedy is dismissal of the charges.

"That is our motion, Your Honor."

Judge Pieper was sympathetic, but reminded Vickery when he was first assigned to this case, he had a conference call with all parties and told them he was prepared and ready to try it the next week. But nobody wanted to try it that week. There was also some scheduling controversy as far as getting Mr. Pittman's family to come in, and several other reasons he remembered for the delay, but the judge didn't think Christopher's rights to a speedy trial had been violated.

The last prong of the preliminary hearing involved Craig May and the Pfizer documents. Vickery had accused Pfizer within two months of the Pittman murders of unilaterally interjecting itself into the case. He claimed they had contacted the solicitor Justice, and the Pfizer litigation attorneys were submitting selective information to the prosecution's expert witnesses. Vickery claimed that fact had never been denied by Pfizer.

Defense Attorney Karen Barth-Menzies had a history of a long and ongoing battle with Pfizer. Barth-Menzies, California's Lawyer of the Year in 2004, had served as the lead attorney in dozens of antidepressant violence and suicide cases involving Zoloft and Paxil, making a name for herself as an expert in the field of antidepressants. The slender and athletic forty-year-old attorney had played basketball in college and was a ferocious competitor.

Barth-Menzies told the judge, "What is important about those adverse event reports, Your Honor, is that they are not anecdotal case reports as described by Pfizer. These are, in fact, adverse event reports that came out of clinical trials. They are controlled clinical trials. Pfizer itself admits that the way to determine causation or a link between drug and side effect is whether it is from the data you get out of the clinical trials. We have in the notebook, you will see, testimony from one of their own experts that established that. The 'prosecutor's manual' that Pfizer totes around the country, and gives the prosecutors when they want to protect their drug, talks about the best way to determine if there is a causal link is through double-blind placebo."

Pieper asked, "Is there any kind of study or evidence that suggests or indicates that the use of these drugs increases or causes violent tendency?"

Barth-Menzies assured him there was.

"And what study exactly are you talking about?"

"It's the analysis that Pfizer did of the adverse events out of the combination of the clinical trials of Zoloft."

Craig May told the judge that Pfizer had been served with a subpoena right after Vickery and Barth-Menzies got involved in this case. The subpoena asked for nineteen broad categories of documents and was really designed more like the normal civil discovery request Vickery and Barth-Menzies tend to serve in their civil plaintiffs' cases against drug companies, where they make their living.

"These discovery requests were hugely broad and incredibly burdensome, and they gave Pfizer two days' notice to comply. Understandably, Pfizer moved to quash that subpoena, and there was a hearing in early June, I believe, to discuss some of this.

"It was Pfizer's position then that, in addition to the burden and the timing issues, there was the legal problem because there was no proper authority for this discovery, no basis in the law, no basis in the fact, and this was essentially a fishing expedition.

"In addition, Pfizer is not a party to this action, and Pfizer is very concerned that the strategy of the defense here is not to try their client, but to try Pfizer in absentia in a quasi–product-liability case here before the court. And Pfizer is not here—it has both of its arms tied behind its back. If it's put in that position, it has no ability to appear here.

"Pfizer is also concerned that the evidence or the documents that were subpoenaed provide no scientific basis whatsoever to exculpate, which is their word, the defendant here. There is no scientific evidence in Pfizer's possession and Pfizer isn't aware of any that shows that Zoloft causes people to murder other people and that is not in the documents that they have subpoenaed and Pfizer is not aware of it anywhere.

"Quite frankly, Your Honor," May added, "Pfizer is very concerned about the precedent there that someone who is on a drug does something, is charged criminally, and in an effort to try to exonerate themselves, they serve broad civil discovery-type subpoenas on a drug company saying, 'Do you have any records anywhere ever that might temporarily associate the taking of this drug with anything that is anywhere close to what the criminal defendant did?' And I don't know if it is an emerging trend or not, but Pfizer has faced this before."

May told the judge that Zoloft had been approved as safe and effective in the United States in the treatment of seven different indications, serious mental illnesses, including depression, post-traumatic stress disorder, obsessive-compulsive disorder, and it helps millions of people every year to cope with those very debilitating serious disorders. Each year, there were adverse event reports filed both with the FDA and with Pfizer, but there was not any scientific evidence that the use of Zoloft causes people to murder people.

May continued in his defense of Pfizer.

"The point of all this, Your Honor, is the case reports are not admissible evidence or proof. They are not the sort of evidence that experts can rely on in this field. And so really they are just there to try and prejudice the jury and take everyone's eye off the ball and try Pfizer, rather than the defendant in this case. It is the statements that we have heard and read in here that make it sound like there are secret documents that Pfizer has been hiding from everybody that will prove everything, and it is simply not the case. And Pfizer is worried that it's going to be a major theme of the [Defense's] case here in this courtroom. And with cameras and press and everyone, things would get written down and publicized, and that is simply not the case, Your Honor, that these documents show that. It is simply not the case that Pfizer has been hiding anything from the FDA, and Pfizer is very concerned that that becomes the issue instead of the guilt or innocence of the defendant."

"What can possibly be done to Pfizer in this case that would create some estoppel of preclusion issue in some other litigation that does involve Pfizer, merely because documents are turned over by virtue of a subpoena?" Pieper asked.

"Your Honor, the fact that we have two lawyers who make their living suing pharmaceutical companies on cases involving antidepressants is not a coincidence here. And they are doing it pro bono, and I respect any lawyer who takes a criminal case pro bono and seeks to assist those in our judicial system, because I know how burdened our judicial system is where I normally practice, and I'm sure South Carolina is no different.

"But the fact that we have *those* lawyers here in this case is not coincidence, and it is because this is a part of the effort by the plaintiff's bar to continue to poke and poke and poke until they get some rulings that they like that they can then travel around the country with and continue to stoke additional cases."

May would have sounded nicer if he had said Vickery and Barth-Menzies traveled around the country in a gypsy's wagon and sold snake oil. He let it be known in the courtroom that the defense had been a thorn in Pfizer's side for a long time and he believed their motive for being involved in this trial and bringing Pfizer in with them was future civil litigation.

It was Pfizer's position through Mr. May that the FDA was requiring drug companies to change the warning language on their labels. The FDA did a study and asked all of the drug companies that had done studies of children, pediatric patients, to provide information about that. The FDA evaluated it, and then made a blanket determination, Pfizer believed, not based on the data or the individual drugs, such as Zoloft, but blanket determination that all antidepressants, even ones that they hadn't studied at all, may increase the risk of suicide to young people.

However, all of May's protesting and arguing before the judge did not change Pieper's position on Pfizer. "Based upon the arguments presented, the briefs filed and a review of the documents presented to the court, as well as the narrowed request by the defense, I'm going to deny the motion to quash," Pieper announced. "As I indicated, or as I'm now indicating, it seems to me that there is a potential for some evidentiary relevance to these documents. The court is not indicating in any way whatsoever that these documents are admissible or that they establish causation. But I think that a review of those documents may be necessary to assure the due process rights of the defendant. I don't find that any of the production of these documents will in any way be cumbersome or oppressive or that they are just engaging in some sort of fishing expedition. I think that they do not otherwise have these documents available to them, and, therefore, the motion is denied."

Vickery and his lawyers smiled at each other like heroes who could now hang their medals across their chests. It was a hard-fought victory against a longtime enemy.

Darrell Duncan, Cherokee County law enforcement officer, was the first prosecution witness to take the stand. Duncan had helped to coordinate getting enough people in place for the search, making sure the K-9 team and SLED's helicopter were sent to the correct area.

The last two witnesses, Lucinda McKellar and Scott Williams, were the two officers who interviewed Christopher when he confessed to the murders. Everything they had to say about Christopher would be repeated again at trial.

When McKellar was asked had there been any further investigation of the case, she said she had traveled to Florida after learning about an incident involving Christopher and a bull. In the incident report that she had obtained about the bull, police had mentioned in the narrative that prior to this incident Christopher had used a BB gun to shoot and cause damage to a neighbor's mobile home. McKellar talked to the owner of the bull, who said Christopher and his playmate's throwing the dart into the bull was no schoolboy prank. It was a vicious act that required a police officer before the dart could be removed from the bull's throat.

Solicitor John Meadors began his counterargument with information about Christopher's "voluntary statement." He told the judge how both officers described his demeanor.

"You know, they said it was like an adultlike conversation. I think that is fair and accurate. They were sitting there talking. They didn't have a problem talking to each other. He had described someone killing his parents and can respond and tell them, says he was under control.

"And, at this final statement, Judge, the issue as to voluntaries, which we think is the only thing relevant in this hearing. He understood his rights. They offered to get him a lawyer. They offered to call the parent and the guardian. Actually, his guardians were dead. His guardians are Joe and Joy Pittman. He didn't ask for anybody to call them. He killed them."

Paul Waldner challenged the officers and tried to poke holes in their stories. He accused them of taking advantage of Christopher in a vulnerable situation, violating his rights, and using their positions and training to clicit a confession. "[Christopher was] a twelve-year-old, a sixth grader," Waldner argued. "Someone who can't even watch a PG-thirteen movie without an adult's consent; that that age is, we would submit, a very serious consideration in this case."

Judge Pieper's opinion, however, was that Christopher had the ability, in spite of his age, education, mental capacity, as well as the medication he was taking at the time, to understand the nature and meaning of his statements, as well as the effect of any waiver of his rights.

"The defendant's statements were freely and voluntarily made without promise, duress, coercion, or influence. That is the preliminary determination by the court.

"The first two statements were made when the defendant was not in custody, and the third was made while he was in custody. And I find that in regard to any statement made while the defendant was in custody that he was afforded the procedural safeguards and rights afforded by *Miranda* versus *Arizona*, but I also find that he understood those rights and freely and voluntarily and intelligently waived those rights under the Fifth and Sixth Amendments of the Constitution."

Pieper was especially concerned that Christopher had been in jail for three years and had not been at a bond hearing.

Hank Mims was ecstatic. That had been a goal of his when signing aboard this case. "His grandmother has absolutely no hesitation whatsoever. Christmas is coming, Judge. I think it would be a good time for him to go home. You've still got him under your control."

Pieper made it clear to Christopher's lawyers that he wanted his bond hearing to be a priority matter and that they have the bond hearing on this ASAP.

With all things said and done, the determination of the court was that Christopher Pittman's trial in a Court of General Sessions would be a two-week jury trial.

CHAPTER 27

Christopher Pittman's trial had been scheduled for late January 2005, and due to the intense pretrial publicity, it was moved to Charleston, some 180 miles south of Chester County. Once word got out that a trial date was set and his lawyers were still claiming his medications had triggered his crimes, the fate of Christopher Pittman drew national attention. As expected, it rekindled a national debate on the dangers of antidepressant use in children and teens. Since Pittman's case involved Zoloft, a widely prescribed antidepressant, it stirred emotions and feelings on both sides of the coin.

On one hand, there were those who believed Christopher was a cold-blooded killer and wanted him locked away in the jailhouse for the rest of his life. On the other hand, there were those who believed he was temporarily insane when he committed his crimes and they contended what he needed most was not imprisonment, but psychiatric treatment.

Antidepressant drugs, such as Prozac, Paxil, and Zoloft, had been at the center of controversy for years over their effects on children, and Pittman's charges against Zoloft put the issue of antidepressant use by children back into the public spotlight. Karen Barth-Menzies, one of Pittman's four lawyers, told the press the focus of defense argument was "involuntary intoxication." She and her team of lawyers planned on presenting evidence in court that confirmed Pittman took on violent, personality-altering tendencies after taking a regimen of Paxil and Zoloft. They claimed he had murdered his grandparents during a psychotic episode.

Despite the FDA hearings and its recommendations for blackbox warnings, Pfizer still denied its widely prescribed drug Zoloft was harmful and vigorously fought cases claiming it caused suicidal or violent behavior. They had squared off many times against Andy Vickery, Paul Waldner, and Karen Barth-Menzies, and weren't afraid to do so again. Bryant Haskins, Pfizer's company spokesman, publicly declared, "Our studies show no increase in such tendencies in children or teens who take the drug for the first time or even when dosages are increased."

Pittman's murder trial was the first in South Carolina history where a defendant had claimed insanity to a crime after taking a prescribed dose of medication. His case began receiving significant media attention immediately and proved enormously interesting to the public. Locally Jason Cato's series of printed articles in the *Rock Hill Herald* followed the developments in Pittman's case, as well as the controversy over the correlation between those antidepressants and suicidal actions or violence among younger patients. Other local coverage included several stories in the *Charleston Post & Courier*, the *Charlotte Observer*, and then national coverage, with a front-page story in the August 23, 2004, *New York Times* and a September 3, 2004, interview of Christopher's maternal grandmother and his lawyers on *Good Morning America. CBS 48 Hours* had been filming portions of the case for some time and were planning to air a full show after the trial. Court TV already had announced it was planning on broadcasting portions of the trial live.

Pittman's defense team had the reputation of having the heart of the shepherd boy David, who, through vast experiences, had battled the drug Goliaths in civil suits. However, they were also known for grandstanding and using the courtroom to showboat their cases against the pharmaceutical giants. The media had already predicted Andy Vickery and his cohorts would use their expert witnesses during the proceedings as a rallying cry for the pitfalls of antidepressants and their potential side effects. The stakes in this case were high not only for Pittman, but also the drug companies that manufacture antidepressants and the doctors who prescribe them. If the jury found Pittman innocent and that Zoloft did drive him to commit murder, the contra coup from the verdict could send Zoloft and other antidepressant prescriptions into a rapid tailspin.

Although Judge Pieper had made it clear in an earlier hearing that the Pittman trial would not become a platform for civil litigation, he was very accommodating with the press, even scheduling a special meeting with them to learn how the court could accommodate and update interested parties. Deputy solicitor John Meadors said his office wasn't thrilled with all the media coverage and indicated they might even seek a gag order, but indicated until then they would respond to proper media inquiries, as long as they did not in any way jeopardize their ability to find a fair and impartial jury.

The now fifteen-year-old Christopher Pittman faced not one but two trials: the first one on the double murder charge of his grandparents, Joe and Joy Pittman, and the second one on arson for setting their house aflame. Just how much of the "Zoloft-made-me-do-it" defense would be allowed in his trial remained unclear, but how else could his attorneys prove he was not a ninety-six-pound monster without saying that his sense of right and wrong had been clouded by a heavy dose of the antidepressant Zoloft?

Early Monday morning, January 31, 2005, the media trucks began arriving in Downtown Charleston and setting up shop in preparation for Christopher Pittman's double-murder trial. In 1996, the CCJC's location on Broad Street was chosen as the perfect site for a number of economical factors, as well as cultural and historic values. Adjacent to Charleston's three-hundred-year-old refurbished courthouse, the center would guarantee viability to this downtown area as a working court of law. Over half of the eleven hundred Charleston Bar Association members and associated businesses occupy these historic buildings along Meeting and Broad Streets. The buildings they occupy not only convey great dignity, but display some of the nation's finest examples of nineteenth-century neoclassic architecture in America. The people who do business within walking distance of the Four Corners of Law bring great strength and character and help maintain this area as a vital commerce, legal, and banking center. The construction of the Charleston County Judicial Center on Broad Street ensured that same ambience would remain for the next three hundred years or so.

The media trucks had arrived early that morning, avoiding the traffic and giving themselves extra time for setup. Christopher Pittman's double-murder trial was not only the hottest show in Charleston, it was the hottest show anywhere—as all eyes of the nation's legal and medical communities closely watched to see how the events would play out. Inside the CCJC, security officers inspected handbags and briefcases as thoroughly as a nun would search teenagers' coolers at a beach party. Spectators were led through a monstrous metal detector on the first floor; then their pockets and pants legs were checked—just in case the machine failed to detect any paraphernalia. They were then directed toward the fourth-floor courthouse, where proceedings for selecting jurors in the *State of South Carolina* versus *Christopher Frank Pittman* were under way.

A respectful, subdued crowd—consisting mostly of Christopher's family, news reporters, and court staff—waited in the lobby outside the courtroom, pacing on

polished, decorative tile floors, and sat in elegant upholstered settees. On the walls, in front and behind them,
were gilded-framed oil portraits of former judges and
politicians that the Charleston Bar Association had hon-
ored. When the bailiff waved the crowd through two
large mahogany doors, they instinctively divided themselves among the four wooden pews. Those who thought
Christopher was guilty—well, of course, they sat behind
the prosecution's table. And those who thought Christopher was innocent—naturally, they sat up front and in
the first pew behind the defense table on the other side.
Everybody else filled in the middle.

The day—and ultimately the entire two weeks of court
as the lawyers would learn—belonged to the Honorable
Daniel P. Pieper. A tall, thin, and relaxed man, with curly
black hair, he sat in the catbird seat, his chair perched
protectively inside a dark mahogany wood platform. As
if to remind court participants what all the hoopla was
about, his chair was positioned so that at all times there
was the American flag on one side and the South Carolina flag on the other side, and a large reproduction of
the state seal attached on the wall behind. Without ever
having said so, spectators in the courtroom took bets
that Pieper had something to do with the design of that.

Currently a law professor at the new Charleston Law
School, Pieper was one of the most intelligent judges in
South Carolina. He also kept a very civil and quiet courtroom, and meant for everything to go as planned. A very
meticulous judge on issues, the law was gospel and carried as much weight as if it had been delivered through
the burning bush. He was a very confident judge, who
monitored every single word of the trial via a link between his computer and court reporter Holly O'Quinn's
computer. "I see every word of it in front of me," he'd
remind the attorneys and witnesses. "I can assure you, if
I need to stop something or review something, I can pull
it up quicker than you can."

South Carolina had made an excellent choice in picking

Pieper's jurisdiction and selecting him to rule on these complicated issues.

To Pieper's left was the jury box, three rows of six mint green upholstered rocker chairs in each. More than enough to accommodate the twelve jurors and three alternates who would serve, should any of the jurors become ill. The jury would become Pieper's friends and allies in this case.

As in all opening days of trials, jury selection dominated the activities and much of the afternoon. Due to the already extensive media coverage of the case, Judge Pieper's first item of business was that the trial begin with a fair and an impartial jury. Earlier that morning, a jury pool of about three hundred persons was seated in the jury assembly room, where they were questioned by Pieper. Less than one-fourth of their group admitted they had seen or heard about the Pittman case on television, or read about it in the newspaper, and said it would not affect their ability to give the defendant a fair and impartial trial. A few of the potential jurors stated their children or grandchildren were taking Zoloft or other antidepressants, and they had been active readers of this case; some had even followed it in the media. Those who stated they could not be fair and impartial in this case were excused and reassigned to a jury pool for possible selection in a civil case on another floor in the courthouse. Ultimately a group of about seventy-five potential jurors was asked to report to courtroom 4C.

As Pieper questioned the pared-down group of jury candidates, strangely, no one admitted they had ever taken any prescription drugs that had noticeably altered their behavior. A little less than 10 percent of the panel did recall, however, experiences they had had with a friend or family member who had been prescribed an antidepressant, or divulged knowledge about these various drugs they had read about in the newspaper or watched on television. Panel members cited the antidepressants they had the most experience with were the big three: Prozac, Paxil, and Zoloft. Only a fistful of candidates claimed any training, education, or experience in pharmacology.

In just a few hours, the court's striking process ultimately rendered twelve jurors and three alternates. Nine of those were women. Seven of the main jury were white; five of them were African American. The list of impanelled jurors included an accountant, a music professor, a Wal-Mart employee, a parking attendant, and a retiree. In any other case, they would have been just fifteen good old Americans who hadn't figured out how to get out of jury duty. But, not in this case. What both the prosecution and defense were hoping they had found were twelve angry jurors.

The Pittman trial promised to be one of the most influential trials in court history, and no one sitting in the courtroom envied their position. Jurors were required to listen for two weeks to nearly 138 witnesses, many of whom were professors, physicians, psychiatrists, pharmacologists, and psychopharmacologists, and digest all they would be saying about the human brain and the negative effects of an antidepressant medication on a young boy who had lost his sense of right and wrong.

As members of the newly selected jury panel entered the courtroom, they strained to get a look at the defendant, Christopher Pittman, who was seated next to his attorneys at the defense table. When the young boy, who claimed an antidepressant had caused him to murder his grandparents and burn their house down, was asked to stand and face the jury panel, he looked different from the picture of the twelve-year-old they had seen in the newspaper and the images they had seen flashed across their television screens.

Before the trial began that morning, Christopher was driven to the Broad Street Barber Shop to get his buzz cut evened out. Dressed in a white shirt, blue tie, and navy blue pants, he was taller and heavier, much more mature, than jurors had remembered.

During the early-morning session, Christopher seldom lifted his head. Instead, he focused on the floor or the lawyers' table in front of him, wiping his face and dabbing his eyes with a tissue. When the judge asked him a question, he'd stand and speak in a deep but barely audible voice.

That afternoon, Judge Pieper admonished the jurors, as he would at the end of every court day, and told them not to discuss this case in any way with anyone—friends, family, or otherwise—and not to conduct any kind of research or expose themselves to any media coverage. Then he dismissed them until 3:00 P.M. on Tuesday.

Before the jury returned to the courtroom, Judge Pieper heard from attorney Carl Muller, who represented Pfizer, Inc., and their employees James Hooper and Dr. Stephen Romano. The two men had been subpoenaed by the defense. Muller filed a motion on behalf of Pfizer to quash the subpoena, as well as two affidavits. One was on behalf of Hooper, a lawyer for Pfizer, and the second one was for Romano, a physician for Pfizer. Muller had also submitted a memorandum and a reply memorandum in response to the subpoena.

Pfizer and other drug manufacturers had already conceded that while antidepressants helped the majority of users, there still existed a small number of people who might be negatively affected by the drug. It was Pfizer's position that if the jury found Pittman not guilty—and, for some unknown reason, he proved to be one of those rare persons—then the decision and the publicity surrounding this trial could open the doors for an untold number of lawsuits and initiate a backlash against the widespread use of Zoloft and other antidepressants, especially by children. Faced with those challenges, Pfizer had a more than vested interest in the outcome of Pittman's trial. It was not surprising to see Pfizer's representatives in the courtroom lobby and sitting in a pew behind the prosecution at the trial, knowing they were not only watching this trial carefully but fighting for their own interests.

"The affidavits made clear, Your Honor," Muller stated, "that neither one of these gentlemen has any knowledge that would be relevant to this case from the standpoint of a lay witness. Neither one of them knows the defendant, the victims, or any family members, or was in South Carolina during the year that the alleged crimes occurred. From an expert witness standpoint, surely the attorney cannot offer anything as an expert witness in this case. . . . There is nothing that either of these gentlemen can testify to. I ask that they be released from the subpoena."

Andy Vickery was adamant that Hooper and Romano were both people with tremendous knowledge of relevant facts. "On January 18, 2002, less than two months after this incident happened, Hooper, on behalf of Pfizer and someone else that Pfizer proffered, provided information to Dr. Pamela Crawford, a forensic psychiatrist with the South Carolina Department of Mental Health. Crawford had been appointed by the court shortly after the crime in 2001 to examine Pittman and determine if he was mentally capable to stand trial and aid in his own defense. I'm concerned not only with what information Hooper had provided Dr. Crawford, but, more importantly, what he had failed to provide her," Vickery told the judge. "They may not know about the facts as we point out in our response of this incident, but they certainly know about the facts that bear on the question of Zoloft-induced violence. And they decided on their own volition to come to South Carolina the week before last, I understand to meet with various members of the media."

"What do you mean by saying they certainly know about Zoloft-induced violence?" Pieper asked with a quizzical look.

"Both Hooper, from his years of defending Pfizer against very similar claims, and Dr. Romano had been chosen by Pfizer to testify before the FDA panel on September 13, 2004. What Hooper could testify to is what he sent to Dr. Crawford—what we contend are highly selective documents that they sent to Dr. Crawford. He can also testify to documents they chose not to send. There was a conscious choice in that process. And Mr. Hooper, as we pointed out in our brief, has been at the heart of [what materials have been] provided prosecutors and their witnesses for a number of years."

Pieper listened to further arguments from Vickery, hoping he would hear exactly what Vickery wanted to do with these particular witnesses, insofar as the jury was concerned, and why would he need that information to be offered. After a lengthy round of questions and answers, he announced any decision on the matter was postponed until the presentation of the defense's case. Eager to let the games begin, Judge Pieper lit the torch and asked for the jury to assume their positions.

After meticulous instructions on how the trial would proceed and a thorough explanation of the court's procedures, Pieper nodded toward Barney Giese, signaling him to begin his opening statement.

"[On] November 28, 2001, Joe and Joy Pittman were living the good life, the American dream," solicitor Giese began. "They were in their sixties. They lived in a two-story house, had some property in Chester in the woods, a beautiful piece of property. They lived there by themselves alone for several years.

"On the twenty-eight of November, after coming back from church, the Pittmans, as they normally did, went up to their bedroom on the second-floor loft, laid down in their bed, together, next to each other. As they lay in their bed, someone armed themselves with a four-ten shotgun, deliberately and slowly walked up those stairs to that loft, took that shotgun, shot Joe Pittman with that shotgun in the mouth, killing Joe Pittman.

"That person who fired that shot didn't stop with Joe Pittman. As Joy Pittman lay in bed, in her sixties, in her own home, someone, that same person, took that four-ten shotgun, put it to the back of her head, and fired it, killing Joy Pittman.

"But, you know, that person wasn't finished yet. That same person went down the stairs, went through Joy Pittman's—who is lying dead in her own bed—purse and took money, went to the arms safe, where Joe Pittman kept weapons, unlocked it, took weapons, took money from Joe Pittman also. And that same person, that same person put them all in the truck and then that person set fire to that house. That person set fire to that house so that person could have some lead time to escape and that person left Joe and Joy Pittman to burn so that their bodies and the evidence couldn't be identified.

"That person, ladies and gentlemen, that person who did all of those things and then left as that house burned, is none other than their grandson, Christopher Pittman."

Christopher hung his head and stared somewhere near the table in front of him. Giese waved two pieces of paper in his right hand. He told jurors they were the two indictments for murder in the *State of South Carolina* versus *Christopher Frank Pittman*, then read each of those. His face reddened as he gritted his teeth and scowled at the jurors. Giese stated it was up to the state and through his office to prove the elements of those two indictments. And if they didn't do that, then the jury had a duty to find Christopher Pittman not guilty.

Giese explained to the jury how the prosecution intended to prove Christopher Pittman guilty beyond a reasonable doubt. He addressed some of the facts from the case and explained how they would go about proving them. There was so much information for the jurors to absorb in one hearing, Giese knew he had to hold back a lot of the facts. His strategy was not to overwhelm the jurors, but wait until they heard the entire story and then start dropping in the smaller pieces, one by one.

"It's pretty basic," Giese assured jurors, "that Chris Pittman took a shotgun and killed Joy and Joe Pittman, shot them, and that shooting caused the death of these two individuals. And, most importantly, that shooting was done with malice aforethought.

"Now, His Honor is going to tell you at a later time what malice aforethought is. But suffice it to say that malice is a dark heart. It's an evil heart. It's a heart fatally bent on mischief and devoid of all social duty. It's a heart bent on mischief."

Giese was passionate in his remarks. The defense had expected him to be aggressive, but he surprised everyone in the courtroom when he outright labeled Christopher as "evil." The defense had imagined other descriptive words the prosecution would use to define Christopher's character—cold-blooded, calculated, devoid of feeling, without conscience, or antisocial—but evil was not among them.

Giese was showing a lot of dramatic gestures in his opening statement. He believed the facts of the case demanded it. Certainly, the Pittmans' deaths provided more than enough pathos for the average juror, and he was determined to use that to show how horrific these crimes really were. He was asking the jury to make a quantum leap. As opposed to saying Christopher was a bad person, he wanted jurors to believe he was "pure evil."

Painting the defendant as demonic was a very risky move. Giese's accusation could blow back on him like spit in the wind and easily become an issue in an appeal, but it was a risk he was willing to take. As he related the sequence of events in a concise, step-by-step manner, he saw the incredulous looks on jurors' faces. He assumed some of them, to this moment, had never imagined such things could occur with someone as young as Pittman.

"Now, we can't cut Christopher Pittman open and look inside him and see whether or not he had malice in his heart, in his mind, when he committed the offense. But what can we do, and how can we prove malice? Well, you are going to hear witnesses testify on the witness stand. They are going to swear under oath to tell you what they know about this case.

"Ladies and gentlemen, the state submits what could be more evil, what could be more devoid of social duty, than taking a shotgun to some sixty-year-olds who are laying in bed asleep? The state submits if, in fact, the state proves that Christopher Pittman pulled that trigger, the malice is overwhelming—overwhelming—and that will not be an issue, the state submits."

While Giese pointed at Christopher and called him names, Christopher sat somberly between Vickery and Hank Mims, with his head hung down. The look on his face betrayed the hope he had placed in his attorneys. He and his family looked upon his legal team like some modern-day Moses, who was going to lead him out of bondage and into the promised land.

Vickery and Mims both leaned in toward Christopher, trying to shield him like they would a boy in a plastic bubble. For the first time during any of Christopher's three-year hearings, he choked up. All through Giese's opening statements, he cried. Clutching a tissue in his right hand, he sobbed gently and stared at an imaginary spot on the floor in front of the defense table.

Giese unveiled the prosecution's line of attack. He told jurors the murders were set in motion after Christopher was disciplined for fighting on a school bus, then turned and stared at Christopher again. Vickery placed a protective arm around Christopher's shoulders and patted him on the back, as if to convey, "There, there, it's okay. You don't have to be scared of him."

Giese asked the jurors to follow the boy's calculated actions, which included setting fire to his grandparents' house, stealing money and a car for his getaway. In an agitated and broken voice, he stated, "The Pittmans on the twenty-eighth disciplined Christopher Pittman. They disciplined him verbally and, possibly, physically with a paddle. Christopher Pittman could not and would not take that discipline."

Giese turned toward the defense table and jabbed the papers in his hand toward Christopher.

"Even though the state submits it was well-deserved, he would not take it. And he lay in bed in his room and waited until the Pittmans went to bed, and he waited and planned exactly what he was going to do that night. And that night, Christopher Pittman, after his grandparents went to bed, got that four-ten shotgun and killed them both."

Giese moved in closer to the jury, then lowered and evened his voice. He had requested to show them pictures of the Pittmans' burned bodies, but the judge had denied his request. Giese believed the pure violence of the crime frozen in those pictures proved there was malice aforethought in Christopher's head when he committed the crime.

Christopher kept his head down. At one point, he took a deep breath, then put his face in his hands. The expression on his face said, "Okay, enough is enough."

Giese continued his fiery monologue, asking jurors also to ponder Christopher's calculated actions after the murders.

"After he left and after he burned that house down, Christopher Pittman fled. And he made it thirty-five miles in that truck until he got stuck in a ditch. Ladies and gentlemen, *that*, the state submits, is this case. This case is about Christopher Pittman and his actions."

Still holding the copies of the murder indictments in his right hand, Giese wanted the jurors to know that all evidence pointed to Pittman's actions being premeditated. Giese told them to focus on his immediate actions after the killings and consider the story Pittman told authorities once he was found. He did not reveal what Pittman had said, for he preferred for them to find out during the trial that Pittman had blamed the killings on a black man, who, he said, had kidnapped him.

Giese warned the jury that it would need to remain "focused" on the real issue. "Now, the defense in this case are relying on a defense called 'insanity.' They are claiming that Christopher Pittman is not guilty by reason of insanity. They are saying that Christopher Pittman did not know what he was doing was wrong and that's the law in South Carolina. . . . When we're done, there will be no question that Christopher Pittman was sane, and knew the difference between right and wrong when he committed those horrible, horrible offenses."

Giese took a step backward, paused, and let those words echo in the jurors' minds. After he felt the jurors had taken it all in, he stepped up toward the jury box and advised them, "Ladies and gentlemen, this is not a case—this is not a trial—about Zoloft. This is not a case—this is not a trial—about Pfizer. It is not on trial. They are not on trial. Christopher Pittman is on trial. And the state asks you to focus on Christopher Pittman and what Christopher Pittman did that night."

As if on cue, Andy Vickery stood and walked toward the jury box. Vickery had gone over this same scenario time and time again. This moment burned in his memory many nights before this day, and caused him to lose sleep and rest uneasily. His challenge was to show the jury the strong bond between Christopher Pittman and his grandparents, show the life they had lived together before the killings and somehow convey to the jury that Christopher's behavior after the shooting was not reflective of his character. He was convinced once these twelve jurors heard about the frayed ends of Christopher Pittman's sad life and how much he loved and depended on his grandparents, that information would prick their hearts and help them understand he was a "modern-day pharmaceutical tragedy."

Spectators and reporters in the gallery recognized Vickery, the high-profile lawyer, as competent, ethical, and honorable. He had, no doubt, examined every minuscule part under the auspices of one of the most respected law practices in his field, personal injury and civil trial litigation. He had probably constructed his defense as painstakingly as a child would construct the Eiffel Tower with toothpicks, and when he got his chance, he would make it all stick. But how could a defense lawyer, even one as talented as Vickery, build a defense to stand in a case that seemed so irrevocable as this one?

"Ladies and gentlemen of the jury, I introduced myself before. My name is Andy Vickery, and in this courtroom, I speak for this young man. 'I had no malice in my heart or murder in my mind.' The solicitor thinks this is a simple case about murder, malice aforethought. I submit to you that this is a case about one drug that has taken three lives. And when you hear all of the evidence, you will have the power to give one of them back."

Vickery admitted Christopher had shot both his grandparents with a shotgun—he wasn't denying that—but he was saying the shootings weren't murder because he didn't have "malice aforethought," a necessary component that reduces the charges of murder to manslaughter or being innocent by reason of insanity. The defense's case would show that a massive dose of Zoloft had put Christopher in such an uncontrollable rage that he was unable to distinguish right from wrong.

At that moment, Vickery was feeling ten feet tall and bulletproof. He laid out for the jury bits of evidence that would bear out Christopher had no malice aforethought. He could not have murdered his grandparents because he had no malice aforethought. First, he spoke of Christopher's grandparents as the people Christopher loved most in the world. He had no reason to kill them. Secondly, he was a shy twelve-year-old, a ninety-six-pound decent boy, acting under the influence of a powerful mind-altering drug. It was the Zoloft that triggered the involuntary intoxication that resulted in psychosis. Christopher was hearing voices commanding him to do things, telling him to "kill, kill, kill," and he lost touch with reality. He did not know right from wrong. And, lastly, Zoloft caused him to be violent, homicidal. That increasing doses of Zoloft over the course of less than a month so affected his brain that he did things he had never done before. Zoloft triggered Christopher's violence toward others. He choked a second grader on the school bus; then a day later, he shot and killed his grandparents.

Christopher looked up at his attorney with wide eyes that conveyed to jurors this might be the first time he had heard in its entirety this set of facts analyzed in relation to his crimes and used to explain all he had done. Vickery invited jurors to travel with him on a sentimental journey through Christopher Pittman's life before he began taking Zoloft a few weeks before the killing. Pictures from a PowerPoint program flashed on a projection screen. There was grandfather and grandson fishing. Pop Pop, on the couch playing video games. Christopher, Pop Pop, and Nana smiling into a camera at a church function.

Upon seeing the photos, Christopher dropped his head low and put his hand to his forehead, as if seeing the images again pained him greatly. He wept silently at the defense table.

In a calm, soft voice reminiscent of a high-school science or chemistry teacher, Vickery described Christopher in terms of before and after the murders. With a Texas twang, he told the jury how Christopher was prescribed Zoloft for depression several weeks before the killing, and when relatives noticed he was becoming agitated and appeared "wired," he went back to the doctor, who upped the dose. On the day before the murders, Christopher had gotten into a fight with a boy on the school bus and tried to choke him.

"Christopher is a shy, decent boy, who was acting under the influence of a powerful, mind-altering drug," Vickery explained. "The drug caused him to suffer 'command hallucinations' that told him to kill his grandparents."

Vickery paused, then stepped closer to the jurors. "But once he stopped taking the antidepressants, he became a changed person."

Vickery turned away from the jurors and walked toward Christopher. Christopher looked up and glanced toward him, then at the jurors, and back at Vickery again.

According to Vickery, Christopher Pittman was one in a collection of America's youth in whom there had been an increase in violent or suicidal behavior because of antidepressants and other drugs. He told the jury Christopher was simply following doctor's orders when he took the prescribed drug of Zoloft three weeks before the killings. Then, a short time before the killings, his dose doubled and he began to suffer from those voices that told him to kill his grandparents.

Vickery then talked through a list of expert witnesses and persons testifying who would help the defense prove that Christopher was temporarily insane due to the effects of Zoloft when he murdered his grandparents. They would say it was the medication that had fed him the urge to harm his grandparents. "But once he stopped taking antidepressants, he is a changed person," Vickery countered in his soft voice, smiling approvingly at his client. "He's no danger to this society or himself. He's a fine boy."

Christopher dropped his head, then looked up with his big, brown, puppy dog eyes. He looked as pitiful as an old beagle that had gotten lost in the woods and couldn't find his way out and back home.

"In summary, the defense is that Zoloft triggers violence," Vickery concluded. "The doctor gave an unapproved drug, a mind-altering drug, to a ninety-six-pound, twelve-year-old boy. He had an involuntary violent reaction, which is called psychosis, to the Zoloft. He did not know right from wrong. He did not have malice aforethought. He did not have an evil mind. He had a mind that had been tampered with chemically."

And just like that, the drug Zoloft, like Christopher Pittman, was now on trial. As Vickery hoisted his ship's flag for the jury to see, he proclaimed that Zoloft can cause certain patients to become violent, possibly homicidal. He claimed there was already a lot of evidence showing that the drug causes agitation, irritability, hostility, and mania. Was it too far-fetched for the jury to believe it could cause someone to kill? If so, Vickery promised to show them a collection of Pfizer documents and to call a battery of psychiatric experts to the stand and help prove this could happen.

After spending only five hours in selecting a jury and giving opening statements, the prosecution was ready to call its first witness. Someone in the gallery joked that Michael Jackson, whose jury selection in his sexual molestation trial had begun the same day as Christopher Pittman's trial, but was predicted to last almost a month, should count his blessings that his case was not being heard in a South Carolina court of law.

CHAPTER 28

It was the opinion of the majority of persons seated in the courtroom 4C that the prosecution would have no problem proving Christopher Pittman shot his grandparents. All the defense could do in response during this part of the trial was damage control.

The prosecution's case began not with the police, but with the West Chester volunteer firemen. Andy Martin, assistant fire chief, was notified he would be the first witness to testify for the prosecution. In his rush from Chester to Charleston, Martin forgot his black tie. The trial was being televised by Court TV and he did not want to take the stand, dressed in his official blue fire-department jacket and a white shirt, without wearing a black tie. His old $8 tie was very convenient in that it was already knotted and easily joined across the back of his neck by a strip of Velcro. But it was still lying across his bed, back home in Chester.

Referred to a downtown men's clothing store off Broad Street, Martin felt better about his situation when the store clerk responded to his repeated taps on the door and invited him in. The polite man showed Martin a nice silk black tie and even agreed to tie it for him. When Martin saw how nice the tie looked on him, he told the clerk he'd take it. And if it wasn't too much trouble, he'd like to purchase a tie clip as well.

Martin swallowed hard when the store's cash register flashed a total of $125. Most of the suits he owned cost less than that, but he was too embarrassed to protest. He thanked the clerk, paid for the tie and tie clip, then hustled back to the courtroom.

Andy Martin took the stand wearing his newest black tie and tie clip. He stated on the night of November 28, 2001, the West Chester Fire Department received a call at 11:52 P.M. and was en route two minutes later at 11:54 P.M. He also recalled details from the night of the fire, identified photos, and told jurors how the Pittmans' bodies had been found.

Christopher choked back tears and dabbed at his eyes with a tissue as Martin related events of that fateful night. His sobbing got visibly worse when Fire Chief James "Red" Weir followed Martin to the stand and related more of the same. Weir had gotten older and was missing a few strands of hair and a couple of teeth.

Weir told the jury he was not only among the first people to arrive at the fire, but he and his wife, Lucy, were good friends with Christopher's grandparents. Red had gone fishing numerous times with Christopher and his grandfather. The defense got to rebut prosecution witnesses and show how well Christopher and his grandparents had connected as a family unit. On cross-examination from Karen Barth-Menzies, Weir confirmed the affection between Christopher and Joe Frank Pittman. He said Christopher and his grandfather used to go fishing together. At least one time, he remembered, they went fishing in his pond. When Barth-Menzies asked Weir if he was surprised to hear Christopher had admitted killing his grandparents, he said he was. "They seemed to get along so well," he stated. "They were just like a loving family. I didn't see anything unusual about Christopher."

"What was Christopher like?" Barth-Menzies asked.

Weir shrugged. "He was just a normal kid."

Christopher struggled to keep his emotions in tow. After Barth-Menzies dismissed Weir from the witness stand, she took a seat next to Christopher and placed a comforting arm around him. Much like an older sister would nurture a younger brother, Barth-Menzies moved in closer to Christopher, whispering encouragements and assuring him everything was going to be okay.

Court TV's commentator Nancy Grace was quick to point out that Barth-Menzies's motive for adopting such a protective attitude was just a ploy.

"All this getting close to him," Grace critiqued, "the petting, picking lint off his shoulders, whispering to him . . . it conveys to the jurors, 'See, I can sit next to him. He's so sweet. He's so innocent. I got my arm around him and he hasn't hurt me.'" Grace criticized Barth-Menzies for her behavior and said she must have learned that from attorney Leslie Abramson in the [Erik and Lyle] Menendez trials, that she wanted the jurors to see, "If [Christopher] only had the proper nurturing, he would be a safe boy to be next to."

But the truth was that Lyle Menendez was twenty-five and Erik Menendez was twenty-two when their double-murder trial began in 1993. Christopher had just turned fifteen, and had been locked up since November 29, 2001. During these last three years, all the major players in his case had changed: the judge who recused himself when he learned his wife owned stock in Pfizer, Inc., the original Chester County prosecutor, who suffered from heart failure and transferred the case to solicitor Giese's office, and his court-appointed defense lawyer who dropped off his case when his new lawyers came aboard. And throughout all this time, Christopher had sat, waiting and praying to be released on bond. Yet, when it finally came in December 2004, his family could not come up with enough money to post his bail. Now, in this little window of time, it looked as if he were going to be denied bond and would never again have the opportunity to be with his family. It was way too much trauma for a young mind.

Outside the jury's presence, the lawyers discussed legal issues. In particular, the prosecution objected to the blown-up picture cutout of Christopher Pittman.

"This is a picture of him taken in 2001, Your Honor," Andy Vickery made clear. "I brought it to the attention of the solicitor and deputy solicitor before we asked to use it." Vickery held up two pieces of paper. "I hold in my hands the two incident reports from the police, both reflecting the five-foot-two [Christopher Pittman]. This is a picture of him at five feet two inches, the most recent one we had, which was suitable to blow up to life size. And whenever there's someone, like the hunters—a witness who reports to make an ID—we want to ask them, 'Which one was it? Was it the five-foot-two twelve-year-old or the six-foot fifteen-year-old?'"

"If that's an accurate representation, then I'm not going to stop you from doing it," Judge Pieper responded in a quiet voice.

Already on his feet, John Meadors argued the cutout was not an adequate representation. The prosecution didn't want that picture in front of jurors because it made him look too childish—like he was a baby. In response to that, they proposed to provide a picture showing the defendant and his grandfather, which clearly showed how tall he was.

Pieper told the attorneys they could argue about the picture when the time came. Meadors conceded, but asked if the defense would keep the picture turned over and on the floor, until they had such a need for it.

While prosecutors portrayed Christopher as a bright, articulate preteen who understood the consequences of his actions, the defense worked to draw a different picture for the jurors. Each prosecution witness was shown the cardboard cutout of Christopher, and the defense used every opportunity to remind jurors that Christopher was just a boy then, not the tall young man they saw in court today.

Defense cross-examination went to the crux of their argument: was this the same boy—the same little boy—they saw in 2001? But, unless the prosecution stumbled very, very badly, their case against Christopher Pittman was pretty close to a slam dunk. To bolster their case, prosecution called Andy Weir, who was now working as a special deputy with the U.S. Marshal's office. Weir had spent nearly all of his life sniffing around fires—approximately 679 fires since being employed with SLED—and was also the instructor at the Federal Law Enforcement Training Center in Glynco, Georgia. The night of the Pittman fire, he and his dog, Trixie, were there, working for SLED's arson teams, attempting to determine the origin and cause of the fire, as well as detect any accelerants that had been used.

Weir described how he and SA Scott Williams had investigated the fire. He said, eventually, when they discovered the two charred bodies, a backhoe was called in and a harness was used for removing the bodies off the second floor. He then related after finding blood on the victims, they knew a homicide had been committed and they had to preserve the crime scene. Even though he was not allowed to let the jury see the pictures that Meadors was handing him, he described what he saw perfectly.

"Can you, based on your training and your experience, describe this fire?" Meadors asked after they had gone through all the pictures of the fire. "Was it a fast fire or a slow-burning fire?"

Weir had a deep, scratchy voice, understandable after knowing all the fires he had sucked down. "I would describe it as kind of a slow built-up fire. It was not accelerated. When you accelerate it with some type of something—gasoline or kerosene—it will make the fire actually speed up. But this was not like a produced fire. This was a slow building-up fire, and based on any

observations from the scene, this fire originated near
and on the second-floor loft area and started burning up
and consumed the roof and started burning down.

"And by the main floor being still intact during our investigation and the mere presence of the canine not
alerting to any type of accelerants, this was not accelerated to the point that any—if any had been used—any
amount at all, the main floor of the house would have
been gone."

"So, it was a slow-burning fire based on your experience. Could there have been a small amount of accelerant
and it just burned off?"

"It could have been, yes, sir," Weir concluded. "It
could have been just available materials you use such as
newspapers, cardboard boxes, things like this."

Pieper decided the trial was at a good stopping point.
He dismissed the jurors, but asked them to flip their writing pads open, write their name on the first page, and
give the books to the bailiff.

"When you're back in the jury room, they will secure
them overnight and return them to you this next day,"
Pieper put in plain words. He made another point to
remind the jurors, again, not to discuss this case in any
way or expose themselves to any type of media coverage.

After the last juror had left the courtroom, Pieper
asked for any additional business from the attorneys.
Christopher's champion crusader Hank Mims stood and
challenged his client's bond, for yet another time. "The
case had been called, Your Honor," Mims protested. His
face twisted in pain, he remind the judge low long they
had been burdened with this bond issue. "Your Honor,
he has been in jail for three years. Where is he going to
go? There is no risk that the state is taking."

Meadors was on his feet. He had incidents to prove his
contention. "Your Honor, the prosecution believes he is
a flight risk."

"*Oh, come on.*" The words slipped out and painted
Mims's frustrated face. "He put some tissue in a door. Is

that what you are talking about?" he interrupted to say, referring to a prior incident at DJJ. "Your Honor, Christopher will be in legal custody of his grandmother and his grandfather and his aunt. They're not going to allow him to do that."

Pieper agreed. "I will be prepared to allow him to be released under that bond with the additional proviso that he have satellite monitoring. If you can arrange that overnight, I will consider it tomorrow. But the defendant will be detained overnight."

A long day in trial just got longer for Christopher Pittman. His family's had leased a condo near Charleston, anticipating Christopher would be granted bail, but the lease expired on February 12. Christopher's time of freedom was growing shorter by the minute.

CHAPTER 29

Christopher Pittman's defense team was aware before coming to trial that the facts of the case clearly belonged to the prosecution, but they were doing an admirable job in the cross-examination of witnesses. Solicitor Giese had put a lot of effort in building his case in his opening remarks. It was unthinkable to believe he had not struck a sympathy chord with the jury when he described Joe and Joy Pittman as a vibrant couple, who were living the good life and trying to do the right thing by taking in their troubled grandson. But the defense also believed they had an ace or two up their sleeves that could change the whole complexion of this case, and there was a lot of green between now and the end of the trial.

It's no secret that criminal defense lawyers are notorious for shifting the focus on to someone else. Third-party guilt, they call it. Defense lawyers are always looking to find the "evildoer," pointing a finger at another suspect or telling jurors there was a villain overlooked by the police.

In Christopher's case, the big, multibillion-dollar drug company Pfizer was going to be the bad guys. In the eyes of the defense, it was this insensitive corporate entity whose sales representatives provided the doctor with samples of brain candy to pass out on a whim. The defense

believed wholeheartedly it was Pfizer who wore the black
hats and that Christopher was only a victim of horrible
circumstances. No doubt, he had been neglected and
abandoned, and had had more than his share of family
issues, but it was a lot easier to point the finger at a company like Pfizer—who already had admitted that Zoloft
had caused manic episodes and violence in some of their
patients—than at Christopher's dysfunctional family. Just
because the prosecutor had labeled Christopher evil, he
was still a twelve-year-old child. He was a little boy who
had lived a troubled life, but without any major indications he had this type of violence—until he swallowed the
Zoloft. If the jurors believed the defense's viewpoint, they
could easily see Christopher Pittman may have had some
difficult times, but he was not the murdering type.

The defense agreed with the prosecution's facts as
stated in this case, but they did not agree with what the
prosecutor said the facts meant. They planned on playing their cards from a hand of worn tactics that surely
would reduce the impact of the prosecution's information. It wasn't beyond them to try every legal and
reasonable opportunity to have Christopher acquitted.
Because they believed there was scientific evidence to
support a link between Zoloft and Christopher's behavior, the decision was made to admit Christopher had
killed his grandparents. Pfizer already had made the ad-
mission concerning side effects of Zoloft, and that was
a very compelling factor that could convince the jurors
he was innocent. The defense would avoid the hammer,
so to speak, that they knew would fall sooner or later.
They would agree to the fact Christopher had committed the deed, and let the chips fall where they may.

At that moment in court, the defense believed their
stipulation that Christopher had committed the crime
would take the prosecution by surprise and steal the
wind right out of its sails. It would also prevent them
from going into the gory details of the murder. It was a
calculated move, but it would force the prosecution to

refocus on what the defense thought was the actual details of the case anyway: Pfizer and the medication they manufactured.

In the presence of the jury, Judge Pieper read the statement prepared ahead of time by the defense. In a calm voice, hoping to downplay the significance of the statement, he informed the jury that both parties had stipulated that Christopher Pittman, on November 28, 2001, killed both his grandparents with a shotgun and then set the fire that destroyed their home.

The prosecution had expected all this. Both sides had ample opportunity to analyze the case and study each other's style and courtroom techniques. The way the prosecution saw it, the defense had just brought them one step closer to the heart of their case.

Pieper asked Christopher to stand. He wanted to know what he thought about all this. "Mr. Pittman, have you discussed the stipulation with your attorney?"

"Yes, sir."

"Now, you understand that in the normal course of a trial that the state would have the burden of proof as to all the elements of the offense. Do you understand that?"

"Yes, sir."

"They would have to prove all of the elements of the offense beyond a reasonable doubt. Do you understand?"

Christopher said he did.

"Now, insofar as this stipulation indicates that you did, on November 28, 2001, kill both of your grandparents with a shotgun and then set the fire that destroyed the home, those facts will be accepted by the jury as true as the court is going to say it is a stipulation to be accepted as true. Do you understand?"

"Yes, sir."

"And to that extent, the state will not have had to prove those facts by virtue of your stipulation. Do you understand that?"

In a voice that was clear and loud enough to resonate throughout the courtroom, Christopher said he understood.

"Do you need any more time with your attorneys to discuss that?"

"No, sir."

When the jury returned, Judge Pieper published the stipulation. He informed the jurors that "a stipulation was an agreement as to certain facts, and they should accept those facts being true and consider them in such a manner as they deemed appropriate in their consideration of all the issues in this case."

Having said that, Pieper dismissed the jurors and returned to hearing arguments from the attorneys. He hadn't ruled on the issues related to Pfizer and evidence about the documents on the drug Zoloft. The prosecutors wanted to keep everything related to Pfizer and Zoloft out of court, but the judge knew it could easily become an issue on appeal. How would a higher court perceive this point on appeal if jurors knew this drug may have been responsible for what happened to Christopher Pittman, and they didn't hear about it?

Of course, the defense wanted the judge to rule that Pfizer executives and their chief physician, Dr. Steve Romano, take the stand. This, too, was no shock to the prosecution. From the very beginning, the defense had been very clear that this was a case against Pfizer and Zoloft. They wanted those defendants actually to be in the courtroom and on trial—not Christopher Pittman. They were determined to show it was Pfizer's drugs that caused Christopher to have those evil thoughts and blur his vision of right and wrong the night he killed his grandparents.

The prosecution believed the Zoloft defense was ludicrous, more like a first cousin to the so-called "Twinkie defense." The facts of Dan White's 1978 murder trial had been exaggerated into a story of how the defense lawyer got White off with an absurd argument that White's judgment had been impaired due to his consumption of Twinkies and other junk foods. White, a former San Francisco city supervisor who had recently resigned his position, shot and killed both the mayor and another city supervisor. Even though he entered the San Francisco City Hall carrying a loaded gun, climbed through a basement window to avoid metal detectors, evaded the mayor's bodyguard, shot the mayor, then reloaded and walked across City Hall to find and gun down the supervisor, the jury found that White's acts were not premeditated. White's legal team had mounted the successful defense claiming that White was depressed and his depression had diminished his knowing right from wrong. White's attorney argued White's eating of Twinkies and other sugar-laden foods was symptomatic of his depression. Thus, somehow the phrase "Twinkie defense" came to represent the efforts of defendants to avoid responsibility for their actions by claiming that some external force beyond their control had caused them to act the way they had.

The prosecution could never imagine something similar happening in this trial. They saw Christopher Pittman as a very troubled young man—with troubled life circumstances. Granted, killing his grandparents didn't make a lot of sense, but even though his murders were a paradox, Christopher was not. He and his family knew enough about his condition to see to it that his medication was taken in accordance with doctor's orders. The evidence indicated he had been given some sample medication by a physician and the orders were written across the front of the package for him to follow. If Christopher was noncompliant, then that was *not* the fault of Zoloft or its manufacturer. There was an equal amount of things that he did that didn't make sense, but the prosecution believed it was his actions after the murder that showed planning and intent. They were willing to show these were the acts of someone who was thinking clearly. The way the prosecution understood it, there were a lot of hurdles the defense had to jump before they could prove Zoloft had been responsible for the Pittman murders.

Christopher was now one of a new breed of criminals existing in the United States—juveniles committing serious crimes. There were so many violent crimes being committed by young offenders, it was commonplace and believable he could have had his own reason or purpose for killing his grandparents. Obviously, one had gotten stuck in his mind.

It was a horrible case, but, nevertheless, it was true. The prosecution knew that Christopher had performed lots of bad acts in his life before the Zoloft, and to say Zoloft had caused him to murder, in their opinion, was more than a stretch. They just didn't see how the Zoloft defense would ever take wings and fly. The scientific evidence just did not show there had ever been a link between Zoloft and homicidal behavior.

Andy Vickery and the defense team, however, were not deterred. On that first day of trial, he tried to get the judge to admit evidence through taking "judicial notice" of four findings by the FDA on the effects Zoloft. He cited that the most recent warning from the FDA had been of an increased risk of self-violence and suicide after having taken the drug.

The judge also had heard the motion from Pfizer to quash the subpoenas for their company doctor and lawyer to testify at Christopher's trial. Vickery protested, arguing that Pfizer had sent their company doctor and their company lawyer to South Carolina to meet with the media about this case, and he availed himself of the opportunity to subpoena them. He told the judge he could provide evidence and show the jury that Pfizer gave sanitized information about the drug to the first child specialist who interviewed Pittman after the crime. Judge Pieper delayed any decision on the matter until a later date in the trial.

"Your Honor"—Hank Mims wanted to address the court before the jury returned—"we went to visit

Christopher yesterday. We were on this side of the glass, and he was on the other side. Every now and then, I have got to tell Mrs. Menzies, 'Hold on just a minute because somebody has opened the door to listen to us.' There is always a guard walking back and forth at DJJ. They don't have the facilities for somebody to talk to his lawyer. They told us that unless they can make special arrangements whenever they can, the guard said, 'This is the best you're going to get.'"

Pieper sat back in his chair and listened to Mims's plea for his client.

"I understand that is the way it is," Mims conceded, "but we've got to do something better. Your Honor, you don't have to take any risks with this boy. All we're asking is that you let this kid be on the outside during the trial. This is how you can help us help him."

Pieper declared that if the paperwork was filed with the Charleston County Clerk of Court and the bond company guaranteed it would put Christopher under house arrest, then he had a chance of going home with his family on Thursday.

When all the lawyer talk was concluded, the jury was brought back in. The prosecution opened their arguments with an idea of just how calculated Christopher was on the day after the shootings. They planned on exposing Christopher's behavior after the murders and hang their case on the fact that he acted like a regular murderer. They would move their case along from the house fire on Slick Rock Road and the discovery of the charred bodies to Christopher being found in nearby Cherokee County. They wanted jurors to hear what Christopher said about being kidnapped and the ultimate confession he gave to the police.

In the previous day's opening statements, Barney Giese told the jury to focus on what Christopher had said had happened the morning he was found, but Giese did not tell them what Christopher had said. He teased jurors there was testimony he wanted them to hear that would be much more telling than Christopher's claim that an antidepressant caused him to kill. Giese deliberately held on to the grandiose story where Christopher blamed his troubles on a black man; it was their proverbial ace in the hole. Now assistant prosecutor John Meadors rolled it all out on the table for everyone to see.

Because five of the jurors were black, Meadors repeatedly blasted jurors with Christopher's fabricated story about the fictitious black man. Like many a defendant who has been on trial, Christopher's words would come back to haunt him. Christopher's reference to the fabricated murderer/kidnapper and his race would be mentioned at least thirty-five times, with the vast majority of those allusions spewing from Meadors and his witnesses' mouths.

Roland Pennington, one of the two hunters who had found Christopher in Cherokee County on November 29, 2001, testified that the boy had told him he'd been kidnapped and brought to the remote wooded area.

"He said it was a black guy," Pennington said in his Southern accent, thick as molasses. "He said the black guy had killed his grandparents and burned the house down."

Terry Robinson, Pennington's hunting partner, followed him to the stand and corroborated Pennington's statement: Pittman had emerged from the woods, announcing he was lost and had been shot at by a black man.

The prosecution believed Christopher's lies would shoot straight as an arrow to the heart of their case—that the jury would see he knew right from wrong when he loaded his pump-action shotgun and committed murder. Wouldn't the jurors recognize that the energy Christopher put into fabricating a lie about a six-foot-two black man, and blaming him for his actions, show he was "of his mind" at the time of the killings?

Defense attorneys did not dispute the facts that Christopher had blamed the killings on a black man, but they wanted jurors to believe his thoughts were clear evidence that he was *not* of his right mind at the time of the killings.

They claimed it was the adverse reaction after a dramatic dosage of Zoloft that caused him to become manic, which led to his violent behavior and subsequent falsehoods. Vickery made several references to the "crazy story" about a black man in the woods. But whether it was a "black man," "black male," or "black guy" in the woods, the prosecutors kept insisting their witnesses describe Christopher's demeanor while he was telling this story.

"Did he look strange?" Meadors asked Pennington in rapid-fire succession. "Did he act as if he was under the influence of anything? Did he understand what you were saying to him? Did he do exactly as you told him?"

"Yes, sir," Pennington answered to all his questions.

Meadors wasn't through driving a wooden stake through Christopher's heart just yet. "My question is when you told him to get in the truck, did he get in the truck?"

"Yes, sir. He got right in."

"In your opinion, did he understand your request?"

"Yes, sir, he understood."

"And did he do that (get in the car), right after you asked him?"

"Yes, sir."

"And, at that point, how would you describe his demeanor? Did he appear to understand your question?"

"Yes, sir." Pennington paused as if to consider the impact his answer might have upon the jury. "He . . . he understood me."

"Did he appear to be under the influence of anything?"

"No, sir."

During Pennington's testimony, Chris kept his head down and his lips rolled out. He looked as if he were pouting, like he had been caught committing a school prank and his friend Pennington was up there on the witness stand, spilling all the beans to the school principal.

Hank Mims didn't waste any time setting Pennington up so he could utilize Christopher's cutout poster. After validating Pennington's eyesight and ability to see the finer details in dense woods, Mims asked Christopher to stand.

Normally, when an attorney calls a witness to the stand, it is business as usual to ask that he or she identify the defendant. But one of the problems for the defense was that Christopher, now fifteen, had grown into this six-foot-one young man. He did not look anything like the person that was going to be identified in court. In order to give the jury an idea of what their client looked like at the time of the killings, the defense positioned the life-size cardboard cutout of Christopher that stood five feet two inches, exactly his height as listed on his arrest report, in front of the defense table and toward the jury. Mims pointed to the picture and asked the witness, "Isn't this the person you saw at the time of these terrible events and not this six-foot person you see sitting in the courtroom?"

The point Mims was making was another calculated defense move to put into the jurors' minds that this six-one moping young man, wearing the white slacks, the dark blue shirt, and matching tie, was quite different from the image of the five-two, ninety-pound smiling boy, wearing an aqua T-shirt, shorts, white tennis shoes, and holding a stick bigger than himself. If it is true "a picture is worth a thousand words," then Christopher found himself sitting in the courtroom, face-to-face, with a blatant reminder of what his life used to be like before he killed his grandparents.

When Terry Robinson, Pennington's hunting partner, took the stand and finished the rest of the story in relation to Christopher being lost in the woods, he reiterated, among other things, that Christopher had told them he had been kidnapped by a murderous black man. Yes, the boy plainly had said a black man had shot his grandparents, burned their house down, forced him into their truck, and then drove him out to the woods.

On cross-examination, Mims asked Robinson, "You

don't know what normal demeanor is for Christopher, do you?"

Robinson admitted he did not.

"Was Christopher talking to himself?"

Robinson said he didn't know.

"So, sometime before the shot that you described for us, you heard talking?" Mims asked.

"Right."

"This was in the area of the SUV?"

"Correct."

Mims looked away from the witness and toward the jurors. "So who was Christopher talking to?"

Robinson paused for a few seconds. He held out his hands protectively in front of him, then shook his head and said, "I have no idea."

Mims raised his voice, as if to admonish Robinson for not knowing the answer to his question. "Are you telling this jury he was talking to himself?"

"He could have been," Robinson said, hoping that would explain it all. He thought about his answer, then attempted to clarify it by saying, "At the time, I didn't even know he had a dog with him."

Mims stepped in closer and bore down on the witness. "So, you think he may have been talking with the dog?"

Robinson shrugged. "He may have."

"Was the dog talking back?" Mims asked quickly.

Robinson smirked. Before he could respond, Mims apologized to the court. A chuckle erupted in the court-room. Pieper quickly restored order.

Mims started over. "Was this a conversation?" he asked, trying to pinpoint an answer.

"Like I said, I just heard talking," Robinson begged off. "I couldn't tell what was being said."

During television breaks in the live trial, Court TV's commentator Fred Graham was telling his viewers that he understood Christopher had been taking large amounts of Zoloft, and the dosage had been doubled shortly before the murder. He said Court TV was getting hundreds of e-mails during the broadcast from people who were taking the same drug as Christopher. They were providing firsthand knowledge and personal experiences with Zoloft. Graham made a point to say that the drug's side effects may be related to the dosage and obviously this little boy could have been experiencing monstrous side effects if he was taking huge amounts. "What had happened to Christopher Pittman," he contended, "appears to be consistent with what was going on with others."

Christopher Pittman was a great case for Court TV to air, program editor Graham boasted, because it put forth a lot of issues with this "involuntary intoxication" type of defense.

The first issue was the prosecution's witnesses testifying from all outward appearances that Christopher didn't appear to be under the influence of any substances. Both hunters said he was acting just like a little boy lost in the woods. Yet, the defense was making the point that this twelve-year-old boy was lost in the woods and was talking to himself. By all standards, these were good points the defense was making. They were holding their own ground in counteracting the hunters' testimony. There were so many facts the prosecution had brought out during the hunters' testimony that the defense couldn't counteract all of them, but they could address a few. Among them were the age and size of Christopher when he was found in the woods and the fact that he was talking to himself in the woods. Mims related during the cross-examination of the hunters that talking to yourself may be normal to everyone else, but it might not have been the norm for Christopher.

Spectators and reporters in the courtroom were becoming fascinated with this interesting defense known as involuntary intoxication. The way they understood, it was more of a form of insanity, a little more serious than an alcoholic stupor when one wakes up in the morning beside some stranger one had picked up in a

bar the night before. The defense was adamant that
Zoloft—an involuntary substance—could affect the way
certain people thought and behaved. It remained to be
seen, but supposedly Zoloft had controlled everything
Christopher Pittman did and said on the night of, and
after, the murders.

The prosecution said that was hogwash and aimed to
make mincemeat of the involuntary-intoxication defense. They likened it to those who claimed they'd had
a whacked-out outer-body experience that made them
behave like some kind of Zoloft zombie who had spotted
Elvis at their dinner table last week.

During the hunters' testimony, the prosecution laid
the groundwork for their argument that the boy knew
what he was doing at the time of the murders when they
asked the hunters about Christopher's demeanor. He
seemed normal enough, both hunters testified. They
saw nothing unusual about the boy lost in the woods.
Only Pennington made reference to any emotional response when he told Mims that Pittman appeared
"skeered," like a little boy lost in the woods.

The prosecution was certainly getting in its licks and
scoring lots of points with the jury. First they were able to
show the jurors that Christopher had lied, basically, to
cover up his crimes. They pointed out this is not characteristic of someone who had done this involuntarily. Not
once had the hunters described him as manic, crazed,
delusional, or aggressive. And wouldn't you expect someone who is intoxicated by a drug to be at least a little wild
and crazy, knowing now that he had shot his grandparents less than nine hours earlier? These were very
important factors for the jury to consider.

There was a lot of talk in the gallery about why the defense was not objecting to the prosecution leading their
witnesses with inflammatory questions. Normally, the
prosecution wouldn't have gotten to first base with this
kind of aggressive leading of the witnesses, without objections and repeated requests for sidebars from the

defense. But with his first witnesses, Meadors was scoring points at will.

The truth was, from a legal standpoint, it really didn't matter that the prosecution witnesses were testifying over and over about Christopher murdering his grandparents, since the defense already had entered into a stipulation to these acts. Although spectators in the gallery believed the prosecution was blowing the defense's case to bits with testimony about Christopher's lies, the real battle had not begun. This case promised to get interesting only when the defense had its turn to level the playing field by blaming the murders on Zoloft and turning it into a battle of hired guns. And when it came time for the defense's expert witnesses, the jury would discover how Andy Vickery and his partners had earned their reputation as tops in the field of civil litigation against drug companies and their products.

Court TV's Lisa Bloom predicted not only a fascinating trial, but told her viewers they were going to learn about juvenile defendants and how they were going to be treated, as well as learn about drugs and their effects. As Bloom closed her program, she quipped, "The Zoloft defense isn't the Twinkie defense, in that it is a little less tasty, but it's a whole lot more controversial."

CHAPTER 30

Another witness in court that same day, Cherokee County detective Darrell Duncan, testified that when he interviewed Christopher Pittman at the Corinth Fire Department, Christopher did not appear upset, nor was he crying. When Duncan asked Christopher what had happened, he also told him the same story he had told the hunters about being kidnapped by a black man.

"He said the black man had burned down the house," Duncan informed the jury. "He said the black man had forced him in the vehicle, and it was his grandparents' vehicle and that's how he ended up in the woods."

"Did [you] have any trouble understanding him when he told you all this?" Meadors asked.

"No, sir," Duncan responded.

"So, tell these ladies and gentlemen," Meadors instructed Duncan, clearly leading the witness, "he appeared calm as he told the story. He said he had heard something, ran outside, heard two gunshots, the man located him and burned the house down."

Duncan nodded. "The boy said he had watched the man pour gas all around his grandparents' house, then burn the house down." Christopher's story about his getaway, he testified, was the same one he had told the hunters.

On cross-examination, Waldner asked Duncan how he had classified Christopher the day he was found.

"A young boy who was a victim/witness of a violent crime," Duncan replied.

Waldner, in his gentle manner, asked Duncan to think about the words he used to describe Christopher in the courtroom today, such as "teenager and young man," and how they were not an accurate description of Christopher the first time he saw him. Pointing out that differentiating between this status is very important for people in law enforcement, he asked Duncan, "And is it not true that many of your words you used to label Christopher, 'victim, victim/witness, and suspect,' are really law enforcement words of art?"

Duncan stated it was important because it meant they would use a different protocol for each of the terms.

Waldner asked Duncan to give an example.

"Well, if you refer to Mr. Pittman's case," Duncan said seriously, "if he was a suspect, we wouldn't have called out all of these people that [were] asleep and off-duty to come out to look for a black male in the woods, get the SLED helicopter up that costs, I don't know how many hundreds of dollars it cost just to run it. And the manpower that we had come in."

That was not the answer Waldner had hoped for.

Giese looked toward jurors to gauge their reaction. Being somewhat a quasi politician, he was familiar with how the public felt about supposedly wasting tax dollars.

Waldner attempted to salvage the rest of the interview. He insinuated the police had not followed the established protocols very carefully in taking a statement from him.

Duncan said he had not taken a statement from Christopher. "I had no reason to believe that he had done anything at that point and time. My investigation focused on a black male that was in the woods that may end up breaking into somebody else's house and killing them."

Waldner asked Duncan if he thought Christopher was coming from his grandparents' home in Chester.

"That I don't know," Duncan replied.

"But based on all the information you received, where did you think he was going?"

Duncan shrugged. He didn't know.

"Okay, I don't, either," Waldner said hurriedly. "Thank you very much."

Meadors objected to Waldner's editorial comment. The judge sustained it, then told the jury to disregard that last comment.

When Duncan was dismissed from the stand, the prosecution followed with another Cherokee County officer, Wes Foster, whose testimony was about the same as Duncan's, other than he actually took the dogs out to look for the alleged suspect. He, too, had had a brief conversation with Christopher Pittman, where Christopher described what his kidnapper looked like.

For some reason, Foster's name had been added to the list of witnesses at the last minute. While the prosecution argued it was important that he be included, Foster's direct examination was heard outside the jury.

"We object to any testimony from Sergeant Foster," Waldner told the judge. "It's cumulative, especially in light of the stipulation that was read to the jury this morning."

Meadors reminded the judge Foster's testimony was directed toward the key issue, the defendant's state of mind. Foster was one of the first witnesses that saw Christopher after the murders, and he specifically could tell the jury that Christopher told him somebody else did it.

"This supports our argument that goes directly to the main issue of 'did Christopher Pittman know the difference between right and wrong?' Your Honor," Meadors argued.

Judge Pieper took time to address that issue for the defense, but ruled against them. "I think the defendant's statement was made freely and voluntarily. It was not under some promise, under conditions of promise, duress, coercion, or otherwise. That it was freely and voluntarily given, and that he was not subject to custodial interrogation at the time.

"I think that all of the defendant's statements to the extent that they may be put together insofar as some detailed plan does go to the issue that the state is trying to project to the jury. Whether or not the jury accepts that is the prerogative of the jury. But the issue that you have postured is one of whether or not he was subject to some influence by virtue of the ingestion of Zoloft, and the capability to focus and plan and provide details, I think, all go into that equation insofar as what will be argued to this jury, so I will allow it in."

Thus, Wes Foster was allowed to testify for the prosecution.

The prosecution followed Foster's testimony with Lucinda McKellar, who had been an investigator with the Chester County Sheriff's Department in November 2001. It was in Christopher's original statement to McKellar that he blamed the fictitious man; then, in a second statement, he confessed to killing his grandparents. She was currently employed with SLED in their computer crime unit, working primarily with child pornography cases.

Neatly dressed in a dark blue business suit, with just enough red lipstick and blush on her face to accent her cherubic features, McKellar made an excellent witness. She was intelligent, articulate, and got the information out where everyone could understand it. When asked to demonstrate how she administered the gunpowder residue kit, she stood in front of the solicitor, instructed him to put his hands out, then had him slowly turn his hands over.

"So when you did this with the defendant, he was lucid, logical, and able to follow instructions?" Meadors asked.

"Yes. He was all of those."

McKellar then was asked to read Christopher Pittman's first statement. She slowly read, word for word, what Christopher had told her at 11:30 A.M., on November 29, the day after the murders.

"Did he appear to understand all your questions?" Meadors asked.

"Yes, sir."

"Did he respond to your questions with this information?"

"Yes, sir."

McKellar stated that as Christopher provided the details, she wrote them down. She and Christopher were in the office downstairs at the Corinth Fire Department when she had written them down. She then asked Christopher to go back and read it, and make sure she hadn't made any mistakes. He did so, and indicated this by signing his initials at the beginning and end of each paragraph.

"I had a mistake," McKellar added, "so I asked him to put his initials on any mistake, indicating that it had changed when he and I were together. When I asked him to do it, he put the right initials in the right place."

Meadors pointed out that Christopher had read each item on each page.

"Yes," McKellar confirmed, "I also said to him, 'Put your initials at the beginning and end of each page. This locks your words in, so nobody can change them.' Chris initialed each page with a 'CP,' then signed the statement, indicating he had read each page."

Meadors wanted the jury to hear more about this first statement that was filled with the lies about the fictitious kidnapping. McKellar was there to oblige.

"At one point, as I normally do with children on their first statement, when Christopher was describing the layout of the house, I asked him to draw a picture. He drew a sketch and labeled different parts of his house. He drew the layout of the house, a two-dimensional map of the bottom and top floors, and I said to him, 'Sometimes I have a hard time understanding, so can you draw a picture of where you were hiding from the black guy, so I can get in my mind what had happened?'"

McKellar said Christopher drew a picture of his grandparents' home and then labeled the area near the woodshed where he hid from the kidnapper.

It was important to Meadors that the jury hear what Christopher did after his original statement to McKellar. She testified he ate lunch and napped for a while, that they talked and played cars for about twenty to thirty minutes, then he lay down again.

"So, he played cards?" Meadors stressed. "He played Go Fish?"

McKellar smiled and nodded.

"Was he pretty good at it?" Meadors asked.

"Yeah, I believe he won several hands." She smiled.

McKellar stated Christopher lay down on the couch again, watched television, and took another nap. When the press gathered around the front and tried to take pictures of him, she asked him to go upstairs. She admitted he also had told her, "I'm on Zoloft, and it makes me sleepy."

"At any time, did you threaten or coerce him?" Meadors asked.

"No, sir."

"Did you do anything mean to him, or anything else?"

"No, sir."

"Did he have access to a bathroom?"

"Yes, sir."

"Did he answer all your questions?"

"Yes, sir."

On the surface, Meadors pointed out, none of what Christopher had done made sense to the prosecution—the killings, burning his grandparents' house down, then blaming it on a black man. But he wanted the jury to see how unreasonable the idea was that Zoloft had made the boy go crazy. If Christopher Pittman were as intoxicated after the murder as the defense claimed, then how could he create such a clear and lucid fabrication of what had happened? Granted, it was a phony story, but if he were psychotic and hearing voices, then how could he sit down with authorities and tell such a convincing, bald-faced lie without batting an eye?

Meadors then asked McKellar about Christopher's second confession, when he finally admitted to killing his grandparents. McKellar read the confession, word for word. The way Meadors ultimately portrayed it to the jury, if Christopher had heard voices, then they were pretty smart voices. The voices knew enough to tell him to burn his grandparents' house down and get rid of the evidence from his crime. Meadors was convinced, and demonstrated through Christopher's own words from his confession, that what he did after the killings was indicative of intent and premeditation: the money stolen from his grandmother's purse, the guns, stealing the car, setting the house on fire, taking his dog with him—this was proof he knew exactly what he was doing, when he did it. He even described it vividly for the detectives. Christopher's actions after the murders fell right along the lines of what Meadors wanted jurors to believe—that he knew all the time what he had done was wrong.

Finally, after McKellar's lengthy testimony in court, Meadors promised, "I'm going to ask you one more time, during this entire time in the process of taking this statement, did the defendant, Christopher Pittman, appear to understand your and Scott Williams's questions?"

"Yes, sir."

"Did he ever appear to be under the influence of anything?"

"No, sir."

"At any time taking this statement, did he say, 'I don't want to talk to you'?"

"No, sir. He didn't."

"Did he say, 'Get my daddy here'?"

"No, sir."

"He actually said he didn't want to see his daddy, didn't he?"

"Yes, sir, he did."

"Did he ask for anybody to come see him?"

"No, sir, he didn't."

"If he had, Lucinda, what would you have done?"

"I would have had to have stopped."

"At any time during this process, did he ask for a lawyer?"

"No, sir."

"If he had, what would you have done?"

"I would have contacted Rick Westsinger with the DJJ, because I don't know how I would get an attorney for him, so I would contact DJJ to see if we could get that started."

Meadors reminded the jurors that Christopher had not been threatened, given promises of rewards, or coerced in any way to confess. At the end of Meadors's direct examination, he wrote a sentence on the board behind McKellar. "What does that say?" he asked her.

"They deserved it," she answered softly.

Trial groupies were saying it was much too early in the trial to choose sides. Vickery and his team of civil litigators had won big judgments against drug companies before and they were fighting very hard to win this one. When it was the defense's turn, Vickery would question McKellar and he, through her answers, would ask her to explain to the jury why it was not normal for a twelve-year-old to kill his grandparents; that wasn't there something outside himself that had made him do it? Vickery assured the jurors if McKellar didn't know the obvious answer as to why this twelve-year-old committed murder, then he would gladly supply one. He wanted them to know it was the Zoloft—no more, no less.

Vickery began his cross-examination of McKellar by

immediately challenging Christopher's statements he supplied to law enforcement. "One of them is sort of this *crazy* story about the black man in the woods and the kidnapping, right? And the second one you would call a confession, wouldn't you?"

"Yes," McKellar answered to both accounts. The first statement taken was while Christopher was not under arrest; then a second one was taken. As a result of his confession during his second statement, he was arrested and charged with double homicide.

Vickery pointed out the significant times of that day were at 11:30 A.M., when Christopher was considered a witness, and again at 3:55 P.M., when he changed to a witness/suspect. Agent Williams came in at 4:02 P.M., Christopher was given his Miranda warnings at 4:02 P.M., and his confession was signed at 5:13 P.M. Vickery looked at each of these statements in detail and compared the times they were taken.

"Detective McKellar, after the case, did you continue to investigate Christopher's background to find out what kind of kid this was, if he had been in trouble before?"

"Yes, sir."

"And tell the jury, if you would, the sum total of everything violent that you found that this young man had done to a person or property, man or beast, prior to November 28, 2001, when he shot his grandparents."

McKellar related incidents involving Christopher stabbing a bull in the neck with a dart and shooting someone's mobile home.

"So, he stabbed a bull in the neck with a dart?"

"Yes, sir."

"And did he shoot a person with a BB gun or an animal or just somebody's mobile home?"

"A mobile home."

"He pinged some BBs off a mobile home?" Vickery said sarcastically.

"Yes, sir."

Using an overhead projector, Vickery reproduced copies of police reports on the screen so the jurors could follow along, then attacked McKellar's conclusions related to each incident. Pointing out the discrepancies, Vickery said, "There was another name, Kevin Rouche, who was involved in the attack on the bull. He was listed as the suspect. Chris was listed as a witness, the one who snatched the dart out. But it was Kevin who threw the dart, and Kevin who went and apologized to the man for sticking the dart in the bull, and the man accepted his apology."

Vickery questioned McKellar as to why she had given testimony earlier about Christopher's propensity for violence, based on this dart incident that was in direct contradiction with the police report from Florida.

McKellar stated she had obtained her information from the owners of the bull, rather than rely solely on the police reports from Florida. She said she didn't feel bad about giving testimony that Vickery thought was contrary to the police records in Florida, but believed this incident warranted further investigation. She talked with the owner of the bull and obtained a statement from him, and that was the information she relied upon.

Vickery wouldn't let her off the hot seat. "You knowingly did that, knowing what the police records said, you knowingly told this court that he is the one that did it?"

McKellar remained silent.

Vickery bantered back and forth with McKellar about her intent and motives in this case, eventually insinuating she should have known how to recognize and/or respond when someone was under the influence of psychoactive medications. "I mean, did you know when he said, 'I'm on Zoloft' that that was a drug designed to affect chemicals in the brain? Did you think that maybe that is something you should have checked out before you asked this twelve-year-old to waive his constitutional rights?"

"No, sir."

"Why not?"

"At the time, I was going by my experience as a law enforcement officer, and he appeared to be coherent—he
appeared to understand me—and I continued with
my investigation."

Vickery questioned her about everything on the statements, from the tiny scratches on the pages to
Christopher's signatures, each time downplaying the
elaborate story about the black guy, saying the story was
crazy and that it didn't make a lick of sense.

A weaker officer would have come apart at the seams,
but not McKellar. She understood Vickery was taking up
for his client, but it was not going to be at her expense.
She told him Christopher's original story *did* make sense
to her.

Vickery was unwavering. "I mean, you are a trained
law enforcement professional, aren't you? And your an-
tennas go up when people tell you things that just didn't
jibe with your own common sense, don't they?"

"Yes, sir."

"Did it make sense to you that a black man would have
murdered both of his grandparents and left him alone?"
Vickery asked in a surly manner.

Meadors leaped to his feet, as if he had been sitting on
a hot bed of coals.

"Objection!" he yelled out. "Your Honor, she answered yes."

The judge recognized McKellar was a big girl and
could fend for herself. "I will allow it. Go ahead, answer
the question," he instructed her.

"This is kind of a broad statement," McKellar continued. "It is really case by case. Every investigation is
different. I can't walk in with preconceived notions or
blinders, because I could miss something. This very well
could have been the truth."

Vickery suddenly switched tactics. Referring to

Christopher's testimony, he became extremely accusatory in an effort to intimidate McKellar. If he were trying to score points with the jury, it wasn't working in his favor. The jury was predominately female and many of them were on the edge of their seats listening to his cross-examination, but when he started bullying McKellar, they slid back in their seats and crossed their arms.

Vickery continued badgering McKellar. "I just want to know whether it made sense to you at the time when he said there is this guy who killed both his grandparents, but then he just took [Christopher] along with him?"

"Is it feasibly possible? Yes."

"That wasn't my question," Vickery shot back, unbending.

"Yes, it could make sense," McKellar answered, calm and still in control. "Yes, sir, because I continued to take his statement and to treat Christopher as a victim-slash-witness."

"Did it make sense to you that when this kidnapper nabbed this kid that he took along his dog?"

"He never said he took along his dog. He said that the dog in the woods looked similar to his dog. 'How did my dog follow me here' were his exact words."

"Correct me if I'm wrong, I sometimes make mistakes about these things. But I thought he said that the dog went with him?"

"No, sir. That's in his confession that he took his dog with him."

"Did it make sense to you that this kidnapper would leave a twelve-year-old boy in a truck with a loaded forty-five?"

"It's a case by case," McKellar answered.

"What does that mean?" Vickery shot back, as if that were the most ludicrous statement he had ever heard. Some spectators thought his demeanor was more damaging than his questions.

"That means it is feasibly possible. I can't tell you that, no, that would never happen. I don't know."

"I know, and I didn't ask you that." Vickery's voice was filled with anger. "I just asked you whether back at the time he gave this to you, if it made any sense to you?"

"It could have, yes, sir."

"Okay. And did it make sense to you that after kidnapping this boy, after murdering the grandparents and kidnapping the boy, that the black man would take him out for a nap?"

"The thing I thought about was, this was possibly a black man that kept him there. It could have been a black man that was scared and kept him with him. It could have been a hostage situation. I did not know. This is this child giving me his explanation of what happened."

Vickery pursed his lips, as if he had gotten a whiff of something rotten. "Agent McKellar, my question was 'did it make sense to you that the information that he was giving you was that he and his kidnapper napped together?'"

"No, sir."

"Did it make sense to you that the kidnapper would throw the keys away?" he asked incredulously.

"Yes, sir."

"That he would get a car stuck or a truck stuck and just throw the keys and run away?"

"Yes, sir."

Vickery asked his partner Paul Waldner for a table. He had McKellar exit from the stand and join him at the table, where he attempted to create a picture of the Cherokee County Sheriff's Department and recapture the ambience when Christopher confessed. After having McKellar describe the room again to jurors, he asked her to sit at one end of the table. He then placed the cutout of Christopher Pittman across from her.

"I can't make him sit, but can you imagine he is sort of sitting at the table," Vickery told McKellar. He pulled out a deck of cards and asked how the card game was played and for how long. After McKellar answered, he posed in the form of a question, "Then was the 'call me Lucy business' and the 'Go Fish' designed to make friends with him?"

Spectators in the gallery groaned. The defense had picked a losing strategy with this move and was going down a path that led to nowhere.

When McKellar eventually straightened Vickery out, telling him all this activity was at a different location and different layout, he put away the cards and the table. Moving forward to his next plan of attack, he then asked about the Scripture verse Christopher had shared with her at the Corinth Fire Department after their first interview. "And let me make real sure I understand. Did you remind him of that Scripture right before he started spilling his guts and giving you the confession?"

Vickery, again, had fumbled the ball.

"Your Honor, I'm going to object to the adjectives he keeps using in his questions," Meadors thundered. "Respectfully, we object to his characterizations that he throws into his questions."

The judge agreed and asked Vickery to please rephrase his question.

"Okay, I'm sorry. What terminology would you prefer to describe—"

"I object!" The cords in Meadors's neck stood out as he jumped up from his seat again.

"Just rephrase as the court indicated, counsel," Pieper told Vickery.

Vickery asked McKellar about the Scripture a second time. Why had she reminded Christopher, who had been to church the night before, of the Scripture verses right before he gave the confession?

"At the time, I realized that he was a suspect and that maybe him telling me that Scripture verse was a way of him communicating that 'this is what I have done.' It was odd that there was a fire with two people that burned and then he says the Scripture verse that ends in 'burning in the fires of Hell.'"

"So, you thought it all had to do with the fire?"

Still bothered about Vickery's previous display of dramatics, Meadors objected to the question, pointed at Vickery, then tossed in, "Is he through with the demonstration at this table?"

Now it was Vickery's turn to be peeved. "I am not," the exasperated attorney responded under his breath.

Vickery then had McKellar read from the Bible, Matthew 5: 21–22: "'Ye have heard that it was said of them of old time, Thou shalt not kill; and whosoever shall kill shall be in danger of the judgment: But I say unto you, That whosoever is angry with his brother without a cause shall be in danger of the judgment; and whosoever shall say to his brother, Raca, shall be in danger of the council. But whosoever shall say, Thou fool, shall be in danger of hell fire.'"

"Those are the two same Scripture verses that you reminded this young man of before he gave his confession, aren't they?" Vickery asked.

McKellar admitted she did not know those Scripture verses. All she heard was the last part "burning in the fires of Hell."

Before McKellar's testimony was complete, Vickery also accused her of providing the prosecution with a motive in writing his statement that day—Christopher had been disciplined by his grandfather. Vickery walked over to the exhibit table and retrieved a charred paddle, then waved it high in the courtroom.

"Your partner Agent Williams had retrieved this paddle at the fire site, had he not?" he asked.

McKellar acknowledged he had.

"Now, if we read this statement, it makes out Christopher's Pop Pop, his grandfather, as a child beater, doesn't it?"

"According to him, yes, sir."

"I mean, it says four or five times he beat him with his

paddle, beat him five or six times with this, back into the room, doesn't it?"

"Yes, sir."

"And he said, 'If you don't go back in that room, I'm going to hit you in the head with it,' didn't he?"

"Yes, sir, according to Christopher's statement, yes."

Over several objections from the prosecution, the judge allowed Vickery to ask Melinda Rector Pittman to stand. "Have you ever had anyone point out to you that this lady is the daughter of Joe and Joy Pittman?"

"No, sir."

"I will ask you to assume that she is. Can you tell her if you have one—"

Meadors objected before he finished. The judge called for a sidebar, but ruled Vickery could continue.

"Agent McKellar, would you please tell the ladies and gentlemen of the jury if you have a shred of evidence to corroborate the statement in your handwriting that Joe Frank Pittman was a child beater."

"No, sir. I didn't get an opportunity to speak to him."

"Okay. You've talked to a lot of folks that know him, haven't you?" Vickery asked.

McKellar said she had, but none that she spoke with ever said anything about Joe Pittman being abusive to his grandson.

When it came time for Meadors's redirect, he immediately addressed the issue of Joe Pittman being a child abuser. He was furious that the defense even would consider such a posture. Clearly in a rampage, he, at one point, snatched a document out of McKellar's hand, marched over to the defense table, and presented it to Vickery.

"Have you ever characterized Joe and Joy Pittman, the couple that good old Chief Red [Weir] described yesterday, as child beaters?" Meadors asked McKellar.

"No, sir."

"You have never described them that way, have you?"

"No, sir."

"Not one time?"

"No, sir."

"They were good people, weren't they?"

Before McKellar could answer, Vickery objected to Meadors leading the witness. Meadors rephrased his question. "After his questions"—he rolled his eyes and thumbed back to Vickery—"were they good people?"

"All the information that I had, yes, sir."

"Would you in your experience as [a] juvenile officer, if somebody spanked somebody, would you consider them child beaters?"

"No, sir, that would take further investigation to determine that."

"When is the first time you learned anything about a spanking?"

"When Christopher Pittman told me [in his second statement]."

"Was that after he had blamed somebody else?"

"Yes, sir." McKellar cut her eyes toward the jury.

"Look at me," Meadors said, sounding like a father admonishing his child in church. McKellar redirected her gaze at him. "And then he blamed his granddaddy?"

"Yes, sir."

On recross-examination, Vickery asked McKellar, "So, all we have to believe about his confession is they are his words, but they are really yours and your partner's words? I just want to know why for his entire life the only thing he ever called his grandparents were 'Pop Pop' and 'Nana,' but in this statement, the word he chose was 'grandparents'?"

McKellar didn't have an answer for that one.

"Why didn't you either audiotape or videotape this statement?"

"I didn't have an audiotape or a videotape with me."

Vickery shook his head in disbelief. "Surely, with all of

the manpower that was out that day—dogs, helicopters in the air—you could have gotten access in that hour and eleven minutes to have tape recorders to tape it so we would have no question in our minds, couldn't you?"

"Yes, sir," McKellar admitted.

After McKellar stepped down from the witness stand, the judge called for a fifteen-minute break. Pieper was well aware that trials become theaters where lawyers are constantly communicating to jurors in all kinds of ways. Objections, staring each other down, shaking their heads—these are all forms of communication and points the lawyers want to make with the jurors. But animosity toward each other was not appropriate and considered a cardinal sin in his courtroom.

"We're going to take a break," Pieper announced, looking directly at Meadors and Vickery. "I suggest you both take a breath of fresh air. As I indicated during your brief trial conference, I'm not going to tolerate any attorney misconduct. Do you understand that?"

Acting like two schoolboys who just got called down for fighting on the playground, the two attorneys stood and said they understood. Pieper then laid out the instructions he wanted them to follow.

"If you have an objection, state the objection. I'll ask for any further elaboration, if I so desire. Do not shout your objection." Pieper raised his voice for emphasis, then lowered it and said softly, "'Objection, Your Honor,' will do fine, and nothing more, unless I ask for it. Do not address any animosity toward each other. I will not tolerate your staring each other down, your grabbing papers, or any other conduct of that nature. There will be no further warnings. Do each of you understand?"

After watching the two attorneys get nailed by the judge, the spectators in the courtroom were trying to figure out just what the heck had happened. One reporter offered her insight: "I believe Vickery was bullying McKellar. He went after her in a petulant manner and it was such a nasty recross that Meadors got offended by this. You gotta be careful who you bully."

"I don't think so," the lady sitting beside the reporter disagreed. "It was the bit about Joe Pittman being a child abuser that got Meadors all stirred up."

Besides the lawyers, there was a lot of intensity in the courtroom. The tables promised to turn when the defense brought their case on, but at this point, listening to prosecution, all anyone could talk about was how the Pittmans took Christopher in, raised him and took care of him, and what did they get for their troubles? Bullets to the head and their dream home burned to the ground.

And now Christopher is calling his grandpa a child abuser?

CHAPTER 31

The spectators felt the passion from lawyers on both sides of the courtroom. For those who were keeping score, both groups of attorneys were evenly matched. They knew their cases inside and out. It was not a case of them fumbling through their papers and stumbling in their examinations of witnesses. Court TV was correct in their assessment of this case—the courtroom drama was making great television play for their viewers.

On the third day, John Meadors continued laying more bricks and mortar to his case in calling SA Scott Williams to the stand. As Williams took his seat, Meadors turned toward the defense table and smiled, as if he wanted so bad to say out loud in the courtroom, "You boys from Texas want motive; then how about trying this one on for size."

Twelve-year-old kids just don't commit murder, Meadors wanted the jurors to know. They run in fields with dogs, play baseball at the park, and pick their noses. But commit homicide? No! By its very definition, young boys have not been assigned this behavior as one of their major developmental characteristics.

"Let's talk about prior to the day of the murders, Agent Williams," Meadors began. "Was there an incident at the school where the grandparents disciplined him?"

Williams confirmed there was such an incident.

"And even Christopher said to you at one point in his confession that his grandparents told him, 'You keep this up and you're going back to Florida'?"

"Yes, sir." Williams remembered Christopher saying that in his confession.

Meadors wanted jurors to know there's not a parent alive who hadn't used the old "you better shape up or ship out" admonishment. And if Joe Pittman had said that to Christopher, and Meadors believed he had, then it was more than likely a precipitating factor to murder. The threat to Christopher meant that he was going to be sent back to less favorable circumstances, where he would move back into his father's mobile home in Florida and fend for himself, and that is what caused his homicidal snap. It wasn't the medication that caused him to snap, but Joe Pittman's cards were on the table and Christopher was not about to be sent back to a place, and another world, where he didn't want to go. That was what really happened earlier to Christopher, the prosecution contended, that caused his rage and to become homicidal.

"Let's focus on his demeanor"—Meadors lured the jury in—"he knew what was going on, right? You had no trouble understanding him or communicating [with] him? He did everything exactly the way you told him?"

"Yes, sir," Williams answered.

The prosecution went to work with SA Williams, and in a rudimentary manner, they attempted to explain the twisted mind of a twelve-year-old who had perpetrated this crime. As predicted, the prosecution had already aligned their strategy beforehand and they made certain that Williams had his ducks in a row. In great and vivid detail, he described the events of the fire, his involvement in Cherokee County, and, finally, Christopher Pittman's confession that he had murdered his grandparents.

Meadors asked Williams to recount how he had climbed on the ladders and found the Pittmans' bodies in the loft of the house. He had him describe the events through photos and assorted pieces of evidence. As with McKellar, Meadors went through the details of Christopher's Miranda warnings, waiver of rights, and confession. His and McKellar's stories matched perfectly.

There were a number of chills up the backs of spectators that day. It started to register in their minds just how two people, sleeping peacefully in their beds one minute, could die a horrible death the next moment.

On cross-examination, Waldner reemphasized that Williams and McKellar should have waited for Christopher's dad to arrive before they interviewed him. He then asked Williams a series of questions, for which he could only speculate an answer: "Do you think that the younger a suspect is, the greater the need for the criminal justice system to protect his rights? Do you think that waiting until Christopher's dad was there would have given his dad an opportunity to make a decision for his son; would that have been one of those protections that we have just discussed? Do you believe his statement about being sent back to Florida was a reflection of a young man who has any appreciation for the gravity of the situation?" Waldner also wanted to know why Christopher wasn't examined when he said his Pop Pop beat him, and why Williams and McKellar didn't do something further when he said he was on Zoloft?

Williams didn't have the answers to all of Waldner's questions, but he gave what information he had.

During Williams's testimony, the defense's cross-examination seemed to indicate there might be a missing day in Christopher's recollection when he gave police his two statements on November 29, 2001. In mentioning the meeting with John Rodgers, the vice principal, Christopher referred to the date of the meeting as "yesterday." There was no mention in the other conversation of the actual day of the bus incident or the day that he went to the vice principal's office. The prosecution cleared that matter up by calling Rodgers to the stand.

In cross-examination of Rodgers, defense attorney Mims asked if it was possible that this incident happened because of something another kid had done. Rodgers was certain it had not.

"One kid threw a piece of paper at the second grader," Rodgers stated, "but the second grader thought it was Christopher. Christopher said he tried to explain to the second grader that he hadn't thrown the paper, but the situation got out of hand. Christopher said the second grader had a sister, who threatened to bring a knife to school the next day and was going to cut him." Rodgers said his investigations revealed there had been a threat, but nothing serious.

When Mims asked Rodgers had he checked to see whether Christopher was on any substances, he replied, "Guidance would have known that."

If there was a dark moment in the prosecution's case, it was Dr. Eric Naumann. Completely open and vulnerable, Naumann came off on the stand more like Mr. Magoo than a board-certified physician.

In recalling for the jury his treatment plan for Christopher Pittman, Naumann's answers were sporadic and brief. Most of the time, he responded with a dull "Yep" or "Nawh." He had a certain flatness of expression and inability to describe adequately what he knew he knew, and that caused the prosecution a lot of heartburn. But, yes, he was the Pittmans' family physician. Yes, he had assessed and treated Christopher. And, yes, he had given Christopher samples of Zoloft to treat his depression.

The prosecution had to work with what they had.

In a soft and noticeably nervous voice, Naumann explained to the jury how he came to know Christopher Pittman, how he gave him a diagnosis, the amount and frequency of medication that he had prescribed, and a follow-up meeting with Christopher only two days before the murder.

When the trial resumed after lunch, defense counsel Waldner started hammering away at Dr. Naumann. Naumann sat there, on the witness stand, dressed in a light blue shirt and dark blue tie, with some kind of outer space planets emblazoned across the front, looking confused.

"Now, did you talk to Dr. Howard Smith?" Waldner asked.

Naumann shook his head. "I don't even know who Dr. Howard Smith is."

"Did you get the records from Lifestream?"

"I—I . . . Could you . . . I don't even know what that is."

"Did you know that he had been in a facility in Florida within the last week-and-a-half?"

Naumann gave a big nod. "Yes, I did. Between he and the grandma, somebody had said it. And it is reflected in the notes." He checked his notes.

"And did you know that his psychiatrist was Dr. Howard Smith?'"

"Nawh," Naumann responded with a wide sweep of his head.

"Have you ever had a situation before, Dr. Naumann, where you had a patient you were meeting for the first time, and who is twelve years of age, and you picked up the phone and called the last doctor he saw? Have you ever done that?"

Naumann paused. He closed his eyes and pondered the question. Resembling a student who vaguely remembered the professor had covered that in class once, but couldn't exactly say when, he finally answered, "Yeah, I think I have."

"You're familiar with the phrase 'continuum of care,' aren't you?"

"Yea-a-h," Naumann said, carefully weighing his answer.

"Maintaining the continuum of care, in general terms in medicine, that's a good thing to do in medicine, isn't it?"

"Yeah," he said, shaking his head. "I believe . . . sure."

"Okay, now to maintain the continuum of care for this young man, and to give psychoactive medication, don't you think it would have been a good idea for you to pick up the phone and call Dr. Howard Smith?"

Naumann sighed. He placed his hand on his chin. "That would be an idea, and certainly . . ." Another long pause followed. He dropped his left hand from his chin and held it out in front, waving it around for emphasis. Then from somewhere out of la-la land, he offered, "I didn't have a number, I didn't have the name of the person, and I didn't ask for it. But the other thing is, more than likely, you know, trying to get medical records. Trying to get medical records on a juvenile who is a psychiatric basis is very, extremely difficult."

"Well, in 2001, you just need a HIPPA release signed, don't you?" the knowledgeable Waldner asked effortlessly.

"Yes-s-s," Naumann acknowledged.

"Ant then you fax it to Lifestream, and then—"

"And hope you get it," Naumann cut him off. "With mental-health records, and with my experience, you usually don't end up getting 'em. I'm not sure why."

Everyone in the courtroom knew it was coming, that Waldner would not let the doctor slide out of this one. Showing no mercy, he asked Naumann, "But you agree with me, Doctor, that when you first saw him on November 5, 2001, it would have been a good practice on that day to at least *attempt* to get his records from Lifestream, and at least *attempt* to talk to Dr. Howard Smith, who was his admitting and attending physician? Do you agree with that?"

Christopher had been sipping water from a clear plastic cup during most of Dr. Naumann's testimony. Mostly, he had looked at the doctor like Naumann were someone who had broken into his piggy bank and had stolen his money. But when he heard his former physician's answer, "It would be a good idea," a wide smile came across Christopher's face. He dropped his head and laughed, then took another sip of water to cover his smile. At least he was enjoying the show.

In November 2001, Naumann said he had made a diagnosis of dysthymia, based on the fact Christopher had been on Paxil, having trouble sleeping.

Waldner pointed out that would have been his biggest reason for requesting the files at Lifestream. The seasoned lawyer was very patient, gently coaxing the physician. It was not a blistering cross-examination, but it was nonetheless very effective.

"Doctor, who gave you the sample pack of Zoloft?"

"I suppose the representative from Pfizer."

"Did the Pfizer representative tell you this could be used in treating depression in children?"

"Probably not."

"Then where did you hear that?"

"Um . . . is it indicated? No. Do people do it? Yes." Naumann asked, then answered his own questions. "We go by the medical letter. Are you familiar with that?"

Waldner said he was familiar with the medical letter, a medical newsletter to doctors. After a brief discussion with the doctor on the publication of the medical letter, he moved on to another issue.

"In your testimony here today, when the prosecution asked for information, you responded, 'Is that enough, John?' Can you explain, Dr. Naumann, just how it is you are on a first-name basis with the prosecution, but you won't even talk to the attorneys for your patient?"

Naumann paused. He didn't know what to make of Waldner's accusation. "Well, Mr. Meadors came to Florence and talked with me. Mr. Zamore had called me two-and-a-half years after the case and I told him I was kind of busy at the time. I learned later he was no longer on the case.

"Then I had somebody else call me up, some woman, in the middle of seeing patients. It was a fairly busy day— you know, I guess it was a busy day. It was a patient day, and she wanted to talk to me, and I said okay. And then she started lecturing me about Zoloft. She didn't ask, 'Could I come, or can I come to talk to you, I want to have a cup of coffee with you and talk about the case?' She just started telling me about Zoloft. I didn't really want to talk to her, sir."

It wasn't washing with Waldner. "Okay. Do you recall saying, quote, 'I would really not be interested in speaking with you' or as lawyers say, words to that effect?"

"Yes." Naumann had no problem admitting that.

"Okay. Does it make you feel awkward, just a little bit, Dr. Naumann, just a little bit awkward, that you were sitting here being called by the solicitor who you have worked with, met with, and spoken to, and on a first-name basis with, and you are not interested in meeting with the attorneys who represent your patient? Does that make you feel just a little bit awkward?"

"Unusual. I don't know if awkward would be the correct word."

"Okay, unusual, right?"

"Uh-huh."

Waldner had nothing but contempt for Naumann. He was especially critical in his treatment of Christopher and for not talking to Dr. Smith, the psychiatrist at Lifestream in Florida. And why he didn't tell Joy Pittman that the drugs were given "off label" was another mystery to him. "Doctor, if the blackbox warning in October 2004 existed in November 5, 2001, would you have handed that sample pack to Christopher Pittman?"

"I honestly don't know. You know, it's a different time."

"With Christopher Pittman, within twenty-four hours from the last time you see him choking a second grader, would that diagnosis be ego dystonic or inconsistent with the behavior that you had observed?"

"It was definitely not the way he had acted in my office."

"And the following day, certainly in the killing of his

grandparents and burning down the house, that wasn't consistent with any behavior you had seen, correct?"

"Nawh, I hadn't seen any of that behavior. That is accurate."

Agent Dewitt McGraw testified he was at the sheriff's office in Gaffney, South Carolina, assisting on another homicide case, when he received the call about the Christopher Pittman case. Cherokee County sheriff Bill Blanton told him they had a situation where a twelve-year-old boy had been found by two deer hunters running in the woods, and the boy was claiming that a black male, approximately six feet two inches, had killed his grandparents, kidnapped him, and driven him to where he was.

McGraw was responsible for coordinating SLED's helicopters and K-9 unit that day, as well as the crime scene and SERT teams. He also had secured the search warrant for the black Pathfinder that Christopher had gotten stuck in the woods. He had helped process the vehicle at the site.

As McGraw testified, spectators in the courtroom watched Christopher's reactions. They wondered if he was still taking his medications. On the first day, he was having anxiety attacks. A real basket case, he wiped his eyes and hyperventilated, and steadily held tissues up to his face and eyes. But on this day, Christopher was in control of his emotions—no longer the pitiful picture in the courtroom, sitting there and looking pathetically hopeless. Several times during the trial, he laughed and joked with his attorneys. Danielle Pittman showed up in the courtroom at midday, and her appearance may have accounted for some of Christopher's sudden change of emotion.

Possibly another reason for Christopher's elevated mood was that Christopher's family and his attorneys had been trying to get him released on bond for the duration of the trial, and Hank Mims finally had found someone who would satisfy the conditions of the bond. Michael A. Smith, of A Bail for You, would handle the satellite monitoring, and a registered bondswoman, Beverly Byrd, had agreed to supply the bond.

Judge Pieper was encouraged by this information. During a break in the trial, he dressed down both Smith and Byrd, charging them in their duties and responsibilities. "And, you understand, you both will be responsible for any defects in the satellite procedure, and if you also sign off on this bond," he said to Byrd.

"Absolutely."

"Both of you will be subject to any penalties or sanctions this court may impose if this bond is violated. Do you understand that, ma'am?"

"Yes, Judge."

In Michael Smith's zest to do a good job, he had taken the liberty of going over to the rented house at Isle of Palms and marking it off. A major vacation locale on the South Carolina coast, Isle of Palms was a 4.5 mile island, only minutes away from Downtown Charleston. The yard perimeter itself at the rented house was pretty small, encompassing 200 by 225 feet. The satellite procedures would not allow Christopher to go outside the perimeter of the yard, which the judge determined was two hundred feet. No other privileges, insofar as the bond was concerned, were granted. Christopher could ride only to and from court, and nowhere else. Absolutely no pizza parlors, no movie theaters, and no shopping at the malls.

Pieper wanted Christopher clear on the stipulations. "Do you understand those conditions, sir, that if I release you on bond subject to that satellite-monitoring proviso, that you will be confined to house arrest?"

Christopher nodded his head. "Yes, sir."

Just for good measure, Pieper asked him a second time and Christopher responded in the same manner. "All right, then, I will approve it," he said to Mims. "But you'll have to process the paperwork with the clerk downstairs before it's final."

Mims smiled. Christopher's release had been a long time coming.

SLED's crime scene specialist David Black followed McGraw to the stand and told the jury he had processed the vehicle once it was towed to the garage area at the Cherokee County Sheriff's Department. At the time of the crime in 2001, Black had sixteen years of service with law enforcement and had investigated five hundred crime scenes. Most of those were death investigations. He was trained in footwear and fingerprinting, and was considered an expert in the general sessions and military courts. In street lingo, Black was *the man* in crime scene investigation.

Black described how he had been called to the crime scene on the morning of November 29 by Andy Weir, somewhere around 9:15 A.M. There was a tarp covering the remains of bedding, bedspring, mattress springs, and the remains of the two victims, Joe and Joy Pittman. The CCSD and SLED agents were already doing the field investigation and arson investigation when he arrived. Black's expertise would be the documentation and collection of any evidence, particularly those things that would have to go back to SLED's forensic laboratory for analysis.

Black stated that during his initial walk-through, he found a number of fired .410 shotgun shells in the drive. He placed little placards with numbers by them and photographed them, as well as a box of .410 ammunition that was found on a drum, between the burned residence and the burned motor home. A fired cartridge case was also located on the ground below the burned trailer, between it and the burned house.

Black had stayed at the crime scene until about 11:30 A.M. He collected other evidence, examined the two dead bodies, and completed the actual collection on the residence. It was then the phone call came through that the grandson had been located in the missing Pathfinder, and he moved to that location in Cherokee County.

"When I arrived on the scene and saw the Pathfinder, it was actually stuck in an area of the swamp. You could see where the vehicle had been backed into a little embankment and some trees. The vehicle was locked. To get entry, once we had the search warrant in hand, we actually had to break one of the windows into the vehicle.

"After I photographed it, I opened the door. The floorboard gearshift was in the reverse position, and the driver's seat was pulled all the way up toward the front. It was so far, it could go under the steering wheel. I saw the gas can in the floorboard on the front passenger's side of the vehicle.

"There were rolls of coins in the car and what looked like the front part of a shotgun. It turned out to be a Remington four-ten pump shotgun. I wanted to photograph it, but had to render it safe and find out what was in it. When I pull the fore stock back, I saw a shell was in the chamber. The shell was removed from the chamber and there were two additional shotgun shells in the two magazines, underneath the barrel, which I also removed.

"A Ruger model ten twenty-two rifle was also found. That was the rifle found on the ground, near a deer stand, where Christopher Pittman came in contact with the hunters. A lever-action rifle and some forty-five-caliber ammunition were found, as well as another box of forty-five-caliber ammunition, a box of twenty-two short ammunition, and an Old Timer's knife and sheath. They were all in the rear seat. Most of these items in the floorboard areas between the driver's seat and the seat that had been dropped in the back."

In addition to all the weapons found in the car, Black was able to identify a partial footwear impression located on the driver's door. When he got a shoe print from Christopher Pittman at the sheriff's office and compared it to the print, it matched in every way.

During that same week in November 2001, Black had

been successful in lifting fingerprints and a palm print off the .410 shotgun, in the area around the trigger. Believing this was the murder weapon, he had to get a court order for Christopher's prints. But when he compared the two, Bingo! Without a doubt, those were the fingerprints of Christopher Pittman on the .410 shotgun used to kill his grandparents.

Meadors asked Black, through a collection of evidence pictures, to identify what he had found from the arsenal of weapons and ammunition the day Christopher was found and the vehicle searched. He then brought in the one gun that silenced the courtroom and turned the air cold. It was the Remington .410 pump shotgun Christopher had used to kill his grandparents.

Holding the shotgun for the jury to see, Black told Meadors, "I was able to lift fingerprints off this gun, which turned out to be the right thumb of the defendant, his right and middle right ring finger." He then introduced the document that showed the comparison and match between the latent prints of Christopher Pittman with the inked prints on the gun.

After lunch, Lieutenant Ira Byrd Parnell, SLED, supervisor of the firearm and tool mark identification laboratory at SLED headquarters in Columbia, since 1987, testified for the prosecution. Solicitor Giese could have spent the rest of the evening reviewing Parnell's qualifications: thirty-two years in the field and qualified in all state and federal courts, he had testified about 850 times as an expert witness.

Standing in front of Parnell, Giese introduced the .410 shotgun into the court again. David Black had examined the .410 prior to bringing it into SLED headquarters. The firearms team then had secured it in the short-term holding area, known as the fire lock. Once Black finished examining the gun, it went straight to Parnell.

Parnell described the .410 to the jury, then told how

he had test-fired it with actual ammo he had gotten from Christopher Pittman's vehicle. He demonstrated how the gun would be loaded and how the gun would fire.

"It would hold a maximum of 4 two-and-a-half-or three-inch shells," Parnell explained to the jurors. "This is how the hammer falls and the gun fires, how you pull the slide, pull the fore-end back.

"It does nothing by itself," Parnell announced, which, of course, was Giese's reason for having him up there.

"But to fire it four times, you have to pump it how many times?

"Four times," Parnell answered.

"Four times?" Giese restated Parnell's words for the jury. "And each time you pump it, after the first one, you are ejecting the used shell?"

"Yes, sir. You are extracting and ejecting a fired cartridge case. And on the forward stroke, it releases one from the magazine tube and puts it into the chamber for the next shot."

"What if you don't pump it all the way up," Giese asked, "what happens then?"

"It won't fire."

Giese reminded the jurors that Parnell had tested this .410, and it was in good working order. The shells David Black had found at the crime scene were some of the same ones that Parnell had fired, and they were consistent with this gun.

On redirect, Giese had Parnell step down from the witness stand and demonstrate how the shotgun worked. Danielle, Christopher's sister, cried when she heard the sounds echo across the courtroom.

Click-clack, click.

Click-clack, click.

Click-clack, click.

Click-clack, click.

Giese's strategy worked. People sat straight up in their seats, wide-eyed and stunned at how penetrating the sounds had been.

In cross-examination, Mims surprisingly demonstrated he knew almost as much about guns and their operation as Parnell. Spectators then remembered Mims saying earlier that he had belonged to a hunting club. But what could he say that would defuse this situation?

Absolutely nothing.

On redirect, Giese had Parnell demonstrate what kind of force Christopher would have to have to fire the gun correctly. In a step-by-step fashion, Giese guided him through the motions: "Didn't take much force to pull that back, did it? Doesn't take a conscious thought to pull that back, right?"

Mims countered that Giese's exhibition wasn't really an accurate demonstration, since there was no recoil in the barrel. He made a valid point when he said to Parnell, "What I'm really saying is, you didn't shoot the gun. It acts a little differently when you shoot it, doesn't it?"

"It's not the same sensation as firing a gun," Parnell admitted.

Mims had won the point of argument, but it was a moot point.

Just as it appeared that a bond had been finally worked out for Christopher, the defense hit another snag. The insurance company guaranteeing the bond was not able to secure an original copy of their insurance certificate. It was a technicality, but the proof of insurance could not be a faxed copy. Until the bondsman could drive to Columbia and hand deliver the original copy, Christopher could not be released.

A phone call was made to Michael Smith, who was waiting for Christopher at the juvenile justice facility outside of Charleston. Smith was told Christopher's bond would have to wait another day.

CHAPTER 32

Thursday morning was rainy and cold, but the courtroom was still packed. Filling the courtroom were a lot of familiar faces, but there were also a lot of people who looked as if they were from drug companies and there in incognito. The question on everyone's mind, especially the drug companies: was the defense going to stave off the prosecution's case long enough to convince the jury that Christopher Pittman did not know right from wrong because of the effects of his medication? If that was to happen, more than likely, there would be an avalanche of lawsuits against the drug manufacturers, and they would be blamed for hundreds of acts of violence, suicide, or aggression.

As John Meadors walked into the courtroom, he pulled two Styrofoam heads out from underneath his arms. They were both numbered: 197 was Joe Pittman and 196 was Joy Pittman. In addition to the heads, he carried a set of blueprints from the Pittmans' house.

Major James McNeil was called as the state's first witness and asked to describe the events of the Pittman fire fatality and the investigation in Cherokee County. McNeil had supervised the investigation from beginning to end, and he was there when Christopher confessed.

"When Agent Williams came out and advised us that

he and Detective McKellar had obtained a statement from Christopher Pittman, I called our solicitor's office and spoke with assistant solicitor Michael Hemlepp. I advised him of Christopher's statement and he informed me to bring him back to Chester, where he could be transported to the Department of Juvenile Justice.

"Agent Andy Weir, Lucinda McKellar, Christopher Pittman, and me all got in Weir's vehicle and came back to Chester. Agent McKellar and Christopher sat in the backseat. During the forty-five minute drive, from the Cherokee County Sheriff's Department to Chester, he didn't say a word. He was relaxed, he may have went to sleep, but he appeared to be okay. Rick Wesley, who is employed with the Department of Juvenile Justice, met with him and did an intake on him. I was informed by my boss, Sheriff Robby Benson, that family members and his father were going to see him. I was in the sheriff's personal office, when Christopher saw his father. His father hugged him and told him he loved him. But Christopher just stood there, he didn't hug back, he didn't move. He just stood straight up, with no emotion."

On cross-examination, Hank Mims recognized McNeil's long length of service in law enforcement and the top-notch training he had received, especially in answer to powers of observation. "Major McNeil, can you tell the jury what somebody looks like and talks like and acts like under the influence of Zoloft?"

"No, sir, I can't."

"What?" Mims feigned a surprised look.

"No, sir, I don't know what that looks like."

Dr. Joel Sexton was the director of pathology for the Newberry County Hospital and served as a consulting forensic pathologist for approximately thirty of the county coroners in the state of South Carolina. A graduate of the University of Virginia and the USC Medical School, Sexton had been doing his kind of work since

1968. Board-certified in anatomic pathology, clinical pathology, and forensic pathology, he had testified as a forensic pathologist over seven hundred times.

Sexton told the jury he had received a call from the Chester County coroner Carter Wright about the Pittman bodies. He requested that the bodies be transported to him just as they had been found, so he could examine them in that context, photograph the bodies, examine the external surface and look for evidence, rephotograph the bodies after they were cleaned up, and then do a complete internal and external examination. In addition, they would collect body fluids and portions of each organ to study with the microscope. They also would take X-rays to see if there was anything that would not be easily recognized by just observing externally.

Sexton wasted no time in getting to the gory parts of his job.

"Joy Pittman was lying on her right side, almost facedown, but more on her right side, along with what I refer to as the right side of the bed. If you are lying in the bed, the portion to the right is what I consider the right side of the bed, so she was on that side of the bed.

"Joe Pittman was lying perpendicularly across the bed, closer to the foot of the bed, with his legs off the bed. He was laying on his back. There was significant burning of the bodies. In the case of Joe, the front of his body was burned to where you could see the internal organs. There was spared skin on the back of the body, which is what you would expect, since oxygen couldn't get to the back of the body because it was against the springs.

"In Joy's case, the burning was primarily on her back and on her left side, with the right side preserved.

"We did identify injuries that were much easier recognized by X-rays than they were by physically looking at the body because of the charring that was present in some areas, including the area of the injury. We did that first external exam outside, and then we carried them inside and we did the X-rays and the rest of the examination. We discovered with the X-rays, there was birdshot in the heads of the victims. In the case of Joy, the birdshot entered a hole to the left side of the back of her head and the pellets were primarily in the front of the brain internally.

"In Joe's case, they entered from the front through the mouth. The X-ray showed that there [were] some broken teeth in the front, but there were no individual pellets in the front of the skull. All the pellets went in through the mouth and into the back of the brain.

"Some of the shotgun shells have a plastic wad with the little leaflets that protect the pellets as they go down the barrel, so they don't get flattened and so they can fully expand truer and give a tighter pattern. That particular type of plastic wad will open up after it comes out of the shotgun, and sometimes it will enter the body. Sometimes it will be trapped on the outside. And in this case, it was in the mouth.

"So he had a shotgun wadding inside the mouth and the pellets in the back of his skull. She had a shotgun wound to the back of her head with the pellets in the front of the brain."

"But when were they killed?" Giese asked.

"When we examine people that are in fires, there are two things that we see if they are alive in the fire. One is black soot in the airway, where they have breathed in soot. Unless the fire is so intense and there is no soot or no smoke, then we just see the effects of the flame in the airway. In this case, neither of those were present. There was no burning of the vocal cords or changes in the airway, and there was no soot present.

"The other thing is in a person that is in a fire—particularly most fires are smoky and the smoke gets to the person while they are asleep before the fire does, and they die of carbon monoxide poisoning, which is a very rapid fatal type of poisoning from gas. And, normally, it is colorless, odorless, and tasteless. Of course, in a fire, the smoke has a color and an odor and a taste. But these people often die from the smoke before the fire gets to them while they are sleeping. So we will see changes of carbon monoxide poisoning, bright red blood particularly in the areas where the blood has settled, but none of that was present. So the indications were that both Joe and Joy Pittman were dead before the fire."

Giese handed Dr. Sexton not only copies of the X-rays, but also the plastic wad and a vial of the birdshot that had been retrieved from Joe Pittman—the wad being in his mouth and the birdshot being the ones in his brain. In one X-ray, Sexton had counted there were ninety-one pellets present in Joe's brain.

Giese showed copies of the X-rays to the jurors and had Dr. Sexton point out the injuries on Joe and Joy Pittman's bodies. Jurors winced as Sexton pointed out Joe's broken teeth, his skull fracture, and the path of the birdshot through the brain, all a result of the gunshot wound at the hands of his grandson.

"Dr. Sexton, did any of them exit the skull?"

"No, birdshot rarely ever exit. And in this case, you can see the skull's fracture and there are a few that are out between the skin and the skull, but there were no exit holes.

"The fact that it went into the mouth and only fractured a few teeth strongly suggests the mouth may have been open because the wadding was trapped in the mouth. So the wadding hit something to slow it down, like the teeth, and some of the pellets did as well. But there were no individual pellets in the front of the skull, embedded in front of the skull. So the blast was close enough to be tightly together and all the pellets went inside. I can't say his mouth was definitely open, but it suggested that it may have been partially open or wide open."

Dr. Sexton suspected the distance between the muzzle of the gun and Joe being shot—and for it to go into his mouth like it did—had to be between three and six feet. Giese had the doctor hold the gun to his shoulder, point it at the Styrofoam heads, and demonstrate that distance, as part of a visual effect.

Giese then showed jurors the X-ray of Joy's skull and the point of entry at the back and to the left side of the head. There were seventy-four pellets found in Joy's skull. Sexton noted that some of the skull when they received the body was missing due to the fire, and that some of the pellets had probably fallen out.

"It doesn't require the pellets," Sexton said. "The shock wave from the blast alone was enough to disturb the brain to render them unconscious and not salvage or not be able to revive them. But certainly the damage caused by the pellets would have intensified that. But, yes, both would have been immediately unconscious and both would have died in a very brief time. In fact, because of the evidence we saw at the time of autopsy, we believed they both died before the fire."

Giese had Sexton demonstrate the blasts from the shotgun on the mannequins' heads. Sexton showed how the pellets entered through the mouth, traveled straight to the rear, then spread out like billiard balls on a billiard table when struck by a breaking cue ball. "Unlike buckshot," he told the jurors, "birdshot is light enough that they remain in the brain, impacting a large force to the part of the brain where they lodge."

When Sexton was passed over to the defense, there were no questions they wanted to ask him. The defense wisely chose not to get into the details of the murders with Dr. Sexton.

"Your Honor," Giese announced, "we have no more witnesses to offer."

At this point, Vickery moved for a direct verdict of not guilty, saying malice aforethought had not been proved. On counterargument, Meadors said the shotgun proved malice aforethought, and that Christopher's own words of "they deserved it" also proved it. The judge agreed with the prosecution.

Vickery also asked that the court remand this case to Family Court, based on the fact that Christopher had a propensity for violence, but the judge denied this motion as well.

Before the start of the defendant's case, Judge Pieper always made it a habit to advise the defendant of his rights. He asked Christopher to come forward and then explained to him he had the right to testify in his own behalf.

"We will reserve that decision until a later point in the trial," Vickery responded on Christopher's behalf.

Pieper again addressed the issue of Christopher's bond with Michael Smith, who was handling the satellite monitoring of this case, and the bondsman who had supplied the bond. Smith was happy to report all the paperwork had been delivered and approved.

Pieper nodded toward the defense table, then boomed out his instructions. "The defendant is subject to house arrest after trial each day. He will remain under the supervision of the sheriff's department. During the court proceeding each day, the defendant must report to court by eight o'clock each morning. That is when the sheriff will take the custody over for the defendant. I did authorize the defendant to have access to his attorneys in their designated workroom during lunch each day. I wish for the address to be provided to the court and to the sheriff's department in writing. But, as of today, I see no reason why the defendant's bail can not be granted."

Christopher broke out in a wide grin, then turned around and smiled at his sister and relatives. Finally, after four years, he was about to taste freedom again.

CHAPTER 33

In jump-starting their case, the defense called Chris
Snelgrove, the pastor of New Hope United Methodist
Church, to the witness stand. Snelgrove was one of the
rare people who saw Christopher before he started antidepressants and after he took antidepressants.

Snelgrove described Christopher as a shy person with
a loving demeanor. He said he was actually one of the
top five outstanding young men he had met in his lifetime. But after Snelgrove saw Christopher when he came
to live with his grandfather, he had to put his hand on
him to calm him in church. He said there was now a big
difference.

The stocky, dark-haired, and bearded Snelgrove was
well-spoken, articulate, and came off as very sincere. It
was a great way for the defense to begin their case. Snelgrove was not only a strong and compelling witness to
show the before-and-after of the Zoloft, but he could tie
in the dates when Christopher was taking Zoloft and
wasn't taking it. His testimony conveyed to the jury that
one could clearly see but for Zoloft we'd be dealing with
a different individual, and Joe and Joy Pittman's deaths
would never have occurred. It was here, the defense was
going to find their reasonable doubt.

In preparing the groundwork for the defense experts

that would follow, Snelgrove told the jury, "No one in the church was aware that Christopher was on Zoloft, but I recognized there was a profound difference in his behavior and his demeanor over this young man I had known for three years, and who had stayed in my home.

"Prior to November 2001, Christopher didn't have any problems sitting still in church. But in November, he did. That was about the same time Christopher was arrested for the murders of his grandparents.

"It has been incredibly difficult in my role as pastor of New Hope Methodist Church in Chester to deal with the impact of their death (the Pittmans') on our parishioners," Snelgrove added. "People have struggled with the things that have happened."

"Did you ever have any concerns or fears or reservations about him being in your home?" Vickery asked.

"No, sir, not at all," the preacher said without hesitation.

"Would you have them today?"

"No, sir, not at all."

"You would take him into your home today?"

"Today," Snelgrove said with great emphasis.

Psychiatrist James Ballenger was a tall, strapping man with white-flecked hair and a beard. He was tall, trim, and tanned, and could easily pass as the captain of some gloriously named fishing vessel on the high seas in the North Atlantic. In March 2004, John Justice had requested permission from the court for him to interview Christopher Pittman. The former director of psychiatry at the Medical University of South Carolina, Ballenger had written thirteen books, four hundred papers, and was one of the leading worldwide authoritative experts in psychopharmacology. The defense had gambled and named Ballenger as one of their witnesses, even though he had been hired by the prosecution to evaluate Christopher—but he would become their worst nightmare.

Vickery began his direct examination of Ballenger

with a discussion of dysthymia and the medication SSRIs, and mania and psychosis with hallucinations. It was obvious that Vickery was attempting to fit Christopher's round peg into a square hole, by saying that Christopher had an SSRI-triggered mania and how it was responsible for his violence.

In direct examination, Vickery asked Ballenger, "Have you ever seen a case, in which your opinion, your professional opinion, a person's criminal responsibility for an assault against someone else should be mitigated or reduced because of SSRI-induced mania?"

Ballenger was very alert and did not hesitate in responding. "I have not seen it in as complex over-time type of crime as we are talking about in this case."

Vickery reminded Ballenger of a case involving Sergeant Bruce Orr. Ballenger had been asked some time ago to evaluate Orr and render an opinion for the benefit of the judge who was attempting to rule on his crime, attempted assault against his ex-wife. It was Ballenger's opinion that the impulsive actions Orr took with his truck and driving it into his former wife's house, that that type of violence was consistent with the fact he had a bipolar manic-depressive illness.

"And at that time, there was lots of other corroborative evidence that Bruce Orr, in fact, was manic at the time," Ballenger said in his defense. "And I did render the opinion that that should be a mitigating factor. But I did it in the form of a report back to the judge."

Giese objected, "We are not trying Sergeant Orr's case. The question as to whether or not he has given that opinion, the answer was yes. He has to move on."

The judge asked Vickery why he needed to go into the details of Orr's case.

"What I have to persuade this jury on, Your Honor, in order to defend my client is that perfectly good people, that are good upstanding citizens, can be caused to do violent things by these drugs. This is a man that was a highly decorated police sergeant in Charleston."

Under those circumstances, Vickery was allowed to continue. He refreshed Dr. Ballenger's recollection about whether he had someone who was a perfectly law-abiding citizen who became manic and assaultive because of SSRI drugs.

On cross-examination, Giese downplayed the case, then used Dr. Ballenger's testimony to annihilate the defense.

"Dr. Ballenger, I know you have just been testifying for thirty minutes. The last fifteen apparently were on some case that you were on some time ago, is that correct?"

"That's true." Ballenger smiled.

"And, in fact, that case has nothing to do with the case we are here today on, is that true?"

"I wouldn't say it has nothing to do with it. I see why counsel brought it up. I think it is extremely different from this case." Ballenger took the time to inform the jury all about the other case and why it was different from this one, then moved forward to Christopher's case. "I don't think there is any evidence that is credible that Christopher Pittman was ever manic, stated simply, in that all of the records . . . there is by six, seven, eight examiners, there is no evidence of mania."

Giese asked Ballenger to explain further.

"When I examined Christopher," Ballenger said in a solemn voice, "what he told me about his symptoms was not credible to me. It sounded like a very upset and excited young man. I mean, the one symptom he had was that his thoughts were going fast. Well, I can well imagine his thoughts were going fast in such an incredible situation, but none of the other symptoms were there."

"Doctor, what is your expert opinion in relation to Christopher Pittman's mania?" Giese asked.

"My expert opinion is there was no mania."

"How about psychosis?"

"The same thing. I don't think there was any psychosis. There was definitely no delusions. I haven't heard any of that anywhere. And I don't think that this few minutes of hallucinations saying, 'Kill them,' 'Don't kill them, leave,' I don't think they were hallucinations."

Ballenger testified that he had interviewed Christopher Pittman twice. Christopher's original lawyer, Yale Zamore, was present during the interviews, as well as their expert, Dr. Lanette Atkins.

"I know Christopher wasn't manic before when he was in Lifestream Hospital, when he saw Dr. Naumann, or when he went to school. The way Christopher described it to me right up to the event, he wasn't manic. My opinion, he wasn't manic during the event. And then there is a great deal of agreement by experienced examiners all with different roles. His doctor at DJJ, or the doctor at the Hall Institute that was treating him, or the forensic examiner, all of them with different roles, they all found the same thing. There was no evidence of mania, at all."

Ballenger expounded further on his conclusions. Jurors sat on the edge of their seats, once again, and started taking notes.

"I believe this case was planned out. It was not committed in a depressive, hopeless fit. Christopher then planned his escape and planned his alibi. He was calm, cool, and collected, more or less. And I say 'more or less,' because he wasn't calm, cool, and collected when the hunters talked to him. But by the time the police get to him there and by the time hours passed, he was calm, cool, and collected.

"When Dr. Sharman saw him at DJJ and a psychologist was assigned to treat him, his description, a day later, was that at the interview that Christopher Pittman was quiet, calm, a low monotone. Not excited—didn't need to talk about the event—distinctly not manic. Even the non–mental-health people who saw him—Agent McKellar said that he told her that Zoloft made him sleepy, as opposed to the hypothesis that it made him manic and active. He told her that it made him sleepy and that it had done that before."

"What else can you tell us about Christopher the day after the murders?" Giese asked Ballenger to tell the jurors.

"The other major issue is the time course of all this. What happened that night is really unclear to me because Christopher had told me two different stories. One that he watched television quietly with his granddad, had a good time, did his homework, and went to church. And then the other story that he was confined to his room from three-thirty to eleven-thirty P.M., he came out and his grandfather beat him. I don't know which of those is true. But the story he told me was that he did his homework. He was upset initially with his grandfather telling him he would have to go back to his father, but he calmed down about that and they had a quiet time watching television until his granddad said, 'I'm sleepy, I think I'll go to bed.' And then, after Christopher was in bed, that is when he says voices started telling him to go upstairs and kill his grandparents.

"That sort of time, and then the event and then leaving, and if you pause it there, from when he laid down in the bed to sometime the next day when people saw him and said, 'There is no mania here.' The police who saw him said that. And that would be the shortest manic episode I've ever heard of. It doesn't happen like that— it just doesn't. More realistically or sort of hypothesizing since he told me that, I don't think they were hallucinations at all. But that they lasted for the few minutes in bed as he went upstairs, and as soon as he did the action, they stopped.

"My sense of that night is that the episode was a tenor- fifteen-minute time course. I don't know that for sure, because I haven't heard testimony about that. But it was short. And then he told me there was one other voice that told him to leave. Now, that would have been sometime after he collected the money and the guns and the truck and his dog, and those kind of things, and that would have been later. But we are still talking about half an hour, maybe forty-five minutes.

"If you are manic, you are not going to be well for six weeks, at least. Mania—in some analogies I have always used, have been it's a forest fire. You can't put out a forest fire in ten minutes. You have to dump a lot of water, or medicine, if you please. You have to do this for a long time, and you have to keep watering after the fire is out and the ground is smoking. So, it is a long process."

Giese kept the doctor's testimony flowing with direct questions, but Ballenger needed no encouragement to continue.

"I didn't see any evidence of mania, psychosis, or hallucinations. There are true hallucinations, and then there is actually a category in this book of pseudohallucinations, false hallucinations, hallucinations that are not really hallucinations. They are like when you have been walking down the street and you hear somebody call your name. It is not a hallucination. It just happens. And a classic example is when you look in a store shop window and you think you see somebody, but then it is gone.

"True hallucinations have tremendous diagnostic importance to us. If a patient tells me and convinces me they have a true hallucination, I almost don't need anything else, or whatever the DSM says, to tell me I have got a very serious problem. Hallucinations just don't happen except in a serious illness or when a person is on drugs.

"True hallucinations are classically where the person hears two people across the room talking about [him or her]. Again, that is across the room, two people talking about [him or her]. If it's not them, it's frightening, you know. They think somebody else is in the room. They do things. They leave the room. They try to get away from it. It is very, very frightening, if you think about it. It's two people talking about you, often arguing, calling you bad names. That is the classic hallucinations.

"I said to Christopher Pittman, 'Well, try to tell me about those hallucinations,' and he described them at first as echoes in his mind. And he had used that word with other examiners through his repeated exams through the time.

"But then I said, 'Well, tell me what that means.' And he said, 'Um.' I said, 'Was it your voice?' And he said, 'Yeah.' And I said, 'Do you think it could be your thoughts being loud in your mind?' He said, 'Yeah.' And I think that was, at this point, the explanation that he favored because he didn't know what they were, but that one seemed to make the most sense to him. And to me, too.

"The month before is also very pertinent right up to the time when he was seen in Lifestream just a day or two more than a month before. The doctors who saw him there diagnosed him as depressed and put in his note that Christopher agreed with him that he was depressed.

"Now, depression is the opposite of mania. The doctor didn't mention anything consistent with mania. Dr. Naumann did not, either. He describes specifically he was calm, not talking fast, no signs of mania. I don't know about school after that, but I don't think there is any evidence there.

"By Christopher's description of that night, it's inconsistent with a diagnosis of mania for him to quietly watch television with his grandfather, for him to do his homework, for him to go to church. Manics can't shut up. They couldn't possibly sit there and be quiet. They can't. I teach students that you can diagnose as mania from across the street. It's the person who's talking and will not stop and is using their hands, walking back and forth. That evidence is not present.

"Then in Christopher's description to me, he said that he did not have any more energy at that time. He said his thoughts were going fast. And I asked him— knowingly asked him a question—I said, 'Were those thoughts normal thoughts, or were they abnormal thoughts that were going so fast?' And that was the only time in the interview he choked. He couldn't, or he didn't know the answer, what it was supposed to be, in my opinion. And he never answered the question.

"The answer is they are normal thoughts, more or less, that are just coming at him very, very quickly.

"I asked him what his mood was and he said, 'Well, I was more or less like myself.' Now, manics would never say that. Anybody who has ever had an episode of mania would say, 'Whoa, it was incredible.' I mean, 'I had ideas of how to solve the world's food crisis and the Middle East crisis, and I wanted to go there, and I could do this. You know, I have called the president six times today to tell him about how to fix Social Security,' and so on and so on. They literally call the president. And he didn't have any of that grandiosity.

"I asked him if he had had any, and he smiled and said, 'I have always known that I could do things that other people couldn't do. I've always known that.'

"My impression is he is a very smart young man and that was a statement about that. But that was his mood statement, 'I was my normal self.'

"So essentially, he only gave me one symptom that is even consistent with mania and that was the thoughts were going fast. And if you think about a high-stress situation that you have been in, your thoughts, you know, they run pretty fast. So, I don't count that as a symptom of mania. And, of course, you would need many more if you are going to use this approach as well.

"Now, in the same sort of way, he drove off in the truck and testified to the police that he went to sleep during the night. A manic person probably would not have slept. That is not a conclusive difference, but probably not.

"When he got out of the truck walking around in the woods, he shot at a squirrel. Now, a manic person might have done that, but he had been trying to learn how to hunt squirrels. He had recently been squirrel hunting and couldn't hit any. It seems more logical that he was just squirrel hunting.

"But then when he was in custody, the most clear thing is that somebody who saw him twelve hours after the event, he tells Agent McKellar that Zoloft makes him sleepy. He was calm, cool, collected, quiet, not talking fast. That is the opposite of mania. When he goes a day after that to DJJ and Dr. Sharman, a mental-health professional sees him, he says he is quiet, low monotone, and that he looked down during the interview. He commented he was surprised he wasn't talking about the event, because events like this are traumatic to the person who does them, as well as to everybody else. And he said, 'He just doesn't seem to need to talk about that.' So, he's commenting that he's actually talking less than he would have expected.

"And then he's transferred to Hall Psychiatric Institute five or six days later, and the examiner, the child psychiatrists who see him there see absolutely no evidence, not only of mania, but not of depression. And like the doctor in Lifestream, just see support for conduct disorder-type diagnosis. The doctor at Lifestream diagnosed him as an oppositional defiant person.

"I believe he had something of a conduct disorder. It's kids who get into trouble at school, trouble at home, trouble with the police, again and again and again, and can't seem to stop it. Oppositional defiant disorder was the diagnosis Dr. Smith gave him initially, saying that he was generally defiant to authority in all forms, so that he gets in tremendous trouble at school and at home defying authority in all forms. And he gave some examples of him attacking his sister with a baseball bat, a series of items with a golf club, mooning a woman in his own hospital, throwing things in the Lifestream Hospital. He used that phrase conduct disorder.

"It is a very strong diagnosis to make after having met a young boy for a day or two, so he must have been pretty confident of it. So to sort of state that, there is no evidence that any of the examiners see of mania or any other major psychiatric disorder.

"What they see from Dr. Smith at Lifestream, a month before, to Dr. Ramsey in Hall Institute, five, six, seven days afterward, is only conduct disorder, not a major psychiatric disorder like mania or bipolar illness, even depression.

"Now, Dr. Smith said that he thought Christopher was depressed, and I think that was right, actually from the symptoms and the way he described it. The incidents with his sister, that was in Florida, prior to any SSRIs. Dr. Smith's history was before any SSRI, and he was describing this oppositional behavior, defiance of authority in all forms, attacking the sister we have discovered five or six times with a baseball bat, golf clubs. Dr. Smith is describing that history before he comes to Lifestream—remember, he ran away, and after threatening suicide with a hunting knife, [he went] to Lifestream. So, Dr. Smith is describing the history, some of the lifelong history of difficulty before he ever was placed on the SSRI the first time.

Finally Giese was able to sneak in a question between breaths. "So, Dr. Ballenger, is Christopher's hallucinations sort of like himself talking to himself?"

"Yeah, having a real struggle in his mind."

"Saying, 'Don't do it,' that type of thing, 'Leave'?"

"Yeah, and it made sense. True hallucinations don't make sense as these people are yelling and screaming and arguing about whether this person is a bad person and does bad things."

"And there was none of that in this case?"

"No."

"And psychosis is not the same thing as mania?"

"Absolutely not. Most manics never have any psychotic phenomenon. What we know about that is it is a severe form of mania; it's the worst form. We also know that in general it happens late in the course. So, if somebody gets manic and we can't get them out of it, and that does happen. Usually we use a lot of medicines and we can bring people down in the hospital and bring them out of the mania, but sometimes that is very, very hard to do."

Ballenger went through this list of troubles Christopher had prior to going to Lifestream and before any ingestion of SSRIs. "It really describes the behavioral op-positional, defiant of authority," Ballenger opined.

"Doctor, let me ask you this in regard to mania also," Giese asked. "There was a time, and I'm sure in your review of the file that after Christopher Pittman was found by the hunters, he gave a story at that time that someone else had killed the grandparents and that someone else had kidnapped him and driven him to the woods there. Is that consistent with no mania, or what is that specifically?"

"I think that is a well-thought-through alibi. A manic wouldn't feel the need for an alibi. A manic would just be above it and roaring on and doing whatever they do. They wouldn't even notice what they have done in their wake.

"In fact, the story that he gave to me is evidence that there was not mania and there was a mind that was think-ing and knew right from wrong. And because the alibi, not only in choosing a black man as the alleged person who did it, but he covers all of the details that needed to be covered. I mean, he says that the black man used a shotgun, that he told him to get the dog, so there wouldn't be a barking dog left behind. Christopher had to explain those things because he had the dog with him. He had the shotgun. And in that story, he said that the black man burned the house to cover the evidence.

"So, it was a very extensive story that covered all of the details that needed to be covered, one that he knew would need to be covered when he was discovered.

"Now, a psychotic person wouldn't really be even close to being able to do that. A manic person, you know, they still have their wits about them. But as I said, they gener-ally wouldn't. They would just be talking about other things and talking a mile a minute. And so I think it is very, very inconsistent even with mania.

"Obviously, suicide and murder are not the same thing. They are very different, obviously, on its face. Let me also remind you that the overwhelming number of people who have suicidal thoughts never hurt anybody except themselves. The overwhelming percentage of people who hurt other people never commit suicide. The biology of these two groups are related in that people who are suicidal and particularly violently suicidal have low serotonin in their brain. That is why the field has been so pleased with the advent of the SSRIs because what they do is raise serotonin in the brain. And so the reason we are pretty convinced the number of suicides in the world have gone down greatly. With the onset of the SSRIs, for the first time in history, suicide has started going down. In fifteen Western countries, the rate has fallen a third. So it is wonderful, a third less people killing themselves."

Giese asked Ballenger was he ever asked to look into and render an opinion as to whether or not Christopher was not guilty by reason of insanity?

"He didn't describe in any way to me or anybody else that his thinking was right. There is no evidence that he wasn't thinking correctly. There was lots of evidence that he knew what he had done was wrong. From the very beginning, I think he did it because he was very mad, very angry. Even the voices in his head said, 'Do it; don't do it; do it; don't do it.' And then he told me he stood in their bedroom with a loaded gun, arguing with himself.

"And he told me and others, many others, that the reason he set these elaborate fuses to burn the house down—but not burn it down until he was down the road—was because he thought a blaze would be a bad thing for him getting away. And so he set, which I thought was remarkably clever for a twelve-year-old, lighter fluid and paper so that it would burn down and then start a fire after he was gone. It is another example that clearly he knew he needed to cover the crime.

"He tells me he knew right from wrong. He absolutely knew it was wrong. He fled for the same reason. He lied to the hunters and made up this story about a black man doing this. You don't do that unless you think you have got to cover something up. His comment to one of the first officers was, in explaining why he changed his story from 'a black man did it' to 'I did it' was he said, 'I knew I would get in trouble and that you would maybe send me back to my father, which I really don't want to do. That is why I told you that story because I thought I would get in trouble.' That was his initial story, the switch that set it in motion.

"What he told me and other people about whether he is sorry he did it, whether he is remorseful about it? He tells me he knows it's wrong. He had told a series of things. Initially he said they deserved it. 'Well, they deserved it.' That means he knows that what he did has to have a justification or rationale. 'They deserved it, they had it coming.' He had subsequently, at times, been remorseful and cried about it. That tells me he knows that it's wrong, that he should feel bad about it. Paradoxically, his bragging about it, taking a newspaper article around on the wards at Hall Institute and bragging about it, tells me he knows it's something that makes him, he thinks, a bigger and tougher guy.

"This was a well-thought-out, well-planned escape, especially him bragging about it afterward. Also, the alibi, the fire, stealing the car, taking money, and putting five guns in his car afterward—that was all part of it."

"Dr. Ballenger, you have an opinion as to why he did this, is that right?"

"Yes, I do."

"Tell the jury what that is," Giese said.

"I have been a teacher for many, many years; teaching young psychiatrists and medical students about psychiatry. If a resident came and presented the story that I'm going to tell you, in a minute, to me, I would say, 'That's awful, and I understand why it happened,' and wouldn't invoke Zoloft, at all, except that somebody was trying to treat him to try to make a difference as they went along.

"But if you think about Christopher's early life, his mother abandoned him at birth. His father was in the military and gone most of the time, and he shuffled back and forth to multiple households. He told me that he felt horrible that he didn't have a mother. He told Dr. Sharman in great depth that the other kids had mothers, how come he didn't have a mother? It was embarrassing. He was humiliated. And his household was apparently—with lots and lots of evidence from all the records—a very critical household. He described his father as a drill sergeant, that if he didn't make all A's, then he had to do push-ups. And if he wasn't doing enough push-ups and he let down, his father would paddle, him with a belt, paddle, or a two-by-four.

"But his father was gone, and it was different parenting. His mother shows back up miraculously three months before this happened, comes back by herself, sets up in a mobile home, and says, 'I'm back.' He said his heart soared. It was wonderful. She started playing with him. He went over there, she and his sister. It was just fantastic. She talked to him about 'we're going to have a house, I'm getting back together with your father. I'm going to get you a car when you're old enough.' It was just wonderful. And then one day, a couple weeks later, he went over there and she said, 'Don't get out of the car; you can't come in the house; you can never see me again.' He told me that it was horrible.

"Now, he didn't want to talk about that, couldn't talk about that. It was the worst thing. It was even worse than the original abandonment. He had fights with his father and ran away from his father. In his mind, he absolutely couldn't live with his father. He sees his father as very abusive; he was afraid of him. So he walked to South Carolina. Now, he only got fifteen miles. He stole seventy dollars from his sister and started walking to South Carolina.

"When they finally figured out he was missing, the father got the police and they found him in a truck stop playing a video game and brought him back. In that context, his father went outside to see what he would do, heard him saying to his sister that he was going to take a hunting knife and stick himself in the stomach. His father ran in and they hospitalized him at Lifestream. And then that's when Dr. Smith took the history that I referred to earlier, put him on Paxil, then started treating him.

"His father came to Lifestream and says, 'You're coming home with me,' and he screamed and yelled, 'I'm not coming home with you. I will kill myself, if you make me come home with you.'

"Lifestream commented that there are big-time problems in this family, that they need a lot of work in figuring out who is [sic] the parents and what's the discipline going to be. They needed a lot of work.

"But in that context, a legal father can definitely take his son out of the hospital, and he did. He took him to Florida and the Pittmans came, one or two days later, got him and took him to Chester.

"Dr. Smith was right, Christopher was depressed. He put him on Paxil because he had all the risk factors for behavioral problems: bullying, truancy, lying, beatings, destroying other's property. In him, it had started a long time ago and sadly culminated with him burning his life down.

"Dr. Sharman has been working with Christopher to establish a relationship for a long time. He comments that it's very hard to establish a relationship with him and that he had almost no bond with his family, none. He did a lot of work trying to generate some connection to Christopher.

"Dr. Sharman did also say that Christopher said, 'I don't care about my father. I don't want to be there,' but he would also write him. So he had the kind of conflicts that you would expect a young person to have some of the time.

"But then Christopher gets in trouble on the bus and chokes a kid. When Dr. Sharman asked him about the event, Christopher said it started going bad when his grandparents started acting like his father, started being stern, rejecting, calling him a loser, and telling him that he would never be able to be a success.

"And he tells me he started getting paddled. I don't

know whether that is true or not. Apparently, Christopher didn't like corporal punishment. His father clearly did, but Christopher, no.

"But Christopher thought his grandparents were rejecting him, especially when the grandmother said, 'You've been kicked off riding the bus. I can't take you to school every day. I have a volunteer job, which I love. I can't do that. We are going to have to send you back to your father or the DJJ.'

"Christopher said they went to church, and he was misbehaving at church. And the grandfather took him outside and told him he was going to send him back to his father.

"Christopher apparently believed that. Whether it was true or not, I don't know. It might have been an attempt to scare him. But after that, either whether he was locked into his room and beat when he came out or not, after that, Christopher was furious. He was absolutely incredibly mad and decided to murder his grandparents.

"In Christopher's words, 'I decided to do away with them.' Christopher says in his story that when he was being paddled after coming out of his room after six or seven hours to get a drink of water, he said that he tried to get his shotgun when his grandfather was beating him. But either way, when the grandmother went to bed, I think the more credible story is he was furious.

"Now he tried to tell me that he was fine, watched television, everything was okay. And then out of the blue when he lay in bed, he suddenly was manic and hallucinating. But I don't find that, at all, credible. I think he was furious at this grandfather and grandmother. He told me he got up and loaded the gun, jacked it so he could put the fourth shell in, so he knew about the gun to know that one way it would just take three shells, and he needed to put the fourth in. He went out and told me that he fired the first shot at his grandfather from across the room. And then he set the fuses and burned the house down.

"For me, I don't know if you are familiar with the phrase of burning the house down around yourself, but it seemed up to me a sad graphic description of what actually happened. He was killing, as he said, the only people—the best people in the world that loved him. The most reliable people, I think, at least in his mind. Christopher couldn't go back to his father. He had a difficult relationship with him and his sister. His other grandmother is not as close. So, he burned everything down to the ground around him."

Giese was more than pleased with Dr. Ballenger's testimony. It had put everything neatly into perspective for the jury.

"Just one more question, Dr. Ballenger. Is it your expert testimony as to Christopher Pittman's mental status on the night that he killed his grandparents, that legally he knew the difference between right and wrong?"

"Yes."

Giese wanted the jury to know exactly what Ballenger meant. "Legal right and legal wrong, and moral right and moral wrong?"

"Yes, on both counts," Ballenger answered.

CHAPTER 34

Thursday's court day seemed like the longest day in Christopher's short life. Finally, after Dr. Ballenger's testimony, the jury was dismissed and Christopher was released on bond.

Dressed in a long brown trench coat, hanging loosely over his brown prison-issued clothing, Christopher stood in the midst of the dimly lit hall with two uniformed guards and waited on his family. They had rented a home on the Isle of Palms, one of the barrier islands surrounding Charleston. The ocean was only six hundred feet away from the home, and he could almost see it in his mind. Christopher told the guards they were going to eat a lot of pizza and celebrate Christmas and his past birthdays. He beamed. "They're going to give me presents," he said with glee in his voice.

Hank Mims stood by like a proud father. He watched with triumph in his tired eyes as Christopher's family walked with him outside the DJJ holding facility. As they approached the large brick columns, Danielle Pittman kissed her hand and then touched Christopher's cheek. His aunt, his sister, his grandmother, and his stepgrandfather were all smiles as the two deputies escorted him down the walk, then released him to a waiting white Blazer.

Hank Mims said good-bye, and Christopher got in the

backseat between his grandmother and Danielle. Everyone was in a state of continual excitement at his being released. Mims walked toward the car again and looked all around, as if he—the fairy godfather who had helped to make it all happen—could now rest.

Mims stood beside the guards and watched as the Pittmans pulled away. The last they saw was Danielle kissing Christopher, laughing, nodding, and shaking. Sadly, Mims knew it would all be bittersweet and come to an abrupt end if Christopher was found guilty.

Christopher was beside himself. The electronic bracelet around his ankle enabled him to stay with his family, but it also reminded him of how short-lived his visit could be. He knew how the bracelet worked: if he passed certain defined perimeters beyond the beach house, a signal rushed from the bracelet, back inside the house, and into a black transmitter box. The box (he had named it "Phillip" after his half brother who had not been able to attend the trial) alerted the police, who would then come and arrest him. The next day, the judge would revoke his bond and end his long-awaited beach vacation.

Christopher and Danielle talked a lot their first night. While they listened to Christian music, played games, and watched movies, Del Duprey sat quietly and enjoyed her two grandchildren catching up on old times. It was fun just watching them be kids again. For supper, they ordered four pizzas from Domino's. Christopher claimed he ate only five slices, but his family insisted he had eaten a pizza-and a-half, not to mention a MoonPie, a half-dozen cinnamon rolls, a bowl of cereal, and had drunk several cups of hot chocolate. After supper, instead of his routine three-minute shower back at DJJ, he relaxed for an hour in a tub of hot water.

Christopher prayed the night would never end. Like Bill Murray's character Phil in the movie *Groundhog Day*, he wished he could relive those same events—over and over again—until he finally got it right. He and Danielle stayed up talking that Friday morning until about 1:15 A.M. When she nodded off, he shook her until she finally opened her eyes. Not wanting to be apart on their first night together, they continued talking until they both fell asleep in the same bed.

Despite having slept only five hours, Chris walked into the courtroom Friday morning looking refreshed. When Jason Cato asked Christopher how he felt, not surprisingly, he said, "I just feel better . . . happier. I don't feel tired at all."

The first witness of the day was an old friend of Christopher's.

Bill Inmon lived in Mount Dora, Florida, had a master's in criminology, and worked at Florida's Department of Juvenile Justice in a research program that examined the transferring of juveniles into the adult system. Inmon didn't know anything about serotonin or SSRIs, but he knew something about Christopher Pittman. He had known Christopher's father since the fall of 1978, and he knew the grandparents Joe and Joy Pittman.

Inmon was Christopher's Cub Scout leader, Den 3, Pack 72. He had been on many campouts with Christopher, participated in archery and BB competitions with him. Christopher, he said, was always well-behaved.

"I don't know of any problems that Christopher had in Florida before he came to live with his grandparents in South Carolina," Inmon testified, "or any problems he had in school or with police or law enforcement. I'm in direct contact with his father, at least, three to four times a week, via telephone or face-to-face and have been that way since we entered high school. I am very close friends with his dad and was with his grandparents. I've always seen Christopher as very meek, very mild, and very respectful. He has always been very respectful to authority. It is my experience that he did not have a lifelong history of difficulties and I was very surprised to hear what occurred in Chester. I am absolutely shocked, I could not believe it. It was not the child that I knew and that had grown up around me. And to this day, I have a hard time believing the Christopher Pittman that I know could do something like this. He never caused any problems in Den three and Pack seventy-two, and was always the most well-mannered, 'yes, sir/no, sir' kid."

Dr. David Healy followed Inmon to the stand. The fifty-one-year old Healy had begun his training twenty-five years ago, specializing in the treatment of people with a wide range of problems, including children and people who were anxious or depressed, and people who have schizophrenia. In his practice, he had used all of the drugs available on the market, including the SSRI group of drugs.

Healy had been called as an expert witness by Vickery, who stated that the doctor had had access to the full clinical trial data of Pfizer studying this drug in juveniles. His opinion would rest on that foundation, plus a ton of different peer-review writings of his own, commenting on other peer-review journal articles. Healy told the court he had written review articles on his own on these issues, and his methodologies had been reviewed in a peer-review context in that he regularly lectured. He had also been hired to do the reporting by Pfizer and had testified in front of the FDA advisory panel on these very issues.

The motion was made by Meadors for Vickery to proffer Healy's testimony so that the judge might make a decision as to what his scientific method was based on.

Healy told the judge how he had lived in Ireland before moving to the University of Cambridge. He supposedly began working on this group of antidepressant drugs before anyone really had heard about them. The research he was doing during the early 1980s was on what do drugs like this do to the serotonin system in people who are actually depressed. Healy became secretary to a group called the British Association for Psychopharmacology, and held an equivalent Ph.D., was a psychiatrist as well as a neuropharmacologist.

Healy also said he had written fifteen books. Of them, *The Creation of Psychopharmacology* and *The Antidepressant Era* were published by Harvard Press. He also had completed approximately 130 peer-reviewed articles, and written a further 50 book chapters and 150 different kinds of articles. Six to eight of those, he claimed, dealt with antidepressants and violence toward self or others, and the things that led to them.

"The three antecedent conditions that are most suspect in your mind are the very three that Dr. Ballenger said are caused by Zoloft, which are akathisia, emotional blunting, and psychotic decompensation. The argument is that just those three may lead to people actually killing themselves or doing harm to the other people with whom they live or elsewhere."

Healy said he based his opinion on reviewing clinical trial data. He had done a crossover study on using Zoloft, where several volunteers had become suicidal and one of them became violent. He was going to say Zoloft causes children to become homicidal and aggressive. He also was going to say it can cause murder, too. He had written a book on that subject, entitled, *Let Them Eat Prozac*, which centered on antidepressants and suicide.

On direct examination, Vickery had Healy go through the history of neuropsychopharmacology and define the word "akathisia" as restless. Healy used the *Diagnostic Statistical Manual IV (DSM-IV)* to support his definition and his theory that SSRI drugs also triggered akathisia.

On cross-examination, Meadors got Dr. Healy to admit he hadn't read the testimonies of the two hunters who found Christopher the day after the murder, but had relied more heavily on defense expert Dr. Atkins's report.

"A lot of your opinion, Doctor, is based on what she said. You were very impressed with her report?"

Healy said that he was, and why. Part of his answer included: "She came to this case as a person believing the drugs didn't cause a problem and they ended up being traced with the clinical features in the case and changing her mind and thinking that the drug had played a big role. That was extremely impressive, yes."

"Why did you say all of that just then?" Meadors growled. "I didn't ask you about how she came in. You put lot of stock in her report? You think it is a great report, don't you?"

"No, no, Mr. Meadors, let's be quite clear," Healy disagreed. "It could well be that she, as a person, had offered the view that the drug had actually caused the problem, and I wouldn't agree with her at all. One of the issues as an expert in these issues generally—as opposed to his case actually in particular—that I deal with is, I look at the particular time frame of the issues, when did this actually happen; had there been any link to change in dosage and things like that; is it consistent with what we know from the clinical trial literature. Based on things like that, I can make up my mind that there is an issue here that needs to be looked at.

"On the specific issue, just like you, I'm going to go beyond that and say if I'm going to get involved in this case, it isn't just whether I think the drug can cause a problem, because I also think the drug can be awfully useful, I will want some of the people involved in the case to have actually made a very good argument why they thought the drug was involved in this particular case. And if that is an argument coming from a person who hasn't seen all the data that I have seen, who came to the case not thinking perhaps that the drug could even cause this problem, that is influential, yes, for this case."

When Meadors asked Healy for his opinion, the doctor replied, "I'm saying that at the time this particular murder happened, I don't believe he had the mental capacity to know right from wrong. That is what I'm saying, yes."

On redirect, the defense asked Healy if akathisia was sometimes called "restless leg syndrome"? Although he never gave them an answer, they called Shirley Phillips to the witness stand and asked her what had happened at church on November 28, 2001. They were sure she could tell the jury Christopher had this syndrome.

"We were having choir practice," Phillips said. "Christopher was just behind me in the pew. I was trying to play the piano and he started kicking the piano stool. I kind of turned because he was behind me sitting on the first pew. And I just kind of turned and I said, 'Christopher, would you please stop kicking the piano stool,' and he did. He was just kicking it, I could feel him kicking it while I was sitting on it. Repetitively, he did that, until I asked him to stop. I guess he was doing it just to be annoying to me. Then I saw Joe come out of the choir, get Christopher, and take him outside. Christopher looked angry when they came back inside. It was a look I had never seen before."

On cross-examination, the prosecution singled out Phillips's statement, "It was a look I had never seen before." They wanted the jurors to see Christopher's rage the night of the murders lurked in the back of his mind like a black snake in dark shadows. Joe and Joy Pittman had never seen it coming.

After Friday's long and grueling day in court, Christopher looked forward to a relaxing weekend. On Saturday morning, he got up early, sat on the porch, and stared at a sliver of the ocean just beyond neighboring homes. He was afraid if he went out of the yard, he would trip the wire and set "Phillip" off.

During their stay at the beach, Christopher and his family spoke to Jason Cato in a series of interviews. As requested, his story would not appear in the *Herald* until after the jury presented its verdict.

"Christopher, what would happen if the jury finds you guilty?" Jason asked candidly. He was the one news reporter the family trusted wholeheartedly.

After spending all those years in the juvenile detention center, Christopher said he had focused on returning to a life outside the prison—not inside. "I try not to think about my future. My thoughts are about what I'll do when I get out."

Christopher said he had kept himself busy. He had read hundreds of books while in detention, the last one being *The Bear and the Dragon* by Tom Clancy. He also had read his Bible every day and kept a list of his favorite verses and chapters for the darker days. If the jury found him guilty, he'd keep his Bible with him for comfort.

"And what are your plans if the jury finds you not guilty?" Jason asked.

"Nothing in law," he joked. "And definitely not a prison guard."

Christopher said he wanted to work with the prison ministry. He thought about studying chemistry or physics at the University of Florida. Then again, he thought about joining the U.S. Marine Corps and seeing the world. One day, he hoped to visit all those faraway places he read about in books, like Europe, Asia, Australia, and Japan.

"But one place I'd never want to see again in my life," he added, "is South Carolina."

Danielle sat on the couch next to her brother. "I've done a lot of praying, and I have no doubt God has some humongous plans for him," she said, wiping the tears from her eyes. "He was not there for my wedding in December, but I hope he'll be there in May to see me graduate from high school." She put her arms around her brother and squeezed. "I'm really proud of him—about how he's handled all of this. It's amazing."

CHAPTER 35

The court spent the first part of Monday morning deciding what pictures to let in as evidence. A lot of the pictures that were presented of Christopher portrayed him younger than twelve, and those were considered prejudicial.

Defense strategy called for family members to take the stand and testify as to what kind of person Christopher was before the murders of his grandparents. Paul Waldner began with Christopher's aunt Melinda.

Aunt Mindy, as Christopher knew her, told the jury all about Christopher's background. She related those events in his life that had been traumatic, especially those that related to his mother abandoning him, his father's three marriages, and the volatile relationship between him and his father. She also tried to clarify what had been told years earlier to the psychiatrists.

The prosecution—as they had with the other defense witnesses—objected to most of what Melinda Pittman Rector had to say. But several spectators in the courtroom believed the prosecution's behavior was more harassment than anything else, and expressed their disapproval with groans and grunts. So much so, that Judge Pieper dismissed the jury and admonished the protesters.

"All right, I just need to say one more time, I thought

I brought this up on Friday, about those who are partic-
ipating or watching this case in the audience section of
the trial. I understand this is a very emotional case for
everyone involved. The solicitor has an obligation to
bring matters to my attention by the mechanics of an objection. There are people in the audience who are
sighing or acting exasperated every time they hear the
word 'objection.'"

Pieper turned and addressed Rector. "And, ma'am,
you are doing it also." Rector apologized. "I understand
this is very emotional for you and the family and everyone involved, but that is his obligation to seek guidance
from me. And I'm requesting in a very polite way that
you not do that. I'm also asking that everyone in the audience who cannot comply with that to please step out
during this time. This is a case where everyone has the
right to participate. The jury will have the duty to decide
this case based on what has been presented here today.
And I ask that you all cooperate and let everyone do
their respective jobs."

Pieper asked that the jury return to the courtroom,
then warned the gallery, "I will instruct the deputies and
bailiffs that if that takes place again, they ask the individual person to please step outside."

Waldner waited until the jury was seated, then continued his direct examination. "Mindy, did you ever see
your dad beat Christopher?" he asked.

"No, I have not."

"Can you even imagine that happening?"

"No, I cannot."

"What about Christopher and his grandmother, his
nana? What about their relationship?"

"It was good. He would pick on her a little bit, but it
was in fun. She was the one that helped with the bedtime
stories, but he preferred his pop pop."

Waldner produced a slide show for the jury, and asked
Melinda to describe the events as portrayed in the pictures. After the last picture, he asked, "Was there ever

any violence, impulsivity, aggression, or hostility that you saw in Christopher before October 2001 that concerned you or made you even suspect that he was a violent child or a violent person?"

"No. Not at that time, no."

"Are you now at peace with your nephew?"

Melinda looked over at Christopher and shook her head, before answering, "Yes, I am."

"Have you forgiven him?"

"Yes, I have."

Danielle Pittman followed her aunt Mindy to the stand. Danielle and Joseph Finchum had married December 12, 2001, shortly after the deaths of her grandparents. Joseph was in the marines and away on active duty in Iraq. She announced happily they were expecting their first child. Unfortunately, Joseph would not be able to join her in the courtroom until Friday.

Danielle was a petite, attractive girl with chiseled features, olive skin, and compelling brown eyes. A pearl hairpin sparkled in her short, straight black hair, and each ear was decorated with three pieces of jewelry. She was noticeably worried about testifying. No one had really told her what to say or do and she was afraid she might say the wrong thing. As she walked toward the witness chair, her hands began to sweat and her heart pounded.

Paul Waldner gently led her through the events of Christopher's early years and what it was like growing up in her father's home. She took a deep breath, before detailing the change she had seen in Christopher after he had stopped taking his medication.

"Now, that I've spent time with Christopher over the weekend, I can see he is more like his old self," Danielle said. "He has been so happy. We've had the chance to talk about the situation that has happened. And I've been able to put my arms around him, just him and I, nobody else there and tell him that I love him. We've been sharing the same bedroom because it has two double beds in it. We stay up for hours and talk and laugh and just have fun and catch up on the times that we've missed in the last three years."

The defense pulled up more photos for Danielle to identify. They also showed her a starter pack of medication, and with a little help from the judge in coaching Waldner, she was asked if that was similar to the medicine she saw in the particular bag Christopher had at Thanksgiving.

"Yes, it is," she acknowledged.

Deputy solicitor Dolly Justice interviewed Danielle, asking her right away, "Isn't it true that you've told someone in the past that Christopher had threatened you with a baseball bat five or six times?"

"No, I did not say that," Danielle shot back.

"Is it true that you've also told someone that he had you or threatened to hit you with golf clubs five to six times?"

"I have never said golf clubs. I said that he threw a golf ball at me."

"It's also true that he threw golf balls at you five or six times, is that correct?"

"I wouldn't say five or six times, no, ma'am."

"Do you recall telling anyone about that?"

"I believe my father, I don't remember who I told about it, honestly."

"And after these incidents, sometimes, Danielle, would you not suffer from bruises?"

"I don't believe so. I was wearing a shirt that was a midriff. So when he threw the ball at me, it left a red mark there, but it went away."

Danielle added that she sometimes provoked Christopher's retaliation, and the kind of fights they got into were just the normal brother/sister–type stuff.

Dr. Ronald Maris, distant cousin to the famous Yankee baseball slugger Roger Maris, was an adjunct professor in psychology at the Medical University of South Carolina. He called himself a "suicidologist," and had been the past president of the American Association of Suicidology (AAS) since 1981. The AAS put out the only journal in the United States on suicide and other life-threatening behaviors, and Maris had been its editor in chief for sixteen years. In addition, he had written twenty books and a number of articles on the subject. Maris shared some of his wisdom with the jury.

"I have no doubt there is a small number of people who take these drugs and develop what we call adverse effects of the medication that are not intended," Maris answered cautiously. "The adverse effects come from antidepressant medications. And probably seventy percent of the people taking them do have an antidepressant response."

Maris believed he should elaborate, didn't want the jury thinking he might be trying to trick them.

"But a small but significant number of people taking these drugs have other responses, which are highly related to suicide, and in my judgment have shown that these particular cases were caused by this difference."

Maris said he had been saying that since the 1980s. He believed that the same mechanisms that could trigger a kid taking Zoloft to harm himself could also trigger him to harm someone else. As proof in the pudding, he had found several studies that show an association with being suicidal and then later being homicidal.

On cross-examination, Meadors ignored the revelation about suicidality and had Maris admit that everyone who is suicidal or violent does not have low serotonin level. And that the FDA found that there was only a small group that has suicidality. Maris had to agree with Meadors that there was a difference between suicidality and homicidality.

Meadors brought the state's case back in perspective when he asked Maris, "If I just told you, Doctor, that I shot two people, and I meant to do it, that the other guy deserved it, would you think I was describing a homicide or a suicide?"

How else could Maris answer? Meadors was describing a homicide.

Following Maris to the witness stand, Christopher's maternal grandmother, Delnora Duprey, recalled for the defense a number of events from Christopher's life. She said even though he was more mature, Christopher was still the same sweet boy she had always known.

On cross-examination, it was obvious from Meadors's questions that he was trying to discredit Duprey's testimony.

"With all due respect, Mrs. Duprey, how would you know?" Meadors asked with sarcasm. "Isn't it true you hadn't seen Christopher for five years?"

"No, no, I said he was out of my life for a period of five years, that I had been back in his life for about a year-and-a-half before this event happened. I would see him in Florida. I knew about the hat incident (Christopher had gotten into a fight at school with a child who had taken his hat) and I knew about the dart in the bull. But I didn't know who possessed the dart. I didn't see Christopher at Thanksgiving at 2001. The day he came out of Lifestream, he came out that night, I saw him the next day, and then he left with his grandparents over the weekend."

Meadors took another swipe at the witness. "Hadn't Joe Pittman [Jr.] told you you couldn't see Christopher? Had you not been allowed to see him?"

Duprey admitted Christopher's father had forbidden the children to see her at one point, but they had gotten it all straightened out.

"Christopher called you from Lifestream. Could you understand what he was talking about? Did you have an occasion to go see him?"

"Christopher was very, very quiet on our first visit. We

interacted, but he was quiet. The second visit, his brother pretty well kept the conversation going."

Duprey said she didn't remember Danielle and Christopher ever fussing, especially not anything that would have been out of character for kids.

Meadors looked shocked. "Swinging a baseball bat at somebody, would you consider that, as a grandma, out of character for kids?"

Duprey didn't flinch. "The way I see that, Christopher was big enough, he could have caught her if he really wanted to hit her with it."

"Do you consider, as a grandmother—you have eighteen of them, I think—swinging a bat at something to be out of character for kids?"

"No, because my brother and I did the same thing. I mean, he chased me frequently."

"Was he swinging at you?"

Dupery nodded. "Yes."

"Would you think it was out of character, as a grandma, for a kid to swing a golf club at another?"

"I think children do things that they get reprimanded for. My brother used to shoot me with his BB gun."

Meadors took his fangs out, then asked Duprey if she was familiar with Christopher's actions at DJJ after the incident.

"If I may, sir, I've talked with the guards responsible for Christopher, on numerous times when I visited, and they have only had good things to say."

"Well, let me ask you if you had occasion to talk to Officer Meyers?" Meadors said, shifting his feet. "Are you familiar with Officer Meyers?"

Duprey was a bit confused. "Did I meet with Officer Meyers?"

Meadors nodded. "Yes, ma'am. Would you be surprised if I told you that Officer Meyers said that your grandson was telling a staff member to kiss his *A-S-S*?"

Vickery jumped to his feet and shouted, "Objection!"

"What is your objection?" the judge asked.

"Counsel is reading from documents that aren't in

evidence and they're hearsay," Vickery protested. But after a brief sidebar, Pieper allowed Meadors to continue.

Meadors paused, building up the suspense, then asked Duprrey, "Are you familiar with any racial slurs that your grandson made in the Department of Juvenile Justice concerning the KKK and the 'N word'?"

Duprey's face reddened. "I've heard that in court, but I've never heard from an officer from the detention facility tell me that. No, sir."

"So it wouldn't surprise you that Christopher told the officers at DJJ that the KKK was going to kick their 'N' ass? Would that surprise you that your grandson said that in the Department of Juvenile Justice?"

Duprey looked toward the defense table. She didn't want to give Meadors the opportunity to launch into an hour-long accusation about Christopher being racist. Finally she answered, "That would surprise me totally because that is totally out of character for Christopher. And I believe he was still under the effects of the Zoloft at the time, because he was not acting as himself. I find that totally out of character for him. He must have still been under the influence of Zoloft, because he has never been in serious trouble and he does not have any of those characteristics. Something had to have been going, yes, sir, because it was not his character. He must have been under the influence of the antidepressant. I don't know how the long-term effects of that is, but . . . and, like I said, I have not talked with many of the guards. The ones I have talked with on the numerous occasions have only said good things about him."

Meadors had her dangling on a hook, and he knew it. He could see fire shooting from her eyes, and that's the way he liked it. All shook-up. "Did you talk to juvenile correctional officer Blackwell?"

"Sir, I'm terrible at remembering names. I've talked to quite a few of the officers."

"Would you be surprised if he said 'FU, black bitch' to her? Would that surprise you?"

"Yes, it would very much surprise me."

"If Christopher said, 'And I told her to FU, Mrs. Black-well,' would that surprise you?"

"That would totally shock me because that's not Christopher's behavior."

Meadors moved in closer to the witness. Going for the jugular now, he asked, "Wouldn't that be consistent with swinging a baseball bat and throwing golf balls and blaming it on a six-foot-two black man, Mrs. Duprey?"

Duprey took offense. "Sir, I feel as though that's out of context," she responded in anger.

After Duprey stepped down from the witness stand, Vickery asked Pieper if he would keep Meadors at bay. "Your Honor, the rules were for us to stay back at the pulpit, and not to approach the witness—unless there was reason to—and only after received permission from the judge."

It looked as if Meadors had gotten some kind of call at an early age to become a lawyer and wreak havoc on any and all expert witnesses that dared to challenge him in a court of law.

As the trial played out, it appeared the Zoloft defense could engender sympathy for Christopher. At a minimum, the jury could agree Christopher's actions were inconsistent and there was something there that was affecting an otherwise clear-thinking boy. There was nothing else that could be introduced to have had that effect upon him other than the Zoloft.

But this wasn't a civil case against the drug company or Zoloft. Time was running out, and Christopher's freedom was on the line. If the defense could save him, then they needed to score, and to score big. It was time for them to send in their star player.

Dr. Lanette Atkins, a South Carolina native and child psychiatrist, was the expert witness the prosecution had been most concerned about. She was the last big hurdle they had to jump. Her position was made clear in December's hearing, in that Zoloft had caused this homicidal behavior in Christopher, and she believed there was solid and believable evidence to support this.

Over the years, Atkins had been working for the South Carolina Department of Mental Health, performing all of the competency-to-stand-trial and criminal-responsibility evaluations for the juveniles. But when the funds for consultants ran out, and SCDMH wasn't able to employ her any longer on that basis, she went back to dealing with kids full-time.

At the time Atkins got involved in Christopher's case, she had moved to the Department of Corrections and was working in Columbia as a psychiatrist, treating the adult clients in the Gilliam Psychiatric Hospital. After she received the call from public defender Yale Zamore and was told about the case, her first thought was the case seemed pretty cut-and-dry for the prosecution. She told Zamore she didn't think she would be able to help him with this case, but she agreed to review the files.

In November 2002, Atkins began her own evaluation of Christopher Pittman in regard to his competency and his criminal responsibility. She did a very exhaustive study of all the files and records, and interviewed nearly everyone who had a connection to Christopher. Through all this time, she met with Christopher every other week at DJJ, on thirty to forty different occasions, and spent an estimated forty to fifty hours interviewing him. She was aware that Dr. Pam Crawford, a colleague of hers, had also been retained to perform an evaluation on Christopher, and she talked with her as well.

"After several months of gathering information," Atkins recalled for the jury, "I contacted Dr. Crawford and said, 'You really need to go back and look at this kid. You really need to go back and see him again, because this is not the same kid you described in your report.'

"I see a lot of kids in the juvenile justice system, and most of the kids are going to use some kind of psychosis, hearing voices, as an excuse. You walk in and they're telling you the voices made me do it. And usually, you can come up with some way to monitor them and see, are there things consistent? Are they describing something that's not really consistent with what generally you have with auditory hallucinations and things. But they'll stick with, 'Okay, this is my defense and this is why I did it.' But Christopher was so different, because he never told me he had hallucinations.

"What finally convinced me he did is I said, 'Christopher, did you hear any voices?' I told him, 'I don't want to hear terminology that any doctors or anybody else has used. I want you to just describe, second to second, what happened when you went into your bedroom.' He said he sat there and started hearing echoes from inside his head, saying, 'Kill, kill, do it, do it,' referring to his grandparents. You know he tried to resist them, they kept getting stronger. Finally he follows what they told him to do. When you have echoes inside your head, I think most people would realize that is not a normal thought process. It's different for children to describe having hallucinations. It was not a normal process, he went upstairs and killed his grandparents, and that's what we know from there."

Defense attorney Waldner wanted Atkins to tie it all together for the jury. Her entire testimony could be summed up in one question and one answer—which would come after hours of repetitive and technical questions. But it all came down to this. "Based on your training and your experience, and based further on everything that you have done in the discharge of your responsibility to Christopher and to this court, do you have an opinion, given Christopher's age in November 2001, and the fact that he was on Zoloft, whether Christopher Pittman, at the time he killed his grandparents, had the capacity to form the necessary intent based on malice aforethought to kill his grandparents?"

"I do," Atkins replied with confidence galore.

Waldner could hardly wait to get out his question: "And what is that opinion?"

"That he did not have the capacity to conform the malice aforethought with regard to . . ." She stopped in midsentence, then restated, "The fact that he didn't have the capacity to form the criminal intent to kill his grandparents. He didn't know what was right and what was wrong."

Having made that point with the jurors, Waldner asked Atkins to go further out on the limb. "Do you have an opinion as to whether on November 28, 2001, when Christopher Pittman killed his grandparents, he suffered from a mental disease or defect [that] would have rendered him incapable of conforming his conduct to the requirements of the law and incapable of distinguishing between right and wrong?"

"Yes, I do."

"And what is your opinion?"

"He did have a diagnosis that rendered him incapable of telling the difference between right and wrong."

During his questioning of the witness, Waldner had been setting the stage for just this moment. He wanted the jury to believe Dr. Atkins knew something that the other psychiatrists did not.

"He had a mood disorder induced by antidepressant medication. That's not the exact terminology. I don't use this diagnosis as much, so let me look and tell you so I don't mess it up." Atkins opened the *DSM-IV* manual, and read from its pages: "You have depression. You have mania. And in this case, Christopher had a mood disorder, which I believe was mania, in my professional opinion, which was related to the Zoloft, and so it was induced by the Zoloft. And we have a lot in the records, a lot of studies that show antidepressants can induce manic episodes in individuals. And, in my opinion, he had that in addition to the akathisia, which you've heard a lot about."

Waldner then asked Atkins to begin with the events from October 2001 through November 28, 2001, when

Christopher's medication was changed to Zoloft and when he killed his grandparents.

In great detail, Atkins recalled those events.

"Would you explain to us, Dr. Atkins, how if he were influenced by the drugs, then he could have performed those different tasks in the sequence in which he did?"

"Well, first off, I think that you have to look at the fact that the tasks were not something that was organized. It was done very impulsively. He was having flight of ideas. He was having thoughts running through his head. He described impulsively grabbing change. He was grabbing guns. There's a lot of things that don't make sense—why would you grab an arsenal of guns if you're leaving the house? Unless you're having other conduct disorder, kids generally want to go and pull up somewhere and knock off all of the police, which was not what his plan was. He did a lot of things that didn't make a lot of sense.

"We heard earlier that there was this fuse, this elaborate fuse throughout the house. That was the first time I had heard of that when Dr. Ballenger was talking. And, actually, there's no evidence to indicate that there was anything like that in the house. We heard the police talk, they didn't sniff any accelerants. And my experience as a veterinarian—I know about the oldactory system and the dogs. Actually, he had mentioned the poof of the lighter fluid and how it would disappear, and that's probably true, but what the dog smells is not the lighter fluid. What they smell is actually the product that's either burned without an accelerant or burned with it. They smell the breakdown product. They don't smell the actual fuel. The gas or whatever is going to be gone, but they can smell the breakdown produce, like what it smells like after everything burns. We have a lot of inconsistency in the report of what happened exactly that night. Nothing that makes sense."

Meadors objected, stating that Atkins had not been qualified as an arson expert. Waldner redirected her back to the subject at hand.

"Christopher had no real plans. He didn't know where he was going. He just took off driving. That's not the act of somebody that has planned things out and planned ahead to kill somebody—running away. He described being angry and scared. And I think anger is part of the mania, which has been pervasive throughout this whole time since he started on the Zoloft.

"Well, as far as leaving the house, it really makes no sense. I'm not sure exactly what happened as far as how he set the fire. He probably doesn't really recall exactly what happened.

"This is a kid that has grown up with guns, since he was six years old, and has learned all about gun safety. And for him to be waving a gun around the way he was waving it around indicates to me that he was agitated, probably had some akathisia, mania, or manic symptoms, at least, because this would not be the way he would handle a gun. And he was not resistant to authority. As soon as they asked him to hand over the gun, he handed the gun over. If he was aggressive, he would have shot the guy. If he was choosing to be aggressive and had taken all of these weapons we hear about as an arsenal to further kill people, he would have stayed back with his vehicle, where all of his ammunition and all of his weapons were, and he would have waited until somebody came so he could blow some more people away—that would be typical of the conduct of disorder kids. He didn't do any of that. He gave his gun over when he was asked to give it over.

"When you read the confession, they go from one thing to another. It's another indication he was having flight of ideas. He was skipping from one thing to another and it makes no logical sense for one of us to read the confession.

"The other thing that shows me that he had no idea what he had really done is his major concern was being back to his father's home. If he had any idea of the gravity of what happened, then he would have been more worried about the police arresting him and being sent to jail. That wasn't his concern. His concern was going back to his father's house, which indicates he had no idea of the gravity of what happened. He described to me everything happening feeling as if he was being in a television show or watching television shows and being apart of it, but he couldn't stop it. And that's another kind of description of just not being in touch with reality, and being out of control of his own behavior.

"The only part I can tell for sure is accurate is that he killed his grandparents. The rest of it I know is not accurate."

Atkins continued offering the jury her scenario of what had happened and it seemed amazingly simple. The jury found it interesting that so many qualified medical experts could differ so widely in their opinions. Atkins had led them to believe the second verse wasn't always the same as the first.

"Christopher was taken off the medication when he was admitted to William S. Hall Psychiatric Institute, but put back on Paxil the end of December and taken off of it, like in January. My opinion is that a lot of his behavior for the first nine months or so that he was even in DJJ was still based on medication side effects, not due to the akathisia that's a direct side effect of the medication, but due to the mania that was induced and not related while he was in the DJJ.

"I've worked with children who were incarcerated and observed that behavior is definitely changed when you're incarcerated and you're involved in a very structured environment with a lot of other aggressive kids. You have to kind of develop a ranking within the group there. So, your behavior definitely changes there.

"In Christopher's case, I think he continued to exhibit signs of psychiatric illness throughout his first several months while in DJJ. He exhibited some when he was still in the Hall Institute when he was there for his evaluation. He was hospitalized for a relatively brief time for observation and evaluation for competency to stand trial and criminal responsibility. And during that time, he reported he was having some problems. He had some conflicts with staff, some people in the unit. Got into some fights. That kind of behavior, fights, making racial slurs, making sexual comments, those kind of behaviors persisted for eight, nine months after he was off the medications. It is my opinion that all of that behavior was based on the fact that he still had mania.

"One of the things with mania is people tend to be hypersexual. And most of the comments he made might have been directed at black staff, but my experience being in the detention center is that you've got a larger number of black staff than you do white staff. There's no doubt he continued to exhibit bizarre behaviors. He talked about making multiple bombs and selling them for small amounts of money, which is something we know that didn't happen. There were numerous things he did in the first nine months. But then after that period of time, since the last two years, at least, he's been the model kid. You don't see that kind of change from a conduct disorder kid, which is what he's been labeled, where they had long existing problems with authority figures coming in and making a total change like that, and being the kid that, I know, being the polite kid that I know, that is the shy child.

"I relied upon that because I've dealt with lots of juveniles with lots of problems. And the majority of them will go on to have other problems. We know that juveniles, studies of juveniles that commit homicide, generally have a long history of aggressive behavior leading up to the homicide. In this case, we didn't have that. In this case, we don't have that long history of aggression leading up to it. We have the short period, which coincides with the medication. And we have some aggression afterward, which coincides with him still being manic.

"Then we have a kid that gets back to great behavior, is loved by the staff at the detention center, makes all A's, actually, working ahead of his grade level in places and is consistently in a stable mood when I see him. And you don't see that kind of change from a kid that has long-term problems with conduct, over a few months. You don't see them being able to maintain that of over the two years that I've seen him. He's had people come up to him that say it's a very hard place to live. You know, you think about it, you're with all of these other kids that have conduct problems and he's been able to resist getting in any fights. He has consistent good behavior, no significant problems in DJJ, he's getting along with everybody, and having consistently the same mood. He's a quiet, shy boy, which is not what we heard about for the first several months he was in DJJ. There, he was a violent young man, hostile, aggressive, or defiant of authority."

Deputy solicitor Meadors would not begin his cross-examination of Dr. Atkins until the following morning. As predicted, there were fireworks. From the get-go, Meadors was critical of Atkins's assessment procedures. He accused her of talking to a lot of family members from Florida, but he said she didn't talk with any of the South Carolina law enforcement officers involved. He also pointed out for jurors that she had spent as much time in this case as she had in any other case, but the difference was that she was privately retained and her fees were $250 an hour outside the courtroom and $300 inside the courtroom.

"I was being paid through the Department of Indigent Defense Funds, but that has run out," Atkins said in response to Meadors's financial query. "So at this point, I'm not sure if I'm receiving any pay or not, but that's irregardless of the case. This case is something I couldn't ethically just drop."

Atkins admitted she had been paid around $15,000, thus far.

Getting back to the heart of the case, Meadors reminded Atkins that Christopher Pittman told Dr. Sharman he thought about how to get rid of his grandparents. "So, you're saying right now when he told Dr. Sharman on November 30, 2001, that he planned to kill them, he was under the influence of something?"

"I believe that when children have manic symptoms, oftentimes they represent things in a different way from the way they normally would. You know, that is more of a grandiose-type thing he played into. Plus, he, at that time, is in DJJ, where he's with other kids who have problems. This is a child who hasn't been in this type situation of incarceration before."

"Had he been there one day, Doctor, when he told Dr. Sharman that?"

"That's correct. And that's probably one of the scariest days to be there, the first day when you get there."

"So, your opinion is when he told Dr. Sharman he thought about how to get rid of them, he didn't know what he was saying?"

"That's correct. I think he was not thinking clearly at that point."

"What about when he told him he planned the shooting and the fire, waited until they were asleep, and shot them four times? He told Dr. Sharman that on November thirtieth?"

"That's correct. But the indications around the crime were that it was not planned out, that it was something impulsive. He had no plans for doing away with the people he loved the most. It was his only stability, the only place he had where he felt safe. They had been angry with each other earlier in the day, but were not angry at the time he went to bed. The voices or those inside of his head came up once he got in his bedroom. He did go through the act of killing his grandparents. He responded after that he was scared. He was angry, as he had been for weeks. He didn't feel anything but anger and reacted impulsively afterward. And I think a lot of the statements that he gave after he was even locked up indicate he was very angry, irritable. It wasn't his normal state of mind."

Meadors tried to undercut Atkins's arguments. He believed she had traveled way off the main highway.

"I had difficulty comprehending Christopher's actions when I first got involved in this case," Atkins said, sensing a need to defend her actions. "When you first see the case, it looks very horrific until you really get into all the details surrounding things. But when you do, this is consistent with a child who wasn't feeling emotion. This is consistent with a child who has some of the symptoms that we know happen from time to time with this type of antidepressant, SSRIs."

Meadors asked Dr. Atkins if she could provide those records indicating where Christopher was initially prescribed fifty milligrams daily and then increased to two hundred milligrams daily, as noted in her report.

"I made a mistake in the way I wrote that," Atkins confessed. "The records didn't indicate that. In talking with Christopher, the fact that he had more than one of the sample packets of medication that had been utilized indicated to me that he probably had taken the two hundred milligrams as he suggested, because Christopher was able to tell me the exact number of the color of the pills and the fact that he was taking them two times per day. It should have said, 'based on the information I gathered,' rather than based on reports." She said she wished she could have taken that out and reworded it.

Having made his final point, Meadors looked as if he were about to sit down, but he couldn't resist taking one final jab at Atkins. "Your finds are ongoing. Might you change your opinion after we get through?"

"No, sir, I don't think so," Atkins said succinctly.

The defense called Keith Altman from New York, whose summation of his work with adverse-event data of various different types, most specifically pharmaceutical drugs, was brief and to the point.

"The FDA maintains a database of adverse events that

occur on certain drugs and they have been keeping computerized data since 1969. I've had access to that data, pretty much every adverse-event report that the FDA has from 1969 through the second quarter of 2004. Reports come to the FDA through a variety of sources. One of them is direct to the FDA. An individual, a health care provider, or anybody who wants to, can just go on the FDA's Web site and it's a section called MedWatch and you fill in a MedWatch form and send it right into the FDA from there."

Altman had worked for the company that maintained these databases. He would testify that the FDA adverse-event database gave some idea as to the numbers of people that these adverse events were happening to in the real world. He was tendered by Vickery as an expert in the adverse-events reporting of drugs like Zoloft to the FDA and the analysis and evaluation of the same. The tenpenny word for the evaluation and analysis of adverse-events reports was "pharmacy-vigilance."

In Vickery's direct examination of the witness, Altman demonstrated that he had parceled the database into a subset that included adverse events involving kids twelve to seventeen years old where the reports were filed by and from a manufacturer on Zoloft. The reports showed in descending order: thirty-one reports on depression, twenty-seven on agitation, twenty-four on insomnia, eighteen on hostility, twelve on hallucinations, twelve on psychotic disorder, twelve of mania. In each of these reports, Zoloft was the suspect drug. Under the listing of murder, there were three of those. It was a very important piece of evidence for the defense.

Meadors challenged Altman on the terminology and the function of these adverse reports. What seemed rudimentary to Altman sounded all technical and complicated to the jury, and Meadors saw no need to attack those points aggressively and possibly irritate the jury by nit-picking. After he brought out the fact that Altman worked for a law firm named Finkelstein and Partners, and part of what they did was plaintiff litigations—suing pharmaceutical companies—he expounded upon what he saw as the plausible explanation for the flaw in the witness's testimony, and let it go at that. "The reports are unreliable, they were not gathered in a scientific manner, that someone could report it and then lie about what happened," he added.

The truth in Christopher Pittman's trial was beginning to vacillate with the integrity of the expert witnesses and how believable the jurors perceived them to be. Spectators and reporters swapped information on the jurors and speculated as to what information from what experts had proved to be vital. At this point in the trial, it was turning into a showdown of the dueling banjos.

CHAPTER 36

On Wednesday, forty-year old Charleston County police officer Bruce Orr testified as to the effects of antidepressants in his life. At the time of his employment, Orr was on the list for lieutenant eligibility, had fifty-one citations for deeds he had done in Charleston County, received numerous awards, and had been voted police officer of the year in 1993. It was a brilliant maneuver on the defense's part to convince the judge that Orr's own problems with his medication, Paxil, was relevant to Christopher's case. Earlier, Dr. Ballenger had opened the door for Orr's testimony when he admitted reporting to Orr's trial judge that his crimes had been committed while under the influence of Paxil.

"I was going through a divorce at the time," Orr told the jury. "I had driven over to my former residence to commit suicide. My intentions were to die on my back porch, where I spent most of my enjoyable life on my back deck, in the backyard. My ex-wife was not supposed to be home at that time. She ended up being there. I left, turned around, and drove the vehicle into the other vehicle and into the house, hoping that it would explode, hoping the house would fall on me, hoping I would die.

"Yes, I realize it was a wrong thing to do. I was taken to

the hospital, but the best way to describe it was like someone playing a movie with pieces of it missing and the plot not making any sense. I made good judgments as a law officer. I had an excellent career. Later, after the medication, I filed for divorce. I was the one that filed for divorce against my estranged wife. I fired that attorney for filing the papers. There was no rhyme nor reason to it."

Dr. Ballenger had evaluated Orr and had come to the conclusion that he suffered from rapid cycling and SSRI-induced mania. At trial, Orr was then given a lighter sentence.

The jury was surprised to hear such a bleak story from a former police officer. They couldn't help but admire such a kindly bear of a man and question if the same thing could have happened to Christopher.

"Do you have anything in the world to gain from sitting there in that witness stand telling your story?" Vickery asked Orr.

"No, sir. In fact, I feel I've got a lot of things to lose again."

Meadors, attempting to turn the tide, asked Orr, "Did you ever file a civil suit in all this?"

"I approached several different attorneys and was turned down. One attorney told me that, unfortunately, I didn't die or he could have done something."

"So, you attempted to file some civil suits?"

"Yes, I have."

"Did you blame another person for what you did?"

"I blamed me, but it was not me. I was not the person that I ordinarily was. I was not Sergeant Bruce Orr, Charleston County Sheriff's Office. I was not a person that was studying to be an associate pastor. I was not a children's minister. I was not the person that I was. I was Mr. Hyde to Dr. Jekyll, is who I was. . . . I blamed me, the other person that the medication made me."

For a moment, the courtroom was quiet. The witness looked from Meadors to Vickery, then back to Meadors.

"But you didn't blame anybody, did you?" Meadors asked, crossing the space between the two tables.

"No, sir," Orr replied.

"Not your parents?"

"No, sir."

"And not your brothers or sisters?"

"No, sir."

"And unlike Christopher Pittman, you didn't kill anybody, did you?"

"No, sir."

And there it was. Meadors had dropped the hammer. The implication had been pared down to not only his question, but by the obvious relish with which it was asked.

Demonstrating a thorough understanding of Pfizer's testifying in this case, the defense then called Pfizer's representative Dr. Stephen Romano to the stand. The clean-cut, broad-shouldered, middle-aged executive Romano and his testimony were crucial in linking Pfizer and the effects of Zoloft on children and adolescents. As Vickery pointed out, he was the Pfizer doctor who testified before the FDA panel regarding the effects of Zoloft on children and adolescents.

Romano had worked for Pfizer for six years and was the vice president in their worldwide medical organization. Until very recently, he was the therapeutic head of psychiatry overseeing all of the psychiatric products at Pfizer. Zoloft was one of about five or six products that he oversaw. He also had monitored a group of people in the company—statisticians, other physicians, and clinicians that evaluated the clinical trials that Pfizer had done in children and adolescents with Zoloft. They had completed and conducted two randomness trials with depression, and one with obsessive-compulsive disorder. All of this data had been forwarded to the FDA. Some of that data in the form of labeling was included in the U.S. label and elsewhere.

At the second FDA hearing, Romano had presented a summary of the data for the Zoloft that was evaluating the product in adolescents and pediatric children, who had been involved in trials for depression and for obsessive-compulsive disorder.

Vickery was prepared to ask Romano about things his company had or had not done with Zoloft, but Romano wasn't too happy about taking the stand. Meadors, with hands flailing and eyes blazing, objected on the basis that Romano's testimony was not relevant to the issues in the case. Romano had nothing to do with the facts in this case, he argued, yet Vickery was treating him as if he were a hostile witness. Getting a hawkish stare from Vickery, once again, the two feisty lawyers and their volley of verbal exchanges perked up the courtroom a bit.

"There's various internal company documents from clinical trials we are seeking," Vickery said, indicating he was not very interested in the last few words Meadors had spoken. "There are various internal documents where Pfizer had found that Zoloft contributed to the kinds of side effects that we are talking about in this trial. There is the warning in Canada, where Pfzier said, 'Based on our clinical trial data as well as adverse events that there is a danger of hyperarousal that can lead to harm to self and to others.'"

Vickery's words kept coming fast.

"Your Honor, I have no intention of offering him as an expert witness, but I intend to ask him about the material Pfizer fed to one of the state's other experts, Dr. Craw-ford, in this case. Interestingly, the court will find out what they gave Dr. Crawford when she asked for information on Zoloft was ancedotal case reports. But be that as it may, I intend to ask him about that. I believed there are enough relevant issues to have him up there. And I assure you, Your Honor, if I do ask him a question that is not relevant, then the prosecution will object."

A light chuckle broke out in the courtroom. Vickery paused to catch his breath, then continued.

"I think the fact that Pfizer sought to influence a witness in this case long before this defense was raised, long before Mrs. Menzies and I were involved, with the very kinds of information that the deputy solicitor says is unreliable, I think is extremely germane.

"I'm going to ask, has this company that produced this drug been aware of any side effects of Zoloft? Then I want them to show some of their internal documents that have been produced pursuant to a subpoena in this case, and let's look at it. Let's see what it says. This would be useful to help the jury decide on the side effects these drugs can cause.

"In fact, mania and psychosis, there has been no stipulation by the prosecution to that effect. I'm going to ask for the facts of what they have done, and there is no one that is better able to tell us about Zoloft than Pfizer. And this gentleman is the very one that Pfizer chose to go to Rockville, Maryland, and to espouse the company's view about how Zoloft affects children and adolescents, less than six months ago. And so there's not one that can tell us better what the company's view is regarding this drug, and then that can be cross-examined about some of what they didn't tell the FDA."

Vickery challenged Romano on the letter dated January 18, 2002, that had been sent to Dr. Pamela Crawford. At the time, she was evaluating Christopher, and this material was delivered to her before she rendered her report on original responsibility, which was dated February 23, 2002.

Vickery knew he would have to work hard to get this witness in. Romano would be cocked and primed, due to his position with Pfizer, and wasn't about to say, "Everything that happened to Christopher, we just attribute it to the drug." But this was the man, numero uno. He was the anointed one Pfizer chose to send to South Carolina the week before last to meet with various media representatives about this very case.

Vickery was determined not to let Romano walk away from the witness stand. He thought the jury was entitled to have it all from Pfizer—after all, it was the dirty laundry from the laundry hamper. This was the information that hadn't made it into the public domain and that's why Vickery believed that it was important that the jury have the benefit of that knowledge before they decided the fate of this young man.

It was the position of Pfizer, as Romano testified, that was based on the data they had generated in controlled randomness trials, very rigorously performed under blind conditions. The patient was given Zoloft or a placebo, which is a sugar pill, under blind conditions, and neither they, the physician, the investigator, nor the patient knew what they were taking.

Romano stated the trials were all well-controlled and were the only studies at the present. When he and his associates reviewed that data for depression, as well as for the obsessive-compulsion, there was no association in the trials with the drug.

Romano pointed out that Pfizer's position was that Zoloft did not increase the risk of suicide in children and adolescents. Their studies had shown no difference between those patients that received Zoloft and those patients that received the placebo.

"When Zoloft came out on the market, back in early 1992—it was approved in 1991—there had always been a warning on the label about suicidality," he explained. "This was an indication for adults only at the time, and still is, but there was a clear warning about suicidality because it is part of the illness and that was recognized by the FDA and by Pfizer. Our company wanted to share some of the details of the studies that they had conducted on Zoloft, but the FDA did not allow us to do that."

After a lengthy discussion concerning what Pfizer did in telling doctors that Zoloft was not approved for children with depression, Romano laid the foundation for labeling the medication in the United States.

"Mr. Vickery, the content has actually been in the Zoloft label for the past thirteen to fourteen years. It's nothing new."

"Is it not a fact," Vickery countered, "that now the FDA has required Pfizer to put a blackbox warning on the label of Zoloft with respect to the increased risk of suicide in children and adolescents?"

"No, that's incorrect," Romano responded to Vickery's crafty question. "First of all, the blackbox warning from the FDA is based on a pooled analysis of nine drugs, but it applies to thirty-three antidepressants. So even antidepressants for which there was no data in children and adolescents generated, the blackbox warning is applied to all antidepressants. It *does not* say increase in suicide. It *says* increase in suicidal behavior and thinking, which is very different, much more common than that, of course, completed suicides. There were no completed suicides in any of these studies that led the FDA to make a decision about the blackbox warning. So, I just want to clarify that because I think that's very important, particularly for you all, to understand.

"On January 26, the FDA actually issued a final content of what would be included in that blackbox warning for all antidepressants, as well as the warning section for all antidepressants around the use of children and adolescents. They actually asked Pfizer and the other companies to strike the line that said a causal relationship was established. So even the FDA after considering all the data that generated the blackbox warning for both Zoloft, as well as for the other thirty-two antidepressants, the FDA asked us to strike that comment from the label and that was because there was no causal link established. It was a suggestion of an increased risk, which is clearly listed now in the black box. The causal link is not there."

One had to admire the courage of the studious Vickery as he challenged Romano, preparing to fall on his own sword if that was what it took to help his client.

"You pointed out earlier, Dr. Romano, and corrected me,

and I appreciate it, that the FDA, when they finally approved it, took out this sentence: 'A causal role for antidepressants in inducing suicidality has been established in pediatric patients.' Instead, they added: 'Antidepressants increased the risk of suicidal thinking and behavior, suicidality in short-term studies in children and adolescents with major depressive disorder and other psychiatric disorders.' Can you tell me the significance of that?"

The question gave Dr. Romano another chance to demonstrate why Pfizer had put so much faith in him.

"Yes, there was a big difference in they did not say it has a causal link. It says there was an increase in specific events, and they become very specific here and are talking to the events that were more often seen in the pooled analysis for patients treated with all the medications. It, of course, was not true for the Zoloft studies. The Zoloft studies did not show a statistically significant difference. I think it means that an increased risk as seen, but to what extent it was due to the drug or not is not yet confirmed, and that's why the FDA took out the causal sentence before that."

Not nearly as important as the previous witness, the defense called Christopher's guardian ad litem, Milton Hamilton. He would provide the jury another look at the two-sided coin depicting Christopher Pittman.

"I was appointed to see that Christopher's rights were protected, not to advise him as an attorney, but just as an adult to watch after him. . . . It was Monday, December third, when I met him. That was the first hearing in Family Court. The detention hearing, I met him at that point, and was somewhat surprised about his size. He was just so small. Young-looking, very subdued, and almost glassy-eyed. Just trying to talk with him, you got maybe an 'okay.' I think Danielle described him perfectly as just being weird.

"Christopher did stay in some trouble and had problems

in DJJ. [But] over the last year-and-a-half, he is an individual you can sit down with and talk to. He's very responsive. He has certainly matured a lot since he was twelve years old and seems to be getting back to being normal.

"I've never had any threats from Christopher, and I've seen him eight or nine times over the last three years. I've seen him two or three visits here, and I went to DJJ twice. I never witnessed his bad behavior. But I was constantly getting documentation and reports from Yale Zamore as to what was going down at DJJ. He kept behaving pretty badly into about 2003."

Jeanette Mishoe, a gray-haired, matronly teacher at DJJ, was perhaps the best hope for the defense to perpetuate the idea that Christopher was a good kid now that he was off his medication.

"I've known Christopher since August 2001. He was a model student. He made straight A's. No behavior problems with him whatsoever. He's very intelligent. I'd heard of his problems, and that he had problems right after he came there, but I never witnessed any of it. He could control his behavior with me. I heard he had some bad behavior, but I've never experienced it. He's never disrespected me, never threatened me, or never disrupted my class. In fact, I've never heard him curse or threaten another student."

Tony Canzater, another employee of DJJ, was there also to prove the defense's contention that Christopher was a good kid. Canzater reminded the jury that the prison environment that Christopher had been living in was very relevant to his behavior.

"Yes, Christopher talked about the 'N word' and other things that the kids said and did at DJJ. It's an adaptability issue. My argument is what you have done is tossed a white boy in a place that's seventy five percent black prisoners. That's the relevancy. This might explain why he might have been acting the way he was acting.

"I met Christopher the second day he got there. He was slim and small, one of the smaller ones. There might have been a couple of kids smaller than him, but not many. He was twelve. The range of the kids he could have interacted with on his wing were thirteen, fourteen, maybe one or two fifteen-year-olds. When he first got there, he got into a lot of trouble, cursing and fighting. I've never personally heard Christopher threaten anybody, but when the officers talked about name-calling toward them, what are you going to do?"

Canzater told Hank Mims that Christopher was written up for what is called serious institutional behavior—sexual misconduct, rioting or assault on staff. "One time, I wrote him up for two days. One time for possession of weapon, like a little samurai sword, a throwing star. But he never hit anybody with it, never stuck anybody with it. He never threatened anybody with it, but he could have been prosecuted with it, had he hurt somebody with it. All in all, Christopher seems like a sweet, smart, and well-mannered young man. I wouldn't describe him as a perfect prisoner. In the beginning, he was pretty rough, a tough prisoner. But that has all changed now."

Three other witnesses from DJJ and Christopher's friend Shirley Carter testified that Christopher was no problem now, or at least he hadn't been written up lately. The general consensus of the witnesses was that he was treating people with the utmost respect. He now understood the discipline and was behaving by the rules.

On Wednesday afternoon, after the defense's witnesses had testified, the judge decided it was time for a break and called a recess.

The last witness of the day was Dr. Richard Kapit. Born and raised in Long Island, New York, Kapit was a short, florid man, whose dark hair had been styled to stay in place until Jesus Christ's Second Coming. For four or five years, he had been the psychiatrist at the Bureau of Forensic

Psychiatrists in Washington, DC, working for the federal government. His work was similar to that of Dr. Pamela Crawford, in that they were a group of psychiatrists appointed by the court to perform evaluations of defendants and prisoners and people in the criminal justice system. Kapit did competency-to-stand-trial evaluations, criminal-responsibility evaluations, consultations on questions of probation and parole, and dangerousness. He had treated a number of prisoners in the DC jail and also the Lorton Reformatory, which was maintained by the DC government, dealing with a number of persons to determine whether or not they were manic or psychotic.

After leaving DC, Kapit worked with the FDA for sixteen years, working as the medical officer who handled the initial applications on the first SSRI drugs, including Prozac. It was his responsibility to evaluate the safety review of the new drug application for Prozac and investigate the new drug applications for Zoloft and for Paxil.

Kapit said he hadn't practiced psychiatry in about twenty years or seen patients in that time. After retiring from the FDA about two years ago, he had served as an expert witness for a few cases involving some litigation. He said his primary effort at this point was having a second career as a journalist writing on issues involving medications and the health care system in this country.

"I have enrolled in a journalism program at the University of Maryland, and I'm pursuing a degree in that and hope to do writing in that area. I saw an article about this case in the *New York Times* last August about this trial and about the charges. It affected my reason for being involved, that a twelve-year-old boy was being prosecuted for murder and he was on Zoloft at the time. Some of the most important work I did at the FDA was on SSRI drugs. And some of the things that I wrote documents, internal FDA documents, were about adverse reactions associated, based on information from clinical trials. The reviews concerned hyperarousal, hypomania, mania—activation that could be caused by SSRI Drugs.

"And so when I read about the case, it occurred to me that there was a possibility that the drugs that Mr. Pittman had taken could have played a role and it seemed to me that I was in a position to offer to evaluate the history and the situation to see if I thought the drugs played a role. And it seemed like an important case. Since I seemed to be in a good position to do that, it seemed like a case where I ought to try to be involved, and so I e-mailed Mr. Vickery and told him I would get involved if he wanted me to."

Kapit and Vickery met in Bethesda, at the FDA advisory committee meetings on the SSRI drugs. Before he testified and got involved, Kapit was given the opportunity to interview Christopher in South Carolina by himself over the course of two days and to discuss the case at some length with child psychiatrist Dr. Lanette Atkins. Besides talking with her, Kapit reviewed all of Christopher's records and talked to many of the same persons she had interviewed.

Kapit's testimony buttressed everything that Dr. Atkins had already said. He, too, believed Christopher was involuntarily intoxicated by Zoloft and did not have the ability to form criminal intent on that date, due to the intoxication with Zoloft. He said Christopher suffered from a substance-induced manic-mood disorder with psychotic features, the very same diagnosis from the *DSM-IV* that Dr. Atkins had made.

"The antidepressant is not what made him suicidal. It is what made him angry and psychotic," Kapit said on direct examination.

In Meadors's cross-examination, he attacked Kapit's methods and motives to raise doubts about his statements, and attempted to discredit his testimony. In rapid-fire succession, he asked Kapit, "Did you talk with Dr. Bonnie Ramsey who said [Christopher] had no indication of mania? Did you talk to any witnesses who saw him on

November twenty-eighth and twenty-ninth. Did you talk to Dr. Howard Smith at Lifestream, who diagnosed him as oppositional defiant disorder? Were you sitting in court Wednesday of last week, or did you miss Lucinda McKellar's or Scott Williams's testimony? You wish you had, [been here that day] don't you?"

Meadors did everything he could to rattle Kapit's cage. At one point during a heated exchange, Meadors paused, then said with a smirk on his face, "You're not getting angry, are you?"

"I suppose a tiny bit," Kapit answered in all honesty. "I'm sorry, but I will try not to exhibit that anger."

Meadors chewed away at the witness like he was fresh meat. Kapit had a short fuse. After having been accused of not doing his homework by the deputy solicitor, he said in anger, "I'm not going to pretend that I can explain every detail of everything that went on during the whole period of time. Psychosis does not prevent you from doing things like that."

Meadors fielded his answer, then fired another cluster of questions back at him, "Laid in bed and thought about how to get rid of them. That is what he told Dr. Sharman, isn't it?"

"Yes," Kapit answered dryly.

"Planned the shooting and the fire. 'I planned it. I waited until they were asleep.'"

"Yes."

"And he actually told Bonnie Ramsey, 'I knew what I did was wrong,' didn't he? He did tell her that?"

"Yes, he did tell her that."

Kapit could not say for sure when Christopher's acute pscyhotic episode subsided, but apparently it lasted only a day or so. He said his mood remained significantly elevated, manic or hypomanic for some time afterward. But the hallucinations, the acute psychotic phase, probably didn't last more than a day or two, or something like that. And they had started after he had been watching TV with his granddad; they started sometime right before he shot them. Those events that occurred during the day or hours prior to the shooting apparently were the events that triggered the psychotic episode.

Kapit's arguments did not stir a lot of emotion in the jury.

After the witness returned to his seat in the courtroom, Vickery moved for a directed verdict on two grounds: a defendant under age fourteen does not have the mental capacity to commit a crime, and there was no evidence that this twelve-year-old boy had malice aforethought.

The judge denied both motions. He then asked Christopher if he was going to testify. Vickery could never ask Christopher to go up against someone like Meadors, and respectfully declined.

Now that the defense had rested its case, the prosecution wanted to meet head-on the defense's assertion that Christopher's behavior had changed, now that he was no longer taking his medication. To effectively counter that suggestion, they called for their rebuttal witnesses.

For the first time, the jury would be given a bird's-eye-view of Christopher Pittman's behavior at DJJ. The prosecution marched in a parade of witnesses from the detention center to prove to the jury that Christopher was not as the defense portrayed him—some milquetoast-type kid who didn't have an ounce of violence in him. There was a great deal of talk about Christopher's behavior now that he was off the drug, and for the next several hours, the jury would hear from expert witness and forensic psychiatrist Dr. Pamela Crawford.

Another potentially dangerous witness for the defense, Crawford began by establishing Christopher had never been zonked out on Zoloft. Recalling conversations from Christopher and his family from December 2001, she painted the picture of Christopher Pittman as an extraordinary liar. She believed he was dangerous, and she was especially concerned when he started talking about building bombs and blowing up the detention center.

On recross, Paul Waldner defused that notion.

"Just how far do you have to countersink the glass and the cap in the composition to even make a bomb explode?" he asked.

Crawford had absolutely no idea.

"Then how can you tell us if this [was] a sophisticated bomb you [were] looking at?"

"I don't know if that [was] a sophisticated bomb."

"You don't know anything about making bombs, do you?" Waldner droned.

"Very, very little about making bombs, almost nothing," Crawford admitted.

Waldner was doing a good job with this witness. He had what he thought was a couple of clever questions that would come in the back door and catch her off-guard. He quickly launched an attack on her assessment.

"And you saw in the William S. Hall Psychiatric Institute records where for body habitus they put down virtually no subcutaneous fat, emaciated? Did you see that, Doctor?"

"I saw he was very thin. When I looked back, he was actually several pounds heavier than he had been earlier on. I think he was ninety-seven pounds. And I believe, I could be wrong, but I heard testimony that he weighed less than that before."

"Well, that's the body habitus he had when you interviewed him, initially, wasn't it?"

Crawford nodded. "Yes."

"Do you think his grandfather could beat a kid like that, beat a child who weighed ninety-five to ninety-seven pounds?"

"Yes."

"Do you figure that you can take a weapon, a board, a

paddle, and beat a child with, who has no subcutaneous fat, who's emaciated and not leave a mark?"

"I could not answer that. What I can say is that Christopher told me his grandfather hit him—he did not describe this as a beating, as a vicious beating. He said he hit him several times on his way to his room and it hurt. He didn't describe that as a beating of such."

Waldner quickly glanced at his notes, then asked, "If there's insufficient evidence to support a diagnosis of conduct disorder in the child, and if it can be shown that his conduct was influenced and directed by the drugs he was taking, then under those circumstances, using your forensics, then what verdict is it?"

"That still isn't clear. I mean, if this kid was manic at the time and that's something that I looked and ruled out on the basis of a variety of things, including extensive psych testing et cetera. Let's just say if he had been manic at the time, that would not necessarily make it that he didn't know right from wrong or that he lacked the capacity to conform. I was able to rule out mania, let me say that first. With five of us looking at his psychological tests, I was able to, without a doubt, rule out mania. But even if he had been manic, that would not necessarily lead him to meet that criteria. There have been many people who are manic, even psychotic, who would not meet that criteria."

The defense settled for that answer, sat down, and waited for the judge to call for any further business. After the jury was dismissed, and before the trial was recessed until the next morning, Andy Vickery announced he had received the DNA testing that had been done on Christopher's blood with regard to his ability to metabolize Zoloft.

As expected, Vickery stirred up a hornet's nest.

CHAPTER 37

On Friday morning, February 11, 2005, Christopher Pittman's trial reopened with a motion from the defense to present the evidence concerning the DNA testing of Christopher's blood with regard to metabolizing Zoloft.

"There are several metabolic pathways by which Zoloft is eliminated from the human body," Vickery explained to Judge Pieper. "We can think of them metaphorically as gutters. They are in the cytochrome B-four-fifty system of liver enzymes. And the DNA testing reflects that one of the two main ones that is the metabolic pathway for Zoloft is, to speak metaphorically, clogged. That he is a poor metabolizer because of this genetic anomaly that affects the ability of his body to eliminate Zoloft."

The defense had been scrambling since yesterday to find a suitable person who would be available within the court's schedule and the jury's schedule to address the issue. Lo and behold, as Vickery came into the courtroom, he saw someone in the hall who had the credentials to do so. Dr. Joe Glenmullen was a Harvard author who had written a couple of books on these drugs, the first called *Prozac Backlash* and the second called *The Antidepressant Solution*.

In Glenmullen's books, he wrote that patients vary widely in their vulnerability to developing akathisia, and not all patients who develop akathisia will become suicidal. Rather, a subset of patients with akathisia is driven to suicidal or violent behavior in some antidepressant-induced suicides. Glenmullen's research had shown that during autopsy studies, there were patients with low levels of the liver enzymes that metabolize and inactivate antidepressants. And because these patients were poor metabolizers, they had abnormally high levels of antidepressants in their blood, despite being on recommended doses.

The defense believed these issues bearing on Christopher's ability to metabolize Zoloft was significant evidence that might be important to the jury as they tried to determine whether there was a reasonable doubt. Because the tests could have turned out to be self-incriminating, Vickery said they had not wanted to do this while Christopher was in custody and allow the prosecution to use it against them.

Judge Pieper ruled his courtroom with an iron fist. He was a little miffed at the defense for presenting this evidence now and not before resting their case.

Vickery accepted the criticism. "But it would have been foolhardy of me to alert the prosecution by alerting the court of that potential. I didn't want to do anything to violate my client's Fifth Amendment rights. I blame it on the prosecution in that they protested Christopher's release on bond. Had they taken a different view on December twentieth, then Christopher could have been out on bond and we could have had our test."

Vickery said he would have liked to cross-examine Dr. Ballenger, who had very good psychopharmacology credentials, on the fact that Christopher has this genetic anomaly, which puts him at greater risk.

"Why was I not aware of it?" Pieper addressed the defense. "This issue is too important to just ignore it. I'm not a big fan of trial by ambush. If you have figured anything out about me by now, you've probably figured that much out."

Vickery apologized again. When the judge asked for the state's position, Meadors addressed the issue.

"Your Honor, obviously, we vigorously oppose this. This is a blood test, scientific evidence that we were not informed about until last night at five-thirty when we broke court. It was then I was informed by Mr. Vickery, who walks up and says, 'I've got some new testing that I want to introduce.'

"Your Honor, that is not how we practice law here in South Carolina. That is not how cases are prosecuted or defended here in South Carolina. He knows what the discovery rules are here in South Carolina, and he violated those.

"This is—all due respect to the defense attorneys and the defense—but this looks very, very contrived to me. I'm told at five-thirty last night that they have this new test, and all of a sudden, the next morning, they have some expert, a doctor from Harvard, who just happens to be in the courtroom. And I don't watch much TV in the morning—but I was watching TV one morning this week and here is this same doctor up here defending Christopher Pittman on TV. And he just happens to be here today. And he happens to be an expert in the area, and they happen to have his book. Your Honor, that's contrived, the state submits. And this is just not right. This is wrong. And this is not how we prosecute cases or defend cases in South Carolina. They violated discovery rules, and they should not be allowed to put it in."

"Well, as you are aware, obviously, I'm not thrilled about this situation," an exasperated Pieper said to the attorneys. "But whether or not I'm thrilled is not how the situation is analyzed.

"As I explained to you, I like every *i* to be dotted and every *t* to be crossed. This is one of the ways I can go home at night and know that I have done a good job and that everyone has had a fair trial in my courtroom. I have just as much leeway in this situation to deny the request as I do to grant it. I don't agree with the procedure employed. I don't agree with it being last-minute.

"I do think that an order could have been obtained, an order under seal that would not have disclosed any expert or investigative analysis or shed light on any potential defense theory. That is why I used the language 'I'm not happy with the situation as it has been approached.'

"However, the other side of me likes for everything to be out on the table so that a jury can make an informed decision about the matter and so that justice can be rendered in every case that comes before me. And I have to weigh that with the approach that you have taken in this case."

Pieper announced he was going to take a break, and while he was on break, he wanted the lawyers to take the opportunity to ascertain whether or not an expert was even available to address this issue. "I'm not going to let you use the person who has shown up at court today. You need to both be on equal footing in that regard."

The defense and prosecution shot each other nervous glances. The defense felt pretty confident they had found a witness who would convince the jury that Christopher was in that small percentage of patients who could not metabolize Zoloft, and now the rug had been pulled out from underneath them.

Another verbal altercation started between Meadors and Vickery, but the judge called them down.

"I'm not going to let this case turn into that in my courtroom. If you've got comments to make, you will make them to me, not to each other. We're nearing the end of this case and it's not going to take that route as long as I am sitting up here. Do both of you understand that?"

During the break, Vickery contacted medical experts at the Medical University of South Carolina who had significant expertise on this subject. But based on their experiences, they told him they did not believe his evidence would be helpful for the jury. From a trial strategy standpoint, Vickery decided not to put the evidence on and asked the judge to withdraw the request.

Judge Pieper reassured the defense that the court was fully prepared to entertain their request. And if the case warranted it to be reopened, then he would entertain that request also.

When the prosecution was asked for their opinion, Meadors offered what he had learned during break: "There are five enzymes in the liver that metabolize Zoloft. One of these five in Christopher Pittman's case was poor. Two were indicated as 'extensive,' meaning free flowing. The other two actually was a double enzyme and retained even more than the other two. But there were no results on that one other enzyme.

"Judge, he talked to a leading expert in this field last night by e-mail. The expert in the field last night told him it wouldn't make any difference at all. I submit to you he knew that. He's playing for the cameras on this. He's now withdrawing it. I just want the record to reflect that."

Vickery told the judge he didn't appreciate the accusations and the other remarks from deputy solicitor Meadors and said he found it astonishing that the prosecutor knew about an e-mail he sent last night seeking advice on this issue. After calming down, Vickery assured the judge it wasn't going any further. "I apologize again, Your Honor, based on information they had garnered this morning, we do not need to reopen this issue."

The jury was brought into the courtroom and the prosecution continued its rebuttal with psychologist Dr. Julian Sharman. Sharman was asked to recall the history and content of meetings with Christopher Pittman over the last four years. Dressed in a white shirt, tie, and sweater, he was so relaxed and comfortable on the stand that had the theme "Won't You Be My Neighbor" been playing softly in the background, no one would have paid it much attention.

Sharman had talked with Paul Waldner over the phone several times, but had never met him. Waldner's first question seemed innocent enough, but it sure prompted a lot of other important questions.

"If you had to describe your relationship with Christopher from the time you first met him on November 30, 2002, to today, how would you describe it?"

Like other witnesses, Sharman described his relationship with Christopher.

"I would describe it as a good relationship that went through phases. But on the whole, especially the last year, grew much stronger as he [has] gotten older and converses more, we've had good conversations. It's been very positive."

Waldner asked, "If Christopher has been described during most of the first year that he was in the DJJ as being a hellion, would you generally agree with that description?"

"For the security staff, yes. In my office, he never did anything like that. But for the security staff, yeah. I'm certainly aware of the incident reports, the early curfew, the lockup, the disrespectful talk, the scraps he was in."

"Would it be unusual for a child being incarcerated for the first time to go through a period of adaptation?"

"It's not unusual, no."

"Would you describe the environment there in DJJ with the guards, with the rules, the structure, with the lockups, the confinement, would you describe that as a normal environment for a twelve-year-old child?"

"It's not a normal environment for any child. It's a jail," Sharman emphasized. "It's not a normal environment."

"If you have an abnormal environment, would you expect there to be a period of time before the child's conduct would adapt to that environment?"

"For some kids, yes, sir; not all."

"Do you think Christopher was one of those kids?"

"Yes, sir."

Sharman further testified that he saw Christopher routinely once or twice a week. As the trial got closer, more frequently, and he had gotten to know him pretty well. During the last year or two, he stated Christopher was not violent in the context of being at the juvenile detention center. He said he was very respectful, and based on what the doctor he had seen, Christopher was very responsible.

On recross, Waldner asked, "Based on your professional opinion and all the time you've spent with Christopher over the last couple years since he went through that first year, the progress that he's made with regard to his grades becoming straight A's, with respect to the way he treats the guards, the way he gets along with the rest of the kids there, do you think that progress is genuine or contrite?"

"I believe it's genuine, but I also believe that when you have been at the juvenile detention center for a while, you conform to the environment. And I think that's what happens with everyone. They start to learn that it's not much good to oppose the rules and everything, that it just doesn't work. And then when you add in just the maturity factor as well, so, in essence, I would say it's genuine."

"Based on the over one hundred times, Doctor, that you've met with Christopher professionally and tried to help him through this process, are you proud of the results you now have in this young man?"

"I'm proud—I mean, I think he has done a great job in the things that we've talked about, although I feel that we haven't made any headway at all in the issues that started—that I presume started this whole problem, which was feeling or resolving issues with his father.

"Even though we've talked superficially over the last years about the case and everything else, there's a lot of questions that Christopher has for his father and his mother and a couple for Danielle that he had hoped that this forum would answer for him.

"We always talked about that. I always kind of assured him that his day in court would be one where Christopher would be able to get an explanation from his father as to why he treated Christopher the way he had. And he had hoped that his mother would be on the stand and explain to him why she had done the actions that she had done. And he very much hoped that Danielle would explain why she didn't tell DSS the truth, because it made him out to look like a liar.

"These are the things that have not been resolved with Christopher. That is why I say I don't know if he entered the real world there—what has changed in terms of his unresolved feelings about those things. My biggest concern is they have not been touched."

Sharman's words were profound. The heartbreaker was that after all this time, and all he had been through, Christopher was no further along in resolving issues with his family members as he had been the day he ran away from Florida.

Before the day ended, the prosecution brought in their own shoe box of control officers from DJJ. In graphic detail, five uniformed officers shared with the jury a number of incidents at the detention center involving Christopher for the past four years he had been incarcerated. They included cursing, fighting, insubordination, threatening bodily harm, hoarding contraband, possession of drugs, and concealment of a deadly weapon.

At the end of Officer George Blackwell's testimony, Meadors asked, "All these times that you worked or watched Christopher Pittman and the incidents that you had with him, had you ever seen him cry?"

Blackwell, who was the main control operator on Christopher's pod, vehemently replied, "No, sir. The only time I've seen him shed a tear is on Court TV."

The prosecution had made its point without a lot of effort. With little prompting, the DJJ officers were more than satisfied at having been given an opportunity to tell their side of the story. The prosecution's biggest boost came when Giese called Steven Snyder to the stand and asked him to relate the last of thirty-nine incidents that involved Christopher at the detention center.

Snyder told the jury this incident took place on January 26, 2005, right before Christopher was to leave and come down to trial. Two solid metal ink pens had been found in Christopher's room, under his bed. Snyder saw the ink pens could be used as pretty formidable weapons and confiscated them. He knew if Christopher had gotten mad at someone, he could have done some damage with those pens.

When Christopher came back from pill call and realized his pens were gone, he came to his door and started screaming at Snyder. He wanted to know who had taken his pens, and got even angrier when told they had been confiscated.

"And what happened then?" Giese asked.

With a lot of flair, Snyder said, "He knew the rules; he knew he wasn't supposed to have that stuff. And yet, he just flipped out. He flew off the handle. He wanted them back; oh, he wanted them back. He was very upset; he had worked himself up, more and more, as the progression of the yelling and banging.

"Christopher started using a lot of profanity, cussing me, calling me names and all this stuff. But it didn't phase me a bit. His tantrum progressed further and further. You know, he would sit on the floor and put his feet, and just bang against the door. Just *bang, bang, bang, bang.* He would do it at night after curfew. When the other juveniles are trying to go to sleep, he's in there banging on his door for hours, you know, just because he knew it was going to make everybody upset. No one could go to sleep because of his noise. It was very loud. He would hit on his window. They have a little small cell window, where we can observe them in their room. He was hitting on the window with his hand, a book he had in his room, and his shoe, his state sneaker. In my opinion, he was trying to break it.

"He then told me he was going to stab me in the stomach and in the eye and in the throat and then he was going to rape me. The rape part—no, I didn't take seriously. But the stabbing, I knew his history and I wouldn't take any chances. During that same incident, I was sitting down writing up the incident and Christopher had hollered through his door he had done it before, and he would do it again."

Giese asked Snyder about the incident when Christopher held the newspaper article and picture of his grandparents' burned home against his cell window and laughed.

"And he was pointing at the picture?" Giese emphasized.

"Yes, sir. He was pointing at the picture," Snyder said, as if it had just happened yesterday.

"And laughing about it?"

"Yes, sir, he was laughing about it."

"To the other juveniles?"

"Yes, sir."

Giese turned and pointed toward the defense table. "And that is the same Christopher Pittman that's in the courtroom today?"

Snyder nodded. "That's the same Christopher Pittman, only taller."

On cross-examination, Hank Mims attempted to weather the last storm. He asked Synder, "Did you have any problems with his threatening you between November of 2001 when he came in and this May incident?"

"Well, it wasn't really threatening," Snyder responded. "He had other bursts of profanity, and a couple of times, I think, he stuffed his sheets in his commode and flushed the commode till the water ran out on the floor. I mean, there was a lot of little things, but as far as the threatening to kill me, he never threatened to kill me."

"And after that May incident, from then until November, did you have any problem with him of a threatening nature toward you or anyone else, to your knowledge?"

"Not where he physically came at me or verbally

threatened to kill me again. Of course, I never let him out of my sight after that."

In a nonthreatening manner, Mims got Snyder to confirm he was six feet one inch and weighed four hundred pounds, but he looked like a little boy who was in need of a hug at this moment. "And in the spring of 2002, when Christopher threatened to stab you and rape you, he was still a scrawny little kid, wasn't he? About five feet two inches?"

Snyder acknowledged Christopher was small.

Mims's curiosity about this incident was an itch that needed scratching. "Then, were you frightened?"

"I knew he wouldn't rape me, but I knew that if he had the chance, and if he had an object, there is the possibility that he could attempt to try to stab me."

"If you have your back turned?"

"If I had my back turned, and you have twenty juveniles in there, there might be an instance. But all it takes is one distraction. You know, he could have had somebody start a fight, and as soon as I turn my back."

Still looking to scratch his itch, Mims asked, "Mr. Snyder, this whole notion of this little boy stabbing and raping a grown four-hundred-pound man is pretty grandiose, isn't it?"

Snyder stared ahead with a bit of resentment; then, as if the thought had just occurred to him, he tossed back at Mims, "Killing your grandparents with a shotgun is pretty grandiose, too."

Giese smiled and looked over at the jury, as if to say, "Game, set, and match."

CHAPTER 38

Christopher Pittman would stay a total of twelve days with his family at the Isle of Palms. At the close of his double-murder trial, on each of those days, he would return with them to the beach house and live like a normal kid again. While his family rallied around him, encouraged him, and loved him the best they knew how, he ate Gummi Bears and drank hot chocolate until he got sick.

During Christopher's reprieve, family members tried to focus on "staying in the moment" and not discussing what could be his last days of freedom. But as the time for a verdict drew closer, so did their fears of him returning to prison.

Melinda Pittman Rector, Christopher's aunt, confided to Jason Cato, "We all are afraid of getting our hopes up and then having them dashed. We're living for today, enjoying today." Melinda's stress was so overwhelming that two days before the jury would end their deliberations, she would collapse and require treatment at the hospital.

The night before the jury was to announce their decision, Christopher and his grandmother talked about the possibility of not realizing their hope of an acquittal. He was so distressed by the thought that he crawled into bed with

Duprey and his stepgrandfather, and they held hands until he fell asleep.

Final arguments in the Christopher Pittman case began on Monday morning, February 14. The prosecution would speak first and last, with the defense's summation sandwiched between. Court commentators often say this process isn't fair, since jurors receive information most strongly at the beginning and end. But others believe the advantage should be given to the prosecution, who has the burden of proof.

On behalf of the state, John Meadors began his summation.

"Ladies and gentlemen, this is the Pittmans' case. The *Joe and Joy Pittman* case. This is what this case is about. This is *their* day in court.

"And as we go through these closing arguments, I ask you to stay focused on what is important. Keep your eye on the ball. And the eye on the ball is November 28, 2001—the actions of the defendant, Christopher Pittman, his state of mind, and how he acted. That's what this case is about. And the only issue is: did he know the difference between right and wrong? That is what it boils down to."

In a surprisingly calm voice, Meadors alluded to "Lady Justice." He reviewed the prosecution's facts and evidence of the case, then told jurors, "Lady Justice says it is okay to find a twelve-year-old guilty. Shooting them (his grandparents) in bed . . . is there anything more malicious? His statements expressed malice. 'I planned it. They deserved it.' It even proved motive: when disciplined, he gets angry. It's no longer summer vacation. Grandparents are going to let you get away with it no more. Granddaddy says no. But he wouldn't follow the rules. After church, Granddaddy takes him outside and dresses him down. Tells him, 'You might go to DJJ or go back home.' Christopher was angry."

Meadors was so consumed with the rightness of his

convictions, he could barely stand still. Looking over his shoulder at the clock to make certain he had not gone beyond his time, he turned back to the jurors. With great emotion in his voice, he concluded, "Ladies and gentlemen, Joe and Joy Pittman were too young to die."

Andy Vickery held a plastic cup of water in his hand and looked as relaxed as if he were teaching an evening class on elementary law. In a soft, calm voice, he stated, "Lady Justice is not blind to our children. Children aren't mature enough to know right from wrong. When we decide Christopher's fate, we must judge this twelve-year-old. The law says twelve-year-olds aren't capable of determining right from wrong.

"A doctor gave an unapproved mind-altering drug to a twelve-year-old, ninety-six-pound boy. He became involuntarily intoxicated and had an unexpected reaction. He had no malice aforethought because of that. He had no [understanding] of the difference between right and wrong. And because of that, we submit to you that Christopher is not guilty."

Vickery used an elaborate PowerPoint presentation to outline his case, answer the charges from the prosecution, testimony from his expert witnesses, and project pictures of Christopher and his grandparents.

"This case is not about being guilty, but mentally ill," he said. "It's not about insanity. As far as we are concerned, there is no evidence of insanity or any evidence of mentally ill. And we say to you, it is inappropriate to render any of those two verdicts, and we don't ask you to do that.

"Involuntary intoxication is mental illness, but it is something that is drug-induced. In order for that to happen, three things must occur: One, you have to be under a doctor's prescription. Two, it has to be an unintended side effect, and three, as a result, it renders the person unable to distinguish right and wrong.

"A twelve-year-old does not have criminal intent. So the proper verdict, ladies and gentlemen of the jury, is not guilty."

Paul Waldner took the lateral pass from Vickery and began his summation with the rules of evidence and how they applied to law.

"We began this case with a stipulation that Christopher shot and killed his grandparents. If law equated that with guilt, it would have ended at that time. Hopefully, in the last two weeks, you learned that what happened to Christopher Pittman was the result of the psychotropic drug that had chemically altered his brain and changed him into someone that was not him. If you think about it, it is the only thing that makes sense. You don't begin a life of crime by walking up the stairs and shooting your grandparents while they lay in bed.

"We do not convict children for murder when they've been ambushed by chemicals that have destroyed their ability to reason. On November 28, 2001, there were three lives that were lost, and with your verdict today, you have the opportunity to give one back. And when your verdict of not guilty is read in this courtroom, the loudest cheers you are going to hear in this courtroom are going to be from children, grandchildren, the church members and friends of Joe Frank Pittman and his wife, Joy Pittman."

All were excellent arguments. These attorneys were professionals in every sense of the word and knew what they were doing. Any layperson could readily understand that.

The last of the warriors, solicitor Barney Giese, looked exhausted when he stood and approached the jury. In a scratchy and hoarse voice, he started out by correcting the defense.

"The defense has said, 'We, the state of South Carolina, has made Joe Pittman into a child abuser.' But I say to you that Christopher Pittman said that. Those are his words, not our words. He is calling his grandpa abusive, not us. . . . Christopher first said he had been abused by his grandparents and that is why they deserved to die. Then, later on down the road, his story changed to hearing voices and 'Zoloft made me do it.' He no longer mentions anything about abuse."

Giese wanted the jurors to know why Christopher Pittman killed his grandparents. He got a nod from two of the jurors in the courtroom.

"I want you also to know that Christopher Pittman is no different in Florida, Chester, or DJJ. In all three of these places, his behavior was the same. He was an angry young gentleman. Even his family said so. He attacked his sister—she told Dr. Crawford she was scared of him. He shot BBs at someone's house. He shot fourteen BBs in someone's Blazer. Even his father, Joe Pittman, said, 'He is angry. I am having trouble controlling him.' I submit to you, if Christopher is doing so well in Florida, then why did his grandparents have to drive from Chester and get him?

"And, finally, he didn't take discipline well. The result of that was death. After his granddaddy took him out of church and disciplined him, he came back with anger on his face. That anger boiled and boiled, and two hours later it boiled over. Then he waited until his grandparents went to bed. What could be more malicious than waiting?"

Giese had caught his second wind. His voice grew stronger and there was fire in his heart. He walked over to the witness stand and picked up the .410 shotgun Christopher had used to kill his grandparents. Aiming the shotgun at the Styrofoam heads sitting on top of the counter, Giese reenacted the murders of Joe and Joy Pittman.

"He walked to where his poor grandfather was asleep. He fired that shot into his mouth."

Click-clack, click.

"Into his open mouth, he fired that shot." *Click-clack, click.* "Ninety-seven pellets through his mouth and into the back of his head. But he wasn't through yet."

In one of the more macabre moments in the trial, Giese reenacted the crime. All of the lawyers had spent days and weeks, and called their hundreds of witnesses, and argued and harangued, but nothing seemed to matter while Giese held that shotgun in his hand. Giese looked at Christopher and shouted, "That is as malicious a murder as you'll find."

Vickery laid his hand on Christopher's shoulder, but his facial expressions never changed. Either Christopher had heard it so much that it no longer phased him, or he still believed he was not responsible, that the "other Christopher" had murdered his grandparents.

"And the sad thing about it, Christopher did nothing to help them," Giese told the jury. "As his grandmother lay in her bed, dying, he went through her purse and stole thirty-three dollars. He had learned something from his first runaway in Florida—not to leave any witnesses."

With harsh criticism for the defense's star witness, Giese did his best to minimize Dr. Lanette Atkins. "Her testimony was incredible," he said, among other things, looking directly at her in the gallery. "It was the biggest case of her career. She had an answer for all of it. She figured everyone out and where they all fit."

Using printed Styrofoam charts, Giese asked a series of questions, then went through his own litany of counterpoints, using the prosecution's expert witness testimony. Unsmiling and serious, he attacked the importance of the incident where Christopher held a picture of his grandparents' home against his cell window. The stunning revelation was that "he had pointed at the picture, bragged, and laughed about what he had done."

Giese walked over to the jurors and said in astonishment, "He told the correctional officer Steven Synder, 'I've done it before, I can do it again.'"

Giese's powerful and emotional summation sent

Christopher slouching back in his seat. Like a turtle fighting to retreat into his shell, he hunkered down in his seat and lowered his head.

Giese placed his last Styrofoam board on the tripod. With **THEY DESERVED IT** written across the front in bold black letters, he gave the jury what he thought was a huge dose of the truth. It was a tragic portrayal of how one angry child had shattered the lives of the two innocent people who had loved him the most.

"These are Christopher Pittman's words," Giese said, walking away from the board and moving toward Christopher. 'They deserved it.' But I tell you this, they did not deserve to die. They reached out to this boy and tried to help him. He showed them no remorse. Instead, all they got was shotgun pellets in the mouth. They didn't deserve it. They deserved to be happy. They deserved to live out the rest of their lives in dignity."

Giese stepped directly in front of Christopher. Taking a road less traveled, he looked down at him and shouted, "No, Christopher Pittman! They didn't deserve it, they deserved better."

The three men and nine women of the jury filed quietly back into the jury room, where they had spent many hours over the previous weeks. They were eager to finish what they had started two weeks ago, but curious to know if other jurors had interpreted the evidence in similar manners. It would be a difficult decision if they held widely diverse opinions.

This was as tough a case as a jury could find. Even though Lady Justice would assume ultimate responsibility for Christopher Pittman's fate, they were the ones who would cast the initial vote and steer his fate. The jurors, eager and businesslike, spread out around the tables. Before they could vote on Christopher Pittman's fate, they needed to know how divided their opinions were. On the first show of hands, the vote was nine, guilty, to three, not guilty.

After a couple of the jurors explained their votes, the discussion began slowly. There was some debate, focused primarily on testimony about the fire Christopher had set, as well as his own confessions he had given to the police. Was he in his right mind when he murdered his grandparents? Had he tried to cover his tracks and get away with murder?

When jurors compared notes, Dr. James Ballenger, the state witness whom the defense called as part of their case, was the most convincing. Ballenger believed that Christopher knew right from wrong, as shown by his careful planning of his crimes. He said Christopher tried to avoid prosecution and eventual confession. If jurors believed the prosecution, then it was Christopher's strong dislike for discipline that fueled the rage that caused him to murder. He killed his grandfather because he paddled him and killed his grandmother because she did nothing to stop it. Prosecutors called the defense's claim of involuntary intoxication a "smoke screen" and asked jurors to focus on the brutality of the murders.

The problematic question for jurors was not if Christopher had killed his grandparents—both sides already had conceded that—but had he killed them in cold blood, or had an antidepressant clouded his judgment, where he could not stop himself?

The defense wanted jurors to believe Christopher was too young to form the criminal intent to commit murder. Even his account of the murders, his getaway, and his trying to blame it on someone else, they said, was the result of a hostile reaction to the antidepressant. It was more than a "smoke screen," the defense contended. The antidepressants had caused him to go berserk.

The jury did not find the defense's chief expert, child psychiatrist Lanette Atkins, reliable. Atkins testified that although she could not form an opinion about whether

Christopher knew right from wrong when he killed his grandparents, when she testified last year, she now believed he could not have known because of his Zoloft use. The jury couldn't see it.

Perhaps, the biggest obstacle to finding Christopher Pittman guilty was his age. How could someone that young stick a shotgun in his grandfather's mouth while he slept and fill it with buckshot? How could he blow the back of his grandmother's head away, then say they deserved to die? Such thoughts could only originate from a criminal mind, or from the most evil person ever imagined.

Christopher had spent most of his days throughout the trial looking down at the floor. At certain times during the trial, he had gotten emotional. It was hard to believe the twelve-year-old portrayed in the blowup had committed these wicked crimes. Apart from the spectacle of this trial, his age was most disturbing. No one in the courtroom envied the nine women and three men on the jury, who had listened to Christopher's social and medical history and heard expert testimony from criminologists, psychiatric medicine practitioners, psychiatrists, and skilled lawyers. A scene like this was unheard-of forty years earlier. These jurors must now decide whether he was responsible or not. If the tables turned and the court handpicked twelve medical experts, even they would find it nearly impossible.

After almost four hours of continuous discussion, it was evident no decision would be reached that day. Realizing these issues were more complicated than the average jury faced, they decided to adjourn, get a good night's rest, and return in the morning.

By nine o'clock the next morning, the jurors were back around the table with renewed discussion about Christopher Pittman's childhood. No doubt, a troubled young boy whose mother had abandoned him and, according to the prosecution, whose father had been emotionally abusive. He had had a string of bad behavior and a record of not responding well to discipline before taking antidepressants. Could an adverse reaction to Zoloft cause him to experience side effects and become manic and psychotic?

Defense attorneys and experts claimed it could.

The prosecution admitted that Zoloft could cause the emotional blunting and the other causes defense had listed—they had never disputed that. But could it push him to the point where he would commit murder? Just because he was taking prescription medication, did it mean he wasn't responsible for his actions?

The three jurors who had voted not guilty discussed their reasoning. Other jurors tried to answer their doubt about Christopher's guilt. They spent another hour or so discussing the effects of Zoloft. Most felt a decision was near. One by one, the three jurors who had voted not guilty were swayed to the opposite side. The talk continued, with prolonged silences between vocalized thoughts. Then the discussion halted altogether. It was time for another vote. This time the vote was: twelve, guilty; zero, not guilty.

Judge Pieper had given the jury many choices: Guilty. Not guilty. Not guilty by reason of temporary insanity. Guilty, but mentally ill. Or not guilty for lack of criminal intent.

When the bailiff conveyed that the jury had reached a unanimous decision, word spread quickly that a verdict had been reached. Within five minutes, every seat in the courtroom was filled. For the first time in the trial, Christopher's father surfaced. His appearance puzzled those in the courtroom until he stated he did not want his presence to become a distraction, a reference to testimony that Christopher went to live with his grandparents to get away from his disciplinarian father. He told reporters he had spent the night with Christopher at the rented beach cottage, and whatever bad blood was between them was resolved.

As Judge Pieper silently scanned the verdict, Christopher stood between Andy Vickery and defense attorney

Paul Waldner. Each of the men had an arm around his shoulders. Christopher's family sat in the front row, holding hands, and praying for a miracle.

Defense attorney Vickery felt there were multiple ways Christopher could have won the trial through reasonable doubt. Nearly seven hours of deliberations was enough time for the jury to come to a decision of not guilty. As the jury filed out, he looked at the faces of the women jurors. If they had been crying, then that was a bad sign. He figured any woman who was going to deliver a guilty verdict would shed a tear over it. At least, one of the nine would. He saw nothing in their poker faces that would suggest that, and he was still confident their verdict was an acquittal.

Melinda Pittman Rector saw something different in the jurors' faces. She said her hopes of a favorable verdict fade as soon as the jury came into the courtroom. The jurors had been making eye contact, on and off, during the trial with the family, but they never looked their way.

Chris bowed his head and showed no emotion as the court clerk Scott Wilson read the verdict. Joe Pittman sat ten feet away from his son, fighting to hold back his emotion. He put his arm around his daughter Danielle and wept as the clerk of court was handed the jury's verdict.

Andy Vickery held on to Christopher and squeezed his shoulder firmly.

"We, the jury, find Christopher Pittman," the clerk read, "guilty, on two counts of murder." The announcement sent a jolt through the courtroom.

Hot tears began to fall across Danielle's cheeks.

Vickery immediately requested a new trial, stating the jury saw a six-foot-one teenager and judged him, instead of the five-foot-two boy who committed the crime. He argued that the state did not offer sufficient evidence to rebut the legal presumption in South Carolina that people under the age of fourteen cannot form criminal intent.

The judge denied both requests, but he said the case

touched on society's core values when it comes to the treatment and punishment of juveniles in the justice system.

Vickery felt as if he had been shot in the gut. He could barely think, but he couldn't stop arguing his case before the judge. With great passion and humility, and until he was blue in the face, he proposed one motion after another, hoping that one would eventually do the trick. This giant of a lawyer was figuratively on his knees, begging the judge to do what he had not been able to do. "I apologize, I'm in a bit of a dither," Vickery said, looking as if his knees would surely buckle at any moment.

Before Christopher was sentenced, family members paused to gather themselves, then came forward and addressed the court.

"I love my son very dearly," Joe Pittman began, "and I want to ask you for mercy on my son, on his behalf."

Spectators were puzzled over the father they had seen so little of.

"I love my son with all my heart, as I did my mom and dad," Joe continued. "If they were here today, they'd be begging for mercy."

Showing the court a face of human agony, Melinda Pittman Rector approached the bench and echoed the same sentiment. That was not her nephew who had murdered her parents, she pleaded, but someone under the influence of the drug Zoloft. "He's a good kid. We have a family and we miss him."

Christopher's maternal grandparents, Delnora and Will Duprey, stood woodenly and begged the judge for mercy.

And, in a very touching moment, Hank Mims stepped out from behind the defense table and spoke up for Christopher. He, too, was in a stupor and couldn't get his words to come out exactly as he had planned. All he could squeeze out was that Christopher had changed and he was a good kid now.

Before he passed sentence, Judge Pieper requested a

fifteen-minute break. During this entire time, Christopher remained at the defense table, sitting hangdog and pitiful, and never once sought the comfort of his family and friends. He, at first, had said he would not make a statement before the judge. However, when court resumed, Vickery asked him if he wanted to speak, and he agreed. Flanked by his four attorneys, it was his only public statement since being arrested more than three years ago.

"All I can really say is that I know it's in the hands of God," Pittman told Pieper in a low, deep voice. "And whatever He decides on, that's what it's going to be."

Two female jurors looked at each other and nodded. They had hoped Christopher would speak out and show remorse for what he had done—at least for the sake of his grandparents—but when given the chance, they thought he had choked. Their faces conveyed their final judgment: all he thought about was himself.

As the lead defense attorney, Andy Vickery, told the judge that if he wanted to, he could rule that the South Carolina law mandating a minimum sentence of thirty years was now unconstitutional. Given Christopher's age at the time of the murders, the ruling would be appropriate.

"You have a legislative mandate that says you shall not give him less than thirty years," Vickery reminded Pieper, "but you have a constitutional imperative . . . that the sentence must be in light of the full circumstances, including his age."

Pieper was sympathetic, saying this case was a very compelling and troubling case for him, but he was bound by the law. The jury had found Christopher Pittman guilty of two counts of murder. His attorneys had been offered a plea bargain, and there would have been some flexibility in sentencing, but they had turned it down. Now he had no choice but to sentence him within those guidelines set by the state.

"This is a very tragic case, tragic to the victim and tragic to the entire family," Pieper responded. "This case has called attention to the very core values of this society about the treatment of the juveniles and punishment."

Pieper then sentenced Christopher to thirty years for each murder conviction, to run concurrently. It was the shortest sentence possible under the state's mandatory sentence for murder—he could have received life in prison—but still not what Christopher and his supporters had hoped for.

"Good luck to you," he told Christopher in a solemn moment.

Finally the *State of South Carolina* v. *Christopher Frank Pittman* was over. Christopher was taken into custody by court officers, and after saying good-bye to his family, he was outfitted in prison hardware, then whisked back to the South Carolina Juvenile Detention in Columbia. It had taken nearly four years to get his day in court, and it hadn't turned out as he had dreamed. He would never again attend a public school, nor would he grow up through his teen years with his friends. A chunk of his life, a very important chunk, had been cut short. He would never get to hunt again, ride his four-wheelers, or romp through the woods.

Christopher was not eligible for parole in his thirty-year sentence. He was given credit for time served and could be released from prison two months before his forty-third birthday. His old six-by-nine cell on B-block at DJJ probably still had his name on it. But he had a new concern now—on his eighteenth birthday, he would be transferred to live in a prison with hardened, adult criminals.

CHAPTER 39

A trial is often about momentum. A defendant can have it one moment and lose it the next. Having it at the right time usually results in an acquittal; having it at the wrong time results in conviction. Sometimes it is as simple as that.

Christopher Pittman's conviction left his family, his supporters, and his defense attorneys bewildered. Some were sobbing at a time when they thought they would be celebrating. It was a tough pill to swallow for the defense attorneys, who were accustomed to winning cases.

As the camps of supporters left the courtroom, television reporters and journalists were waiting to ambush them. The first response from Barney Giese concerning the case: "I have sympathy for this boy and his family."

Andy Vickery overheard Giese's comment and said in a loud voice to the crowd of reporters surrounding him, "They have no sympathy. No compassion."

Joe Pittman quickly took center stage. He accused the prosecution of being out for blood and explained to the press why he had not attended the trial. "There have been a lot of accusations against me. The prosecution would have wanted to make this case against me. On the advice of my son's attorneys, I stayed away so the jury could focus on my son and his defense." He then pleaded with the governor and the president of the United States to pardon his son.

Vickery assured the press they were people who would not let this case file gather dust. "We will go to every step we need to get Christopher's sentence overturned. . . . We've invested a lot of time in this. We've walked in his shoes, crawled in his hide, and we have broken hearts."

There were already plans for Christopher Pittman's lawyers and his family members to fly out later that day for an appearance on the *Larry King Live*.

The defense promised an appeal, but Judge Pieper was one of the best judges in the state. He had scrutinized the case carefully so there would be no reason for an appeal.

Court TV's Nancy Grace was livid over Pieper's sentence of thirty years.

"I don't care who he is," Grace said after the verdict was announced. "He is a wimp! Here was his chance to take in the statute and do something different. There was enough evidence about the Zoloft to say there was an effect, and the judge had the opportunity to break with the system, to give this boy less than thirty years, and he missed it! I say again, he's a wimp." But, by the time Grace interviewed Giese and Meadors, she had cooled down and seen the light.

"The antidepressant defense was just a smoke screen," a very subdued Meadors explained. "Nothing more than that."

"We're not worried about an appeal," Giese assured Grace. "Judge Pieper was very careful about the legal issues and he knows the law better than anybody. I don't see any reason for an appeal."

Court TV interviewed jury foreman Steven Platt. Platt said the jury's decision to convict pretty much came down to guilty versus not guilty. He said everyone was satisfied with the sentence of thirty years and believed the Zoloft may have caused those symptoms Dr. Ballenger mentioned, but Zoloft did not cause Christopher Pittman to murder.

The jury had rendered its verdict, the judge had reached his sentence, and the people of South Carolina had spoken in relation to sentencing juveniles in an adult court. But those who understand criminal law know that some of the most dramatic moments occur not in the courtroom, but in the hallways outside the courtroom, on the lawn outside the courthouse, or inside restaurants and bars, where people eat and drink and discuss the case.

In a bizarre twist of fate, Jason Cato was eating in a restaurant on James Island the Monday night during jury deliberations. It was here that he overheard jury foreman Steven Platt talking with the bartender about Christopher's case. It so happened that Cato was researching and writing a story for the *Herald* on jury sequestration and he believed Platt's conduct bore the odor of day-old sushi. On Wednesday, he spoke with Melinda Pittman Rector and defense attorney Andy Vickery not only about his position on sequestration, but mentioned his conversation with Platt.

Vickery filed a motion for a hearing, and on February 18, Judge Pieper and the clan were back in court to decide if there had been juror misconduct. Jason Cato was called as a witness, but would appear not as a reporter covering the trial, or as the person at the *Herald* most familiar with the Pittman case. He was present as the potential witness to this juror's misconduct.

On Tuesday morning, March 1, 2005, there was a proceeding held in camera before Judge Pieper. In the hearing, the court heard Platt say he didn't remember giving any opinion about the case or discussing anything of substance about the case. But the bartender said he recollected clearly that he discussed the substance of the case with Platt, who even told him what his vote was going to be.

"Steve said he was a juror," the bartender told Judge Pieper. "He even gave me his opinion on which way he was going to vote. He said he thought the young man was guilty. On Monday night, he said the defendant was guilty, and that the jury was split."

The conversation was very important, not only for impeachment purposes, but also for the substantive purposes so as to know what it was that Platt told Cato. The defense had made a motion for a new trial based on allegations of juror misconduct.

Jason Cato's attorney, Jay Bender, argued that Cato was protected in his news-gathering activity by the South Carolina Reporter Shield Law, Section 19-11, dash 100. The South Carolina General Assembly enacted the shield law to protect reporters from being annexed as investigators for litigants. And it did so to recognize that causing a reporter to be subpoenaed to give testimony, or provide other information, would interfere with the flow of information to the public.

"Even if that is some form of juror misconduct," Bender pleaded, "is it necessary for you, in considering whether or not to grant a new trial? Any testimony from Jason Cato, if it relates to this conversation, it's going to be cumulative to what you already know. There doesn't seem to be any dispute that there was a conversation on Monday night between the juror and the bartender.

"Even if that is so, where is there any showing that the conversation polluted the jury's deliberation? Even if the juror had told the bartender that there was a split on the jury, the world knew that because the deliberations were recessed Monday night. Had there been unanimity on Monday night, there would have been a verdict. The jury would not have been sent home. So there was some sort of split. The numbers didn't seem to make any difference. The jury came back on Tuesday and reached a verdict.

"There is nothing from any juror that suggests that any conversation the one juror had on Monday night tainted the discussions on Tuesday when a jury verdict was reached, or at any other time. So it cannot be said that the testimony from this reporter is necessary to establish—even if it is material or relevant—it's not necessary to establish that there was some misconduct. Certainly, there is nothing to indicate that the reporter has any information about what the jury discussed in deliberations. You have that from the interview with the jurors."

Vickery protested. "I submit that when Mr. Cato imparted information voluntarily, both to me and to Melinda Rector and actually Mr. Pittman, too, as our affidavit reflects, that he was not involved in news gathering. But even if you view that in the broadest terms, that by doing so with respect to that information, at least, he waived the qualified privilege of the shield law. Because what it is designed to do, obviously, is to keep people from hauling reporters into court and making them divulge things that involved their news gathering. This was news imparting." Vickery didn't think there was any other alternative means for the court to know other than that which Platt and Cato had discussed.

"We've heard from one of them, I think that justice requires that you hear from the second one," Vickery stated. He wanted to know more about the discussion of the deliberations and the split amongst and between the jurors.

"But as to Mr. Cato," Judge Pieper responded, "there is no basis whatsoever, insofar as any of the jurors, that some conversation by Mr. Cato and Mr. Platt, in any way, was carried into that jury room. Is that a fair assessment of what we learned today?"

Vickery agreed. "But what that doesn't address is the question of whether misconduct that occurred outside of the jury room was significant enough that the court would exercise its discretion, had it known at the time to disqualify this juror." He did his best to convince the judge that juror misconduct had occurred. "Was it possible that the juror told people who didn't believe that Christopher Pittman was guilty, and who intended to vote not guilty? And in this conversation, did the juror say, 'I'm going to tell them that the law requires that they go with the majority.' And if that occurred, then that would certainly be something of a significant-enough gravity that the court, as you turn back the time, which you must do, to that point and said, 'What would I have done, had I discovered that?"

But Pieper ruled there was no basis to think that was ever said. Christopher Pittman would not get a new trial. His conviction would stand as determined in the court trial.

Because he had been subpoenaed as a witness to jury misconduct in the Pittman trial, Jason Cato was taken off the case and another reporter assigned to take his place. After four years of hustling news and keeping Christopher Pittman's name in the headlines, Cato walked out of the courtroom a wiser and better person for it.

EPILOGUE

The jury in Christopher Pittman's case believed his behavior was affected by Zoloft on November 28, 2001, when he killed his grandparents, but was convinced beyond a reasonable doubt that he knew the difference between right and wrong and acted with malice aforethought. Christopher's attorney filed a motion asking Judge Daniel Pieper to reduce Christopher's sentence to a maximum imprisonment to age 21.

On May 13, 2005, Judge Pieper denied the motion for a new trial in the Pittman case. The court's opinion acknowledged that one juror discussed his potential vote with a bartender before the verdict. The court also noted that two other jurors who voted guilty actually believed that Christopher was not guilty, but voted with the majority because of one, "coercion" and/or two, a misunderstanding of the law, in that one juror thought she had to vote with the majority to achieve unanimity. Yet, Pieper ruled the fundamental fairness of the deliberations or the verdict were neither persuaded nor affected by these actions. Christopher's defense team filed an appeal with the South Carolina Supreme Court, asking the court to reverse Christopher's conviction.

In a touch of irony, Christopher Bernaiche, who was bipolar and convicted of murder, was granted another trial in Detroit, Michigan, on the same day Christopher was found guilty in South Carolina. On December 27, 2002, the twenty-seven-year-old Bernaiche lost at a pool game in a bar, got into a fight, and then returned with a gun. He shot up the bar—firing at least twenty shots— killing two men and injuring three other patrons. Andy Vickery also served as lead trial counsel and argued Bernaiche's antidepressant medication, Prozac, had caused Bernaiche to react violently and ultimately kill. His Proazc had been doubled two months before the shooting. No doubt, Bernaiche's trial will boil down to the same determining factor as was Christopher Pittman's trial: a battle of the psychopharmacological experts.

In August, 2005, the South Carolina Supreme Court agreed to hear Christopher's appeal. The ruling meant his appeal would bypass the South Carolina Court of Appeals, because "[Christopher Pittman's case] involves an issue of significant public interest or a legal principle of major importance."

Christopher remains incarcerated at the DJJ in Columbia, South Carolina. Unless Christopher's case is overturned before April 2006, when Christopher will turn 17, he will be transferred to an adult prison.

According to Melinda Pittman Rector, who maintains a website in memory of her parents, Joy and Joe Pittman's home owner's insurance policy refused to pay for any damages or loss of property to their home. Rector stated the insurance company cited a clause in the contract which prohibited payment when a fire was deliberately set by a "relative resident."

On a happier note, Danielle Pittman Finchum gave birth to a healthy girl. She and her husband, named the baby after her grandmother, Joy Pittman.

Acknowledgments

As every reader knows, it takes a lot of people to create a true crime book, and I am indebted to many. I could never have written this book had it not been for the help of people who provided information, pictures and encouragement.

First, I'd like to express my appreciation to Melinda Pittman Rector, who graciously supplied family pictures and her father's book of memories.

A special thanks for additional information and/or pictures goes to Jason Cato, James "Red" and Lucy Weir, Andy Martin, Sheriff Robert Benson, Major James McNeil, Reverend Chris Snelgrove, Kathy Connor, Shirley Carter, Stuart and Ann Grant, and Holly O'Quinn.

I especially want to thank my writing partner and good friend, Dale Dobson. Thanks also goes to my sister-in-law Rhonda Hucks and new business partner Heidi Herring. I am also indebted to my three biggest supporters: my banker, Richard Causey; my accountant, Morgan Lewis; and my attorney, Ralph Stroman.

As always, nothing is possible without the support and love of my wife, Deborah, and two children, DJ and Deegan. And to my mom, Katherine Hudson. I am always blessed by her continual encouragement and influence.

Finally, a special and deep gratitude goes to my agent Peter Miller and the folks at Kensington for all their help and support.